The Golden Revolution, *Revisited*

John Butler

Foreword by Steve Baker,
Member of Parliament of the United Kingdom;
member of the Treasury Select Committee

ISBN: 978-1-0902-8095-4

For those waiting patiently for the sunrise.

Contents

Foreword

WE LIVE IN THE AGE OF BROKEN PROMISES

by Steve Baker, Member of Parliament of the United Kingdom; member of the Treasury Select Committee

We live at a time of both sensational and terrifying possibilities. This is an unfrozen moment in human history within which the Western world faces profound change, whether for good or ill. How did it come about?

We could discuss the failure of trade policy to defend against market distortions overseas, or the gaping holes in western welfare states through which too many fall, whomever is in power. We could lament the backfiring of the authoritarian identity politics of political correctness, which were imposed in place of common courtesy.

Standing behind and thus above all these problems is a system on which each of us depends each day for everything we do. The people suffering its increasingly evident failures have long known there is something wrong with the world, yet they have not known what it is.

Today, people are beginning to understand that there are one or more fundamental flaws in the prevailing system of money and bank credit. It is a system that permeates everything around us. It pays for our homes and cars. It funds the production of our food. It pays for our holidays and our computers. It is everywhere, but it is not well understood, ironically not even by those operating it.

It is slowly undermining the foundations of our society. For over forty-five years since the end of the Bretton Woods currency system, nominally backed by gold, our money has been a chronically expanding supply of primarily bank-issued debt on which someone always pays interest. Every part of our monetary system today is someone else's liability. At no point can those obligations be finally settled—even bank notes carry a promise to redeem that cannot be kept.

The profits from this long-term process of debt creation have been privatized to the benefit of those in the financial system, but when financial crisis came, the losses were projected onto everyone. Painful state austerity followed.

And we wonder why the political center ground is hollowing out to the populist left and right.

There is little good in the writing of the defunct economist John Maynard Keynes, but he did understand the dangers of debauching the currency. In 1919, he wrote:

> There is no subtler, no surer means of overturning the existing basis of society than to debauch the currency. The process engages all the hidden forces of economic law on the side of destruction, and does it in a manner which not one man in a million is able to diagnose.[1]

Why did we allow this system to evolve? Why, having stumbled into the end of the carefully designed if flawed post-war monetary order, did we tolerate the system which emerged?

In 2011, an important centenary passed mostly unremarked. On 16 December 1911, the UK's National Insurance Act received royal assent. It was a well-intentioned Act that insidiously undermined the

1 John Maynard Keyes, *The Economic Consequences of the Peace*, 1920 edition, p. 235.

friendly societies by establishing and entrenching state welfare. For the past century, due in part to the exigencies of war, the UK has frequently remained in the vanguard of this process now common to nearly all developed countries.

Back in 1911, British government spending was under 15 percent of GDP. The World Wars pushed state spending to around 46 percent and 70 percent of GDP respectively, and the peacetime trend was so established. From about a quarter of GDP in 1920, peacetime spending grew to match Great War levels by 1970.

Now, governments have always paid for themselves through taxation, borrowing and currency debasement. UK tax revenues increased from about 10 percent of GDP in 1911 to 40 percent in the late 40s. After a slight respite in the 50s and early 60s, taxation passed 40 percent of GDP again in about 1970, hitting an apparent upper limit. It has stayed thereabouts ever since, whoever has been in power.

Governments mostly did not restrain themselves: borrowing and currency debasement took over as deficit spending ultimately funded political promises. The pattern was repeated around the Western world. A monetary order ultimately restrained by a final link to gold could not endure.

Nixon ended the Bretton Woods system in 1971, and the world has since had an institutionally inflationary, debt-based fiat monetary system. The UK money supply (M4) grew from a few tens of billions of pounds to c. £700 billion in the spring of 1997, before tripling to over £2.2 trillion in January 2010. Comparable exponential increases in the money supply can be observed in all major developed economies. The associated booms and busts were inevitable.

With so much new money being loaned into existence by the commercial banks, it is no surprise governments have been able consistently to run chronic deficits. The unprecedented global monetary environment of our lifetimes was a deliberate policy choice of welfare states. Former Federal Reserve Chairman Alan Greenspan gave the definitive explanation in his classic 1966 essay, "Gold and Economic Freedom." He wrote:

> An almost hysterical antagonism toward the gold standard is one issue which unites statists of all persuasions. They seem to sense—perhaps more clearly and subtly than many consistent defenders of laissez-faire—that gold and economic freedom are inseparable, that the gold standard is an instrument of voluntary, free-market association and that each implies and requires the other.[2]

The financial crisis and our present political and economic predicament may be seen as the inevitable consequences of using an expansionary monetary system to cover long-term deficit spending. Quantitative Easing makes plain what once was hidden: expanding the money supply conveniently funds the deficit spending necessary to meet the spending promises of the welfare state and its politicians. But at what cost?

I have an atypical sympathy for politicians—after all, these days I am one. Ten years ago, I was so frustrated with politics I decided to stand for election. What I have seen since has been eye opening.

First, despite the enormous spending of the welfare state, even generally affluent areas like my own see enormous human suffering. People too often go homeless and hungry, with the gaps imperfectly plugged by charitable action. Housing is in short supply and unaffordable for working people. Health and social care too often fail to deliver. State pensions are paid to all but provide only a modest living to those dependent on them.

All of this creates huge and genuine demands on the common purse.

Second, hardly any politician engages with the practice and theory of society and social cooperation, politics, and economics. Expedient

---

2 Alan Greenspan, *Gold and Economic Freedom*, The Objectivist, 1966.

"solutions" carry the day. Elected politicians are rarely well-read. The torrent of communication by e-mail and social media becomes oppressive and prevents material consideration of fundamental issues. Public-choice theory takes over as everyone seeks to live at the expense of everyone else while getting on with everyday political life as best they can.

So we stumble forward. The public make reasonable demands for promises to be fulfilled and taxes cut. Politicians struggle to find both revenue and politically acceptable cost efficiencies. Officials and public sector workers ask for higher pay, in some cases with justification. The central banks use ever-more inventive, interventionist monetary policies to keep the enervating train moving.

Sooner or later, this system will blow up, taking with it deficit spending and other promises, which simply cannot be kept. Our economy and politics will become healthier for being honest. The rebuilding will begin.

If there is to be an epiphany among the monetary policy elite, we may yet see state monies return to a sound basis. Meanwhile, entrepreneurs are remonetizing gold and bringing forward crypto-currencies and associated money services. Today, it is demonstrably true that science and markets can provide good quality money through entrepreneurial initiative: we will indeed see Butler's *Golden Revolution*, in time.

The future is therefore bright. A new era of greater freedom, prosperity, and progress founded on honest money is before us. We will reach it when we can pass through formidable political barriers.

The end of the era of broken promises will be marked by a final series of bubbles, as desperate interventions are applied in a futile attempt to defibrillate stagnant economies. At some point, it will become apparent that these interventions cannot prevent some odious combination of default and accelerating price inflation. Rapid action will then be necessary to reinstate a basis for a sustainable and just prosperity based on free-market capitalism without counterproductive intervention in money and bank credit. That will require politicians, officials, and a free public who understand the arguments set out in this excellent book.

For some of us, "diversification" now means owning gold, other real assets, and even bitcoin. For too many people, not understanding why may prove costly indeed. John Butler's book does the great service of enabling anyone to understand why.

Acknowledgements

THIS BOOK IS DEDICATED TO the global gold community, a small but diverse group of individuals which cuts across all countries, cultures and demographics. Since joining this unofficial group in the mid-2000s, while working as a Managing Director at Lehman Brothers, I have come to appreciate its extraordinary diversity. While I have no doubt only scratched the surface, every member I have met has their own personal story to tell about how they came to understand why gold always was, is, and will remain the ultimate, best money and store of value known to man.

Some tell of their parents or grandparents sharing stories of fortunes won and preserved, at least in part, by a small hoard of gold or silver coins, notwithstanding economic adversity, social unrest, revolution or even war. For others, such as myself, the journey was more academic in nature, with some combination of science, economics, philosophy and history providing key insights into the nature of money and the folly of men who assume, wrongly, that they can and should control it.

Notable monetary scientist and firm believer in the importance of sound money, Sir Isaac Newton, explained that he derived his Law of Universal Gravitation by "standing on the shoulders of giants." All of the ideas presented in this book originated with giants, past and present. I am but a mere messenger, one who has sought to combine multiple disciplines and powerful ideas into what I call "The Monetary Cycle of History," of which the remonetization of gold is an essential part.

Thus I would like to thank those individuals who have provided the ideas, examples, patience and moral support that I have found so essential in the production of this book. Of these, James Turk, Alasdair

Macleod, professor Kevin Dowd and Hugo Salinas-Price have played the role of avuncular uncles generously sharing their monetary wisdom. Barry Downs, son-in-law of the late sound money legend and former New York Federal Reserve vice-president, John Exter, has provided an indispensable historical source.

Then there are the fellow travelers, those like I who have found some giant shoulders on which to stand. In no particular order, these include fund and wealth managers Brent Johnson, Steffen Krug, Axel Merk, Shayne McGuire, Ned Naylor-Leyland, Detlev Schlichter, Daniel Lacalle, Ross Norman, Ronni Stoefele, Mark Valek, Jayant Bhandari, Ben Davies and Tim Price.

Although she might not consider herself to be a member of the gold community per se, fellow author Nomi Prins is nevertheless a keen, thoughtful and eloquent critic of our present-day financial and monetary system and she kindly read and commented on an early version of the new section in this *Revisited* edition. Thanks Nomi for your guidance and inspiration.

Steve Baker, MP for Wycombe and tireless advocate for fundamental money and banking reform kindly agreed to write the Foreword and this book is all the richer for his generous contribution.

Finally, in an age of unsound money, reckless finance and fraudulent banking practices it is a rare privilege indeed to pursue a career which aligns seamlessly with the urgent need for reform. Thus I would like to thank my colleagues at Goldmoney for the opportunity to assist them in building their business and realizing their vision for how the world's newest financial technologies, combined with the world's oldest and best money, can help to place the world back on a path of sustainable economic growth and social advancement.

John Butler
London, March 2017

Introduction to the Revisited *Edition*

> "If we went back on the gold standard and we adhered to the actual structure of the gold standard as it existed prior to 1914, we'd be fine. Remember that the period 1870 to 1913 was one of the most aggressive periods economically that we've had in the United States, and that was a golden period of the gold standard. I'm known as a gold bug and everyone laughs at me, but why do central banks own gold now?"
>
> — Alan Greenspan, June 2016[3]

MUCH HAS TRANSPIRED SINCE THE publication of *The Golden Revolution* in April 2012. *The Golden Revolution, Revisited* is thus more than just a new edition. It is substantially expanded, revised, and updated. There have been significant monetary, economic, and political developments during the past five years that have, in their various ways, reinforced or confirmed certain views or predictions and are worthy of inclusion. Yet there have also been unforeseen developments that, nevertheless, relate to the subject of international monetary regime change and, in some cases, provide for a deeper understanding of our current place in what I call the "monetary cycle of history."

Let us begin here: if there is one thing that I hope readers of this book take away it is the perspective provided by the broad study of monetary history. This is absolutely essential if one is to understand what may

3 Former Fed Chairman Greenspan made this (surprising) comment during a 2016 interview on BloombergTV. He elaborates on this view somewhat in his February 2017 interview published in *Gold Investor*, the periodical of the World Gold Council. This can be found at www.gold.org.

seem a truly extraordinary set of contemporary economic circumstances, ranging from zero (or negative) interest rates; a near-decade of hyperactive monetary policies in much of the world; the continuing existence of too-big-to-fail institutions; persistence of government deficits; and, to bring these abstruse topics home to many, the increasingly evident evisceration of the middle class of society. This latter topic, referred to in dangerously facile fashion as simply "inequality" by most, and deserving of a separate book in its own right, is the central topic in the entirely new, first section in this revisited edition.

Also entirely new in *Revisited* is a discussion of the astonishing rise of interest, public and private, in so-called digital- and/or crypto-currencies. While Satoshi Nakamoto's original bitcoin paper was published in 2008, it took the creation of bitcoin in 2009 and several years more for blockchain technology to capture even the imagination of the tech community, much less that of the public at large. But somehow, in early 2014, the topic suddenly went mainstream and publications such as the *New York Times* and *Newsweek* investigated and reported on the bitcoin phenomenon and its potential implications.

About one year later, major central banks, including the Bank of England, began to study the topic in earnest and published extensive papers regarding the potential implications of blockchain, as a more general reference to the technology behind bitcoin, rather than the bitcoin algorithm itself. It has subsequently become a mainstream view that so-called blockchain technology will contribute to the disruption and disintermediation of a wide variety of financial and commercial activities and many so-called FinTech (or financial technology) start-up firms are seeking ways to provide practical applications and solutions. Even banks have come to embrace the technology, with internal working groups seeking ways in which to apply it to realize efficiencies and streamline operations across multiple divisions.

It is a discussion of the implications of FinTech more generally that comprises the final new chapter in this edition. *The Golden Revolution* did touch on this at a few points along the way, but recent developments demand and deserve an expanded and more thoughtful treatment about how FinTech is not only about realizing greater efficiencies in transactions, payments, settlements, and regulatory protocols but about a range of developments which, in my view, are going to facilitate, perhaps even catalyze, a return to a gold-backed monetary system for much if not all of the world. Exactly how this would come about is of course unclear. Of all the various possible scenarios presented in the original edition, the spontaneous, "bottom-up" process of individuals simply refusing, one by one, to use fiat currencies for commerce and to switch to gold instead, seemed perhaps the most far-fetched at the time. No longer. Financial technology could be a game changer in this regard, as I explain at the end of Section III.

It is my hope that this new, revisited edition—nearly a new book some might say—will draw interest not only from the original audience but also an entirely new one that, during the past five years, has become more interested in the future of money, banking, and finance generally. The evidence that the current financial system is chronically dysfunctional is now glaringly obvious amid zero or negative interest rates, poorly capitalized banks, and stagnant or declining per-capita real income growth. The increasingly ad-hoc, strained, even outright illogical explanations of mainstream economists as to why their policies are not as effective as claimed or are producing nasty, unintended, counterproductive consequences, are ringing increasingly hollow. As Thomas Kuhn argued so cogently in his masterwork, *The Structure of Scientific Revolutions*, these are clear and present symptoms of a fundamentally flawed intellectual paradigm, in this case for the understanding the proper role of money in the economy and, by extension, in society. While even now only a comparable few have been willing to consider that it is the use of debt-backed fiat money itself that is the fundamental systemic flaw, their ranks are growing.

For those who have been following developments closely, such as recent calls by senior economic officials in multiple countries that cash should be outright banned, it may still feel as if we are continuing to proceed down the "Road to Monetary Serfdom," to paraphrase Nobel laureate Friedrick von Hayek. However, ahead in that road lies a largely hidden, sudden curve: one that leads back along the well-established monetary cycle of history.

Revolutions represent historical tipping points: as with the road described above, their causes and effects are nonlinear. Each and every individual can make a difference, and the best way to start is to become informed. It is my great hope that all my readers, new and old, find that this book contributes to their understanding not only of the monetary cycle of history but the unique role that they each might be able to play within it. In the words of the revolutionary Karl Marx, "Philosophers have *interpreted* the world, in their various ways. The point, however, is to *change* it."

Introduction: Why a Gold Standard Lies in Our Future[4]

> "More and more people are asking if a gold standard will end the financial crisis in which we find ourselves. The question is not so much if it will help or if we will resort to gold, but when."
>
> — Congressman Ron Paul, Foreword to the Minority Report of the US Gold Commission, 1982

CONTRARY TO THE CONVENTIONAL WISDOM of the current economic mainstream that the gold standard is but a quaint historical anachronism, there has been an unceasing effort by prominent individuals in the US and a handful of other countries to try and reestablish a gold standard ever since President Nixon abruptly ended dollar-gold convertibility in August 1971. The US came particularly close to returning to a gold standard in the early 1980s. This was understandable following the disastrous "stagflation" of the 1970s and severe recession of the early 1980s, at that time the deepest since WWII. Indeed, Ronald Reagan campaigned on a platform that he would seriously study the possibility of returning to gold if elected president.

Once successfully elected, he remained true to his word and appointed a Gold Commission to explore both whether the US should, and how it might, reinstate a formal link between gold and the dollar. While the Commission's majority concluded that a return to gold was both

4 Although this is the original introduction from the 2012 edition of *The Golden Revolution*, it has been amended in order to refer briefly to the additional section and content included in *The Golden Revolution, Revisited*.

unnecessary and impractical—Fed Chairman Paul Volcker had successfully stabilized the dollar and brought inflation down dramatically by 1982—a minority found in favor of returning to gold and published their own report, "The Case for Gold," in 1982. Also around this time, in 1981, future Fed Chairman Alan Greenspan proposed the introduction of new US Treasury bonds backed by gold as a sensible way to nudge the US back toward an explicit gold link for the dollar at some point in future.

In the event, the once high-profile debate in the US about whether to return to gold eventually faded into relative obscurity. With brief exceptions, consumer price inflation trended lower in the 1980s and 1990s, restoring confidence in the dollar as a somewhat reliable store of value. By the 2000s, economists were talking about the "great moderation" in both inflation and the volatility of business cycles. The dollar had been generally strong versus other currencies for years. "Maestro" Alan Greenspan and his colleagues at the Fed and their counterparts in many central banks elsewhere in the world were admired for their apparent achievements.

We now know, of course, that this was all a mirage. The business cycle has returned with a vengeance with by far the deepest global recession since WWII, and the global financial system has been teetering on the edge of collapse off-and-on for several years. While consumer price inflation might be low in the developed economies of Europe, North America, and Japan, it has recently begun to creep higher, notwithstanding growth rates that are very weak in a historical comparison. Stagflation is returning and may well come to exceed that of the 1970s in size and scope before long.

The economic mainstream continues to struggle to understand just why they got it so wrong. They look for explanations in bank regulation and oversight, the growth of hedge funds and the so-called shadow banking system. They wonder how the US housing market could have possibly crashed to an extent greater than occurred even in the Great Depression. Some look to global capital flows for an answer, for example China's exchange rate policy. Where the mainstream generally fail to look, however, is at current global monetary regime itself. Could it be that the dollar-centric global monetary system is inherently unstable? Is our predicament today possibly a long-term consequence of President Nixon's fateful decision to "close the gold window" in 1971?

This book argues that it is. But it also goes farther. The unbacked dollar reserve standard has now done so much damage to the global financial system that it is beyond repair. The current global monetary regime is thus approaching a transformation that will carry it in some way back onto some form of global gold standard, in which monies, at least in official, international transactions, are linked to gold. This may seem a rather bold prediction, but it is not. The evidence has been accumulating for years and is now overwhelming.

Money can function as such only if there is sufficient trust in the monetary unit as a stable store of value. Lose this trust and that form of money will be abandoned, either suddenly in a crisis or gradually over time in favor of something else. History is replete with examples of "Gresham's Law" that "bad" money drives "good" money out of circulation, that is, that when faith in the stability of a money is lost, it may still be used in everyday transactions—in particular if it is the mandated legal tender—but not as a store of value. The "good" money is therefore hoarded as the superior store of value until such time as the "bad" money finally collapses entirely and a return to "good" money again becomes possible. This monetary cycle, from good to bad to good again, has been a central feature of history.

Most societies like to believe that they are somehow superior to those elsewhere or that have come before, although it is only natural that this assumption is called into question during difficult economic times. But there are some laws to history and one of them is that money not linked to some form of physical standard—most often but not always metals—is doomed to a short, ignominious existence. The historical record is crystal clear on this. All purely fiat currencies eventually fall to their intrinsic value of zero.

Why should this be? Is not the story of civilization the story of progress? I believe that it is, but within certain limits, as provided by human nature. We may be civilized, but we are also human. All of us experience feelings of fear and greed at times in our lives, perhaps with respect to our basic needs, wants, and desires or perhaps higher aspirations. There are those of us who might be overwhelmed by such feelings from time to time, those in power in particular, who tend consistently toward corruption regardless of whether they serve the public in a democracy or attempt to rule it in a dictatorship. One need look no farther than several modern, supposedly representative "democracies" now facing sovereign bankruptcy and default to see this potentially dark side of human nature in action.

To understand what is happening in the world of banking, finance, and economics today, please don't read an economics textbook full of equations or other mainstream, Neo-Keynesian claptrap. Read history instead. It may not necessarily repeat but it certainly rhymes. We are deep into a crisis of monetary confidence from which there is no escape without a return, one way or another, to a metallic money standard. The evidence is there for those who care to look. But few are prepared to countenance that some of the more painful lessons of history must be relearned in our time.

There has been much written about why the price of gold is moving higher and will continue to do so. It will. Probably much higher, when denominated in units of dying fiat currencies. But while this is certainly useful advice, it does not fully prepare the reader for the practical reality of the transition to the coming global gold standard, which is going to be substantially different from the fiat monetary and financial regime of today. It is not just money that is going to change. The nature and business of banking will change. So will finance in general. A gold standard will benefit certain industries, markets, and countries but be potentially harmful to others. It follows that investment strategy and asset allocation methodologies must adapt.

A new global gold standard is coming. It is only a matter of time and how orderly or disorderly the transition is. Those who are prepared will prosper or at a minimum protect their wealth during the potentially rough transition period and be ready for what comes next. Those who don't may lose entire fortunes built up with the hard work of several generations. The stakes are high and they are real. It is time for us to leave the false comfort of our fantasy fiat currency "wealth" behind and get on with the business of practical preparation for the inevitable. And don't expect our so-called leaders or representatives in government to help. They are more likely to obstruct than assist in this critically important task.

This book is divided into four sections. Section I examines the deleterious economic and social effects of unbacked, fiat money, in particular how it exacerbates inequality, with monetary inflation acting as a largely unseen, regressive tax falling disproportionately on the poor and, in the event they reside inside a welfare state financed through taxation, on the productive middle class.

The second expands on the points made here regarding why the world is headed inexorably back onto some sort of gold standard. It explores just why the fiat-dollar standard was always potentially unstable and how the seeds of its demise were sowed many years ago, unseen by the economic mainstream. It then demonstrates how recent events, interpreted through the lens of the "monetary cycle of history," imply that a return to gold is not only inevitable, but imminent.

Section III considers what the transition period might look like, including some historical examples of both orderly and disorderly monetary regime changes as well as provocative, hypothetical ones. History provides a rough guide for what to expect, to be sure, although we must give due consideration to the specific structure of contemporary international politics, including major geopolitical rivalries. In this section, we also consider how much the gold price is likely to rise as it becomes remonetized. Finally, Section III takes a look at recent innovations in money and payments technology, including bitcoin and other so-called cryptocurrencies and various other ways in which FinTech firms are seeking to disrupt and disintermediate key aspects of the banking and payments systems. It then concludes with a discussion of how FinTech may also facilitate the spontaneous remonetization of gold.

Section IV explores how the world of banking, finance, and investment will change under a future, technologically advanced gold standard, which industries, countries, and markets are likely to benefit, and which are likely to suffer. Further, it looks at the implications for practical investment strategy and asset valuation. By fundamentally changing the very foundation of the global monetary order, the return to gold will affect interest and exchange rates, yield curves, corporate credit spreads, equity valuations, and the volatilities of all of the above.

The book concludes with a few thoughts on how the future gold standard will impact society more generally. It is this author's strong opinion that a world that has returned to a gold standard will be a far, far more pleasant, productive, peaceful, stable, and moral place than that which we for a time allowed ourselves to be deluded into believing was, in certain respects, the best of all possible worlds. After all, they don't call particularly prosperous historical episodes "Golden Ages" for nothing.

Section I:
The Monetary Sources of Economic Inequality

> "On Thursday [Sept 15, 2008] at roughly 11am the Federal Reserve noticed a tremendous draw-down of money market accounts in the US to the tune of $550 billion dollars being drawn out in a matter of an hour or two. The Treasury opened up its window to help and pumped $105 billion into the system but quickly realized they could not stem the tide. We were having an electronic run on the banks... They decided to announce a guarantee of $250,000 per account so there wouldn't be further panic. Had they not done that their estimation was that by 2pm that afternoon $5.5 trillion would have been withdrawn from the US, would have collapsed the entire economy of the US and within 24 hours the world economy."
>
> – US Rep Paul Kanjorski, C-SPAN interview, 2009

2008: A CRASH COURSE IN MONEY

IN NOVEMBER 2008, FOLLOWING THE collapse of the investment bank Lehman Brothers, there was an unprecedented run on US money-market funds. Frightened that these funds would "break the buck"—fall below par value—due to their extensive holdings of Lehman's and other financial institutions' commercial paper and other debt, investors rushed to liquidate and move their holdings into FDIC-insured bank deposits or even safer US Treasury securities. The result was a near-collapse of the so-called shadow banking system and, were that to have occurred, many believe a general run on the conventional commercial banking system would have followed in short order.

Amid such uncertainty, for the first time since the 1930s, the American public was forced to contemplate what, exactly, money was. After all, although it contained the name, and you could write checks on it, was a money-market mutual fund account really "money"? Or was it merely masquerading as money, concealing previously overlooked credit and counterparty risks? Was an uninsured deposit at a bank potentially at risk of failure "money"? Were multiple large commercial banks to have failed and FDIC funds thus to have been depleted, were even guaranteed deposits "money"? Finally, although few may have asked themselves these next two questions, were the banking system to collapse entirely, would even the US Treasury have been able to continue making payments to holders of Treasury securities? Could the dollar itself have collapsed, rendering even physical cash worthless? To paraphrase the now legendary Star Wars character, Jedi Knight Obi Wan Kenobi, it was as if millions cried out in terror, "What is money!?" and then were suddenly silent, because they didn't have an answer.

For a period spanning from the 1940s to November 2008, most of the US public took the concept of "money" more or less for granted. It was the paper dollars you used to make purchases, or at least it was the basis for purchases, say by writing a check or by using a credit card, and if you had a lot of dollars, well, then, you were wealthy. Indeed, many considered "money" and "wealth" to be the same thing.

In those dark days of November 2008, however, they were anything but the same. The monetary officials at the Federal Reserve didn't exactly help to clarify matters either. They rolled out several emergency lending and liquidity facilities with acronym names such as TALF to inject liquidity into the financial system and eventually TARP to provide banks with wholesale, taxpayer-funded relief from their bad assets. The monetary result of these and other bail-out programs was to create a huge, unprecedented amount of "excess reserves" in the banking system. This liquidity, these excess reserves, are defined as "money" by the Federal Reserve and are thus included in the official US money supply data. But are they really fungible "money" that could, for example, be used to make purchases (as with a medium of exchange)? That someone would consider as a source of "wealth"? No, to call the purely electronic, zero-velocity excess reserves "money" only obfuscates the matter of what money really is even further.

A frightened and increasingly confused public was thus receiving an unexpected and unwelcome crash course in learning what money was, or was not, and were taking matters into their own hands by moving their money from forms that were discovered to be relatively unsafe (e.g. money market funds) to those thought to be relatively safer (e.g. guaranteed bank deposits, Treasury securities, physical cash). In doing so, their actions were making a bad financial liquidity situation worse, as this caused a sharp contraction in the broad money supply that stands behind the commercial lending activities undertaken by shadow- and nonshadow financial intermediaries alike, thereby forcing asset liquidations and escalating the systemic risk so feared by the Federal Reserve.

If public perceptions of safety matter so crucially as to what can be properly understood as "money," and if sudden changes in those perceptions can have a huge impact on the broad money supply, does this help us to answer the question, "What is money?"

Defining money

Let's start with some definitions. Money is generally defined as that which serves as one or more of the following:

1. A medium of exchange
2. A store of wealth
3. A unit of account

In a modern economy, money serves in all three roles and we don't normally consciously consider which of these three our money is carrying out at any one particular point in time. However, it is worth considering that there is a hierarchy in the above roles, that is, that people will most probably resist or refuse to use a medium of exchange that does not function as a reliable store of value. After all, why accept that which is expected to depreciate rapidly in value? (This is one reason why economists generally agree that high rates of inflation are economically destructive, in that they inject a large amount of risk into ordinary, day-to-day transactions, making rational, efficient economic calculation all but impossible.) If a given money is not considered sufficiently safe, as per the discussion above, then it will struggle to meet a strict definition of money. It becomes unclear just what money is when it can vaporize in a bank account or be arbitrarily devalued or defaulted on by the issuing government or other authority. November 2008 illustrates the point, as does 1931–33, when US banks were failing by the hundreds as depositors rushed to withdraw not only their banknotes, but physical gold as well. (Most recently, the Indian government summarily and arbitrarily declared high-value banknotes invalid, igniting monetary chaos.)

The unit of account function, to complete the definition of money, is not strictly necessary, but rather a matter of convenience. In theory, we could all choose to translate our accounts into how many loaves of bread we could purchase; how many months of living expenses we have saved up; or how many years of retirement we can afford. Younger folks might measure their savings in terms of nights out on the town. The fact that people choose instead to maintain their accounts in the legal tender is that it is simply easier that way. There is the notable exception, however, that when an individual, small business, or corporation is preparing their taxes or engaging in other official transactions with a public agency, they are required to use the legal tender as the unit of account.

This traditional definition of money in terms of the roles it plays, which in turn requires a high perceived degree of safety, as shown above, overlooks entirely another way to understand money, however, one that is explored at length by the philosopher and information theorist George Gilder. Money's role ultimately reduces, he explains, to that of a conduit for information. Prices are the essential information that allows a market-based economy to work. As he writes in his 2014 book, *Knowledge and Power*, "Capitalism is not primarily an incentive system but an information system."[1] The single most important form of

1 George Gilder, *Knowledge and Power* (Regnery: 2013).

information, he argues, is prices, and the numerator of all prices is, of course, units of money.

This insight has profound economic and social implications. For if information flows efficiently, an economy can function efficiently, thereby serving society. But if the information is somehow distorted or otherwise flawed, it implies an inefficient, substandard economy that can fail in various ways to serve the society as it should. At worst, if the flow of information basically stops due to a monetary crisis, the economy stops. This is being observed to some extent today in Venezuela and, in recent years past, in Zimbabwe, Argentina, much of Eastern Europe, and the former Soviet states. Post WWI there was a general monetary crisis that spread across most of the European continent, with similar consequences. (The Indian economy may also soon seize up entirely if the current monetary chaos caused by Prime Minister Modi's sudden "demonetization" policies continues.)

In November 2008, the US public suddenly became aware that the money machine, long believed to more or less run itself with a little help from the Federal Reserve, could suddenly stop. In the scramble for safety, the public relearned a little about what money really is. It is a great irony that in a supposedly open, transparent, mature free-market economy an improvement in the public understanding of money became an immediate, grave threat to the very system that money was intended to serve: for it is money that should serve society, not the other way around.

The role of money in society

That money should serve society seems an obvious point, yet one that is far from clear amid sustained unconventional monetary policy and the associated zero or even negative interest rates that penalize prudent savers while encouraging imprudent speculators. The year 2008 may have lifted one veil on money. This book lifts the rest: not only what money is but how it is created and used in practice and to what extent it does, or does not, serve the economy and by extension society at large. I will show that the way in which the monetary system currently operates is the single most important source of rising economic inequality in both the US and around the world. Furthermore, I will demonstrate that the current system is one in which money can continue to function—and even then suboptimally—only to the extent and as long as the public remains mostly ignorant as to what our modern money really is and how the financial system really works.

Such a confidence charade implies an unstable monetary system. Unstable systems are subject to large systemic risks, regime shifts, restructuring, and reformation. Applying game theory to the current, unstable global monetary equilibrium implies that some variation of a fundamental monetary crisis lies in our future, most probably our near future, and quite probably on a scale larger than that which hit in 2008.

Fortunately, this is likely to catalyze a restructuring and reforming of the current, highly suboptimal monetary order. When combined with relatively recent, historical strides in financial technology, this will pave the way toward a far superior monetary system, one in which money serves as a source of economic stability, confidence, and resilience, rather than the opposite. This future monetary system will also reverse the multidecade trend toward economic inequality, increasing the earnings potential of labor-based incomes relative to those that are capital based.

What many claim is an inexorable trend toward inequality—perhaps one endemic to capitalism, or to associated technological advancement such as robotics—is in fact nothing more than a huge, historically unprecedented economic imbalance in disguise, financed by massive, misallocated debts atop a misunderstood, fragile, and now failing monetary system. Imbalances are by definition unsustainable in the long run, and the only way to resolve and rebalance this particular one is for financial assets (capital) to decline sharply in value relative to wages (labor).

In this section, I explain why this is so. In subsequent sections, we then explore how this change will come about, why gold will be at least partially remonetized in the process, and the general economic and financial implications thereof. In doing so, I will also demonstrate how new, nonbank payment technologies will play a key role in all of the above and remain central to the further evolution of money in future. Finally, I will conclude with some thoughts on the salutary social impact of a restoration of stable money, including higher rates of economic growth and the myriad benefits of greater economic balance within and between countries around the world.

Chapter 1: On the Misunderstanding of Money

"[Adam] Smith, far from being the founder of economics, was virtually the reverse. On the contrary, Smith actually took the sound, and almost fully developed subjective value tradition, and tragically shunted economics on to a false path, a dead end."

—Murray Rothbard

"Money is gold and nothing else."

—JP Morgan

For something used nearly every day by nearly every person on the planet, money is much misunderstood. Yet it is arguably the single greatest invention of civilization. Indeed, one could plausibly claim that without at least some form of money, however primitive, civilization becomes impossible. For without some means to avoid direct barter in economic transactions, there is simply no way to divide up labor and capital beyond the close social ties of the family, extended family, or tribe. Without an extensive division of labor and capital, insufficient specialization of both precludes the ability to form the larger social units required to organize towns, cities, countries, empires, and their respective governing institutions. Even if we are to allow for at least the possibility that primitive civilizations could exist absent money, they would almost certainly remain confined to a stone-age level of organization.

Indeed, the history of all the great civilizations, and right up to the present day, is to a necessary extent a history of money. The Sumerians, arguably the oldest of old, invented a monetary unit based on a ration of wheat or barley, the shekel, and specified a corresponding weight of silver to provide the unit of account and serve as the *de facto* monetary base. The Lydians of Asia Minor invented modern coinage, later adopted by the highly commercial Athenians and thereby spread throughout the Hellenistic world. The Roman golden *solidi* and silver *denarii* would in time displace Athenian coinage, until their gradual, multicentury debasement resulted in their own displacement by the Byzantine *solidi,* or *bezants* as they were known in western Europe.[2]

Around the time of the fall of Byzantium in 1453, out of the ruins of the western Roman Empire, arose the great Renaissance. At first Portugal, then Spain, France, the Netherlands, and finally Great Britain provided the bulk of the coinage that would dominate in international commerce and serve as reserves in the relatively simple banking systems of the time. Innumerable local, domestic coins would circulate alongside and be changed and exchanged by weight and purity as required to facilitate local commerce. One silver coin in particular, the "thaler" of Bohemia, would provide the name basis for the Spanish "dolar" or "piece of eight." The United States would adopt this particular silver coin, or at least the specific weight thereof, as the basis for the first official US federal money in the Coinage Act of 1792, which also monetized gold at a ratio of 15:1 vs. silver by weight.

Notwithstanding periodic experiments with paper money and occasional modifications to its coinage, the US would remain on a

2 The common usage of silver as a medium of exchange in the ancient world should on no account eclipse the important role played by gold as a store of value. While it was not as common for gold to circulate as widely, this was most probably due to gold being held overwhelmingly by the wealthy and powerful. In the case of Sumeria, the silver shekel was also defined in terms of the mina (or mené), a specified weight of gold, implying that gold, not silver, was quite likely the ultimate money.

metallic monetary system of some sort until 1971, when by executive order President Nixon brought this convention to an abrupt end in arguably unconstitutional fashion, transforming the dollar into an unbacked fiat currency. (Switzerland would become the last country to formally sever the link between its national currency and gold in 1994.)

Confusing money with debt

The history of money is not only a history of coinage, however. It is also a history of bills, banknotes, and other forms of coinage receipts, which frequently circulated alongside actual coins. As these were explicit claims on coins (or bars) held in a secure vault and available on demand, these did not represent debt but rather alternative, more convenient forms of money, fully backed by actual money—gold or silver most commonly—held in, say, a bank or private vault.

The history of money is, however, intertwined with a history of debt. Indeed, it can be argued that money is simply debt with a zero maturity, one that is simultaneously originated and liquidated at the same moment, as an exchange takes place—when the exchange is agreed, the debt is originated. When the money changes hands, the debt is extinguished. (As the origination and liquidation occur essentially simultaneously this could also be thought of as taking place in reverse order.) But if there is an interim period during which money is not immediately exchanged for goods or services rendered, then a debt remains outstanding, denominated in the monetary unit and perhaps one accruing interest over time.

The topic of debt can lead to potential confusion around money. This is because debts can circulate at a discount to actual money as money substitutes. The size of the discount imputes a rate of interest on the debt. The rate of interest carries with it two components: time value and credit risk. The former is based on the economic concept of "time preference," that consuming goods or services today is always preferable, if only at the margin, to consuming them at some point in the future.

Hence, the rate of interest is naturally positive, if perhaps approaching zero under certain circumstances. (It would be wholly unnatural for the time value of money to be outright negative due to the immutable Second Law of Thermodynamics, entropy. Ask a physicist.)

Credit risk is some estimation of the probability that the lender will not be paid back in full, if at all, when the payment comes due. The higher the perceived credit risk, the higher the interest rate. Other factors equal, credit risk also increases with time, but this should not be confused with the pure time value of money. Rather, it is due to the uncertainty of repayment, which normally grows ever higher as maturities increase. Even the most creditworthy of borrowers tend to have a life span of no more than several hundred years.

Although they might originate out of the same social evolutionary processes, money and debt are nevertheless different. Debt is first originated in exchange for money and is subsequently settled when the principal and interest are repaid under terms of the contract. Money itself bears no interest as it represents the final settlement and any associated claims of either a liquidation of debt, or an exchange of goods. The relationship between money and debt can, however, lead to much confusion, for example, in David Graeber's best-selling book *Debt, the First 5,000 Years.*

Graeber makes some bold claims in his book that on close inspection do not hold up to scrutiny. The one that I will address here is that in the history of civilization, the use of debt long preceded the use of money and that direct barter was, in fact, uncommon. In Graeber's view, debt provided the basis of primitive, altruistic, "gift-based" economies in which favors given at one point in time are subsequently returned at a future point in time, and that the exchange of such "gifts" formed the transactional basis of the ancient civilizations, beginning with ancient Sumeria. While direct barter may still have taken place—it is impossible after all to prove a negative—Graeber claims that it played a relatively minor role, and money arrived on the human scene much later not as a substitute for barter but as a substitute for debt.

Now, I am no anthropologist and I would not presume to question Graeber's observations, only his interpretations and conclusions so following. For example, Graeber observes that in the ancient Sumerian economy bushels of wheat or barley in fixed amounts ("shekels") were exchanged for "gifts" of various kinds, rather than for any actual money. The value of the shekel was, however, linked to an amount of silver, which was stored in the temples and did not itself circulate domestically. But rather than imply a nonmonetary economy this is in fact strong evidence that a relatively fixed amount of silver reserves provided the *de facto* Sumerian monetary base, even if the circulating medium of exchange happened to be that of the bushels themselves.

This is no different in principle to a system of circulating silver-backed banknotes, although banknotes are not necessarily self-liquidating, as with bushels. But as the bushels are constantly being produced into and then consumed out of existence, the "money" supply can therefore be considered essentially stable, when adjusted for the natural seasonality. In any event, the silver provides the monetary base and a specified weight of silver—also known as a shekel—functioned as the official government unit of account, including for use in calculating taxes. The taxes were then also generally paid in bushels—the medium of exchange—but this remains at base a silver-backed monetary system, not one based on gifts or other unsecured debt, although Graeber so claims.

Another important point Graeber makes about primitive commerce is that whereas within a given civilization, what he calls "debt" is used in exchange, when trading with foreigners, actual money frequently trades hands. In the case of the Sumerians, this would mean that in trade with non-Sumerians, not only might bushels be exchanged, but the silver itself. Now, as the silver was held at the temples, then presumably such trade would be primarily official in nature and thus quite possibly for relatively large sums. But that does not in any way diminish the importance of silver backing the domestic money as the ultimate form of settlement. Nor does it support Graeber's claims that "debt" rather than money was the basis for trade. Indeed, foreign trade might have been of great importance at times. But it is understandable why foreigners, operating outside the Sumerian legal system and possibly within quite different social customs, would not trust a "gift"—an offer of credit—from the Sumerians in exchange for goods. Nor should the Sumerians have been expected to trust in foreigners' credit, for the same reasons.

This is an absolutely essential point: real money does not require a third party to verify it and enforce its use and value. It has what is frequently called intrinsic value, that is, value independent of any official agency or specific legal system. However, money substitutes do require some form of third-party verification for acceptance. Debt not only requires such verification but even the reverse, in that debt contracts must not only be verifiable but enforceable by law, or they become worthless.

Graeber's anthropological evidence is clear: where trust is lacking, such as at the international level, real money trumps debt. The implications of how foreign trade ultimately relies on monetary (silver) exchange, or possibly direct barter, rather than on the origination and liquidation of debt will be explored in a more contemporary context in our discussion of international monetary relations and game theory in Section III.

The classical economic view on money

Since antiquity, theologians and philosophers have pondered certain basic elements of what is today defined as "economics." The systematic study of economics, however, only really got going in the 1700s, and is referred to as "classical economics." Adam Smith is considered the father of classical economics due to the tremendous influence of his primary work on the subject, *The Wealth of Nations*. His eloquent presentation of many basic principles of economics, such as the productive power of the division of labor and capital, the self-regulating role of the marketplace—the fabled "invisible hand"—and the benefits of free trade, have rightly earned him a prominent place in the history of economic thought. That said, Smith's thoughts on money, as presented in *The Wealth of Nations*, are relatively simplistic and dangerously misleading.

In contrast to Graeber's revisionist view, Smith was of the belief that the use of money did indeed originate as an alternative to barter, rather than as an alternative to debt. Smith argued that barter was cumbersome and did not allow for much specialization and hence division of labor and capital. The use of money was, therefore, essential to economic progress and to growing the wealth of nations, which for Smith meant total productive potential rather than mere acquisition of specie reserves in the Treasury. He also held that for money to be useful it should be sound, which in his day meant that it had to be something tangible rather than just paper promises to pay (IOUs). He thus also argued against the debasement of money, something that he associated with the rampant, nationalistic mercantilism of the day and that he believed interfered with free and fair trade between and within nations, hence impeding economic progress and wealth creation generally.

Smith's observations above certainly seem reasonable enough and, for the most part, have stood the test of time. But the reader of *The Wealth of Nations* is almost left with the impression that Smith would prefer not to analyze money in much detail. For example, he does not distinguish clearly between the money supply provided by specie and that provided by circulating banknotes, or "real bills"—receipts for circulating goods. To Smith, as these forms of money and money substitutes are all fungible, they are all basically the same in their economic purpose and effects. But surely they are not the same—a claim on specie is not the same as specie itself. This is especially the case in the event that the circulating notes or bills are not 100 percent reserved by the issuer(s). Smith did not perceive, or if he did he failed to mention, that in the circulation of fractionally reserved bills and notes there existed the possibility for pernicious monetary inflation, or for credit risk to creep into the financial system, thereby destabilizing and undermining commerce.

Smith had an equally simplistic understanding of credit and interest, although he understood intuitively that the rate of interest must be linked in some way to the productivity of capital. How else could debt be serviced at a given interest rate, if the capital stock were not sufficiently productive to generate the necessary interest income? As capital productivity increased, so did the rate of interest, and vice versa. The same relationship also held for land and rents. For Smith, the "invisible hand" was just as much at work in matters of credit, interest, and rent as it was in the marketplace for goods. (As a professor of moral philosophy and as a deeply religious Scottish Presbyterian, Smith did support usury laws prohibiting lending to the poor at what he considered to be extortionate rates of interest. In general, however, he had no problem with a free market in credit and interest.)

Unsurprisingly, Smith's somewhat simplistic understanding of money is not considered among his more notable achievements. But it is surprising indeed why this is so. Smith was a close friend of fellow philosopher David Hume, whose price-specie-flow mechanism was a notable step in the development of the historically prominent quantity theory of money. Moreover, Smith cites the work of Richard Cantillon, some of which he borrows nearly verbatim. Yet he essentially ignores Cantillon's comparatively sophisticated views on money, which we will examine in some detail later. Finally, and most surprising of all, in *The Wealth of Nations* Smith fails to include even his own monetary theories in detail, even though these had formed the basis of his previous, documented lectures on money at the University of Glasgow![3]

One possible explanation for Smith's facile treatment of money in his magnum opus is that, at time of writing, there was a major academic and even political dispute regarding the relatively new institution of fractional-reserve banking—regulated with disputed success by the Bank of England—and the wide circulation of banknotes that were

3 Murray Rothbard, *An Austrian Perspective on the History of Economic Thought, vol. II* (Mises Institute: 1995).

claims, albeit unallocated, on specie. Smith may have determined that it was best to present an essentially neutral position on the matter, given that the primary purpose of *The Wealth of Nations* was to discredit the mercantilists, not to advance any specific monetary theory or take sides in what Smith might have regarded as a relatively unimportant matter.

Regardless, notwithstanding the sheer size and scope of *The Wealth of Nations*, Smith had little to say about money, credit, and interest. His successors, including the flamboyant businessman David Ricardo, did attempt to build on his limited insights. But they did so within a monetary framework which was, for those who put so much faith in the "invisible hand" of the dynamic, free marketplace, surprisingly rigid and mechanical. It is as if Smith and his classical successors shared his somewhat puritanical moral sentiments about what money should be—a fair and neutral mechanism for the distribution of economic goods—and allowed this to skew their conclusions about how money in fact functions in the economy and the hidden or not so hidden dangers of monetary inflation and fractional reserve banking.

The quantity theory of money

Although one can trace its antecedents back to ancient times, the modern Quantity Theory of Money (henceforth QTM) was developed during the enlightenment by David Hume and John Stuart Mill. The equation MV = PQ, is the classical expression of a mechanistic monetary framework based on the QTM. By way of explanation:

M = the money stock

V = the "velocity" of money, that is, how many times it changes hands in a given period

P = the price level

Q = economic output

According to the quantity theory, increases in the money stock pass through more or less mechanically and neutrally into the general price level. As for more sophisticated variations, a money injection will first increase Q, the quantity of economic output, but this is due only to so-called money illusion, that is, the misperception that increased nominal demand, following from the increase in the money supply, is in fact increased real, sustainable demand. Once the money injection has run its course, however, real demand slips right back to where it was, with real output unchanged and the price level simply higher to reflect the net increase in the money supply (i.e. more money chasing the same amount of goods).

Note, however, that nowhere in the discussion above does velocity—the circulation rate of money—explicitly enter the picture. Sure, it figures in the equation above, but it does not play an active role; it remains a constant. There is a reason for this: attempts to model changes in the velocity of money have never borne much fruit. This is due perhaps to the highly capricious nature of money demand through history. Occasionally it moves higher, occasionally lower. Abrupt shifts happen from time to time. Sometimes these are so abrupt they defy any rational economic explanation at all.

Take for example the great German Weimar hyperinflation of 1922–23. Yes, money velocity had been on the increase in 1922, but for reasons that may remain forever unknown in their exact specifics, something snapped in 1923 and what had been a gently rising price level suddenly phase-transitioned into a "get rid of money at all costs; buy and hoard anything not bolted down" mentality. Money velocity soared. Germans suddenly began to dump money in exchange for any and all real goods and eschew holding cash balances. This withholding of goods from circulation—a negative supply shock—locked the economy into a self-fulfilling vicious cycle of rising prices and an associated further decline in productive economic output. To use an astronomical metaphor, it was as if the economy had passed the monetary event horizon from which there was no escape from total collapse. Bartering with real goods—including silver and gold but more commonly bread, eggs, milk, or cheese—became the norm.[4]

The Weimar experience eludes any attempt to model what precisely caused the abrupt shift in the velocity of money. Nobel laureate John Sargent once published a paper examining various hyperinflations in history and concluded that there was simply no way in which the quantity theory MV = PQ framework could even begin to explain either how they began or how they ended.[5] What did explain them, he found, were significant, qualitative changes in the composition of the government and the associated impact on fiscal policies and expectations thereof. That is, when a government lost fiscal credibility in the eyes of the public, hyperinflations began. When a new government with sufficient fiscal credibility arrived on the scene, hyperinflations ended.

While this is perhaps an entirely correct assessment, it is a deeply unsatisfying one from the perspective of the modern economics profession, which prefers and purports to be able to model any and all significant economic phenomena according to some equation or set of equations. Those phenomena that do not fit into equations are generally just dismissed from the data set entirely as aberrations, as freak events, as historical developments that are so unlikely to be repeated that it is not worth bothering thinking about them much.

This procrustean academic mentality, that that which does not fit neatly into equations should simply be cut off from the discipline, smacks of the faith-based, "paradigmatic" thinking that Thomas Kuhn disparages in his seminal history of science, *The Structure of Scientific Revolutions*. It is narrow, shallow, and downright dangerous when such thinking informs economic policy, especially at a time when debt levels, economic leverage, and imbalances are all at record levels

4 The economic and broader social aspects of the Weimar collapse receive a most compelling treatment in Adam Fergusson's modern classic, *When Money Dies.*

5 Thomas Sargent, "The Ends of Four Big Inflations," in Robert Hall, ed., *Inflation Causes and Effects* (University of Chicago Press, 1982).

relative to incomes. The risk of a phase transition from a stable to unstable monetary order is clearly high at present, and just because there is no precise way to model the pure uncertainties around just how this could happen does not at all imply that we should not try to consider what the consequences are likely to be, the focus of sections III and IV of this book.

Milton Friedman and the Monetarist "Chicago School"

Regardless of the QTM's obvious shortcomings, this mechanistic, quantity-based approach to modeling money was rebranded, revitalized, and expanded to inform economic theory more generally by Milton Friedman and his fellow "Chicago School" Monetarists of the mid-twentieth century, who reminded the then Keynesian-dominated economics profession that "Inflation is, always and everywhere, a monetary phenomenon." Yes, velocity might be a capricious factor evading attempts to capture it in equations. Yes, prices might also be "sticky," as the Keynesians alleged. And yes, economies do have their other rigidities and imperfections, but to the Monetarists, traditional Keynesian aggregate demand management was so demonstrably unworkable and potentially counterproductive that some other basis must be found to nudge an economy toward equilibrium when necessary.

For the Monetarists, the ideal way to manage an economy was to allow money to fulfill its central, essential function as a source of stability. The growth of the supply of money need only be held more or less constant at a rate commensurate with potential output growth and all other things will, in one way or another, sort themselves out in time. Independent, wise, and capable central bankers, as guardians of the money supply, could ensure that economic cycles were generally smooth and that growth could reach its potential, whatever it was, through some form of monetary targeting. In the event that an economy was to slip into a so-called liquidity trap or other state of structural disequilibrium, there was, somewhere to be found, a workable if possibly radical monetary solution.

Recent attempts to find monetary solutions to perceived disequilibria abound. Since 2008 we have observed a range of monetary experiments ranging from negative real (i.e. inflation-adjusted) interest rates; zero rates; negative rates; quantitative easing; long-dated asset purchases; and purchases of corporate and mortgage securities in addition to government bills or debt. Japan, of course, has been on the search for alternative monetary solutions for a good while longer, with clearly limited if any success.

Indeed, it is fair at this point to pose the question as to whether there exists any workable monetary solution to the general problem of excessive debt and economic leverage at all. But if there is not, then the Monetarists are wrong. If the Monetarists are wrong, then the modern economics profession's understanding of money is wrong. Could it be that, somewhere along the way, perhaps to avoid the uncomfortable difficulties of modeling money velocity and demand, some false assumptions were absorbed into the economic mainstream? Let's look for an answer to this question by going way back, to the preclassical economist mentioned earlier, Richard Cantillon.

The (mostly) forgotten monetary theories of Richard Cantillon

While it is lamentable that Adam Smith failed to incorporate Richard Cantillon's sophisticated monetary theories, it is downright curious that his twentieth-century successors, the Monetarists, have also done so. I have speculated as to the explanation for Smith's neglect. It could be that he simply wasn't interested in the subtle, monetary aspects of economics and chose to prioritize those topics that he believed had a more direct and obvious role in determining the wealth of nations, such as the division of labor and capital. But as the Monetarists have always focused predominantly on money, one would have thought that they would have sought out preclassical works on monetary theory, including that of Cantillon.

The Monetarists also rose to prominence well after economist William Jevons had rediscovered and popularized Cantillon's work in the late nineteenth century. Thus, they should have given him far more serious consideration. That they did not is most unfortunate, because the fact is that, far from holding a simplistic, mechanistic view on money, Cantillon saw it as a dynamic force and potentially damaging source of economic turbulence. Indeed, Cantillon's theories arose largely out of the great French inflation associated with the disastrous monetary policies implemented by John Law.

Given that Cantillon's monetary theories were based in large part on his direct observations of the broad economic effects of John Laws's money injections, perhaps we should not be so surprised to make similar if less obvious or self-evident observations amid the generally inflationist monetary policies in place today. Correlation is not causation, to be sure, but there is certainly enough accumulated circumstantial evidence to form a credible hypothesis. Unfortunately, in the social sciences, including economics, properly controlled experiments are not possible. However, as we delve deeper into the work that has been done on understanding and analyzing Cantillon effects, we shall see that there is strong theoretical support for certain historical developments, including those of today, that might be dismissed by some as mere coincidence.

John Law is one of the more colorful characters in the long (and occasionally rather sordid) history of monetary policy. By all accounts, Law was a genius. He could calculate large sums in his head, including the probability calculations required to win at gambling. Something of a ladies' man as well, in 1694 Law found himself engaged in a duel over a young lady and although he won, he also killed his opponent in the process and found himself temporarily imprisoned. As was not uncommon at the time, some of Law's family relations apparently offered a bribe to secure his release, and Law then escaped English jurisdiction, at first fleeing to Amsterdam and then on to Scotland.

While in Scotland, Law published a paper on money and proposed the creation of a Scottish national or central bank. Although this proposal was rejected it raised his profile, including in France, where he eventually settled. In 1716 he made a similar proposal to the *Banque Generale*, the Bourbons' bank. The plan for the bank included the issuance of currency that was nominally backed by gold, but in fact only fractionally reserved. This allowed for the bank to operate with enormous leverage, lending out large sums to state monopoly companies, including the Mississippi company operating in the New World.

Due to his growing involvement in both domestic and international financial activities, in 1720 state regent Phillipe of Orleans appointed Law the Controller General, giving him effective control not only over banking and currency policy but also state finances generally. This dual role of being both head of the Treasury and of the de facto central bank allowed Law to fully indulge and implement his plans for a financial system of paper currency, backed by credit, and fractionally reserved banking. The associated, huge expansion in the supply of both money and credit facilitated a huge boom, as documented here by the New York Federal Reserve:

> In 1719, the French government allowed Law to issue 50,000 new shares in the Mississippi Company at 500 livres with just 75 livres down and the rest due in nineteen additional monthly payments of 25 livres each. The share price rose to 1,000 livres before the second installment was even due, and ordinary citizens flocked to Paris to participate. Based on this success, Law offered to pay off the national debt of 1.5 billion livres by issuing an additional 300,000 shares at 500 livres paid in ten monthly installments.

> By mid-1719, the Mississippi Company had issued more than 600,000 shares, and the par value of the company stood at 300 million livres. That summer, the share price skyrocketed from 1,000 to 5,000 livres and it continued to rise through year-end, ultimately reaching dizzying heights of 15,000 livres per share. The word *millionaire* was first used, and in January 1720 Law was appointed Controller General.

Everything seemed to be going just fine. But as with all such booms, the rise in asset prices, in order to continue, needs a constant supply of new money and credit. It is not clear whether Law understood this. Regardless,

> ...in early 1720 some depositors at Banque Generale began to exchange Mississippi Company shares for gold coin. In response, Law passed edicts in early 1720 to limit the use of coin. Around the same time, to help support the Mississippi Company share price, Law agreed to buy back Mississippi Company stock with banknotes at a premium to market price and, to his surprise, more shareholders than anticipated queued up to do so. To support the stock redemptions, Law needed to print more money and broke the link to gold, which quickly led to hyperinflation.
>
> The spillover to the economy was immediate and most notable in food prices. By May 21 (1720), Law was forced to deflate the value of banknotes and cut the stock price. As the public rushed to convert banknotes to coin, Law was forced to close Banque Generale for ten days, then limit the transaction size once the bank reopened. But the queues grew longer, the Mississippi Company

> stock price continued to fall, and food prices soared by as much as 60 percent.[6]

In a final, desperate attempt to salvage what was left of his schemes, Law criminalized the sale of gold in hope of stabilizing the value of the currency. When that didn't work, he attempted to criminalize the very ownership of gold itself, something that would not have been enforceable without turning France into a police state. As the pathology of Law's program became ever more apparent to the Duke of Orleans and his advisors, they finally moved to shut it down.

Notice this particular sequence of events as they play out above. At first, fueled by new money and the associated credit expansion, share prices soar. Thereafter, once the money and credit spigot is turned off, the bubble begins to collapse as those who had profited from the share appreciation seek to cash out. But they don't just cash out into cash. The wealthy are generally somewhat clever in managing their financial affairs and, knowing full well that the system was fractionally reserved, they cash out for gold instead.

Law is now trapped. He attempts to salvage his failing monetary and banking system by breaking the link to gold, but, having now made this explicit, even the poor now lose confidence in the unbacked fiat currency as a store of value and they dump it for food, clothing, and shelter—for anything of tangible value. But as the poor were on the final receiving end of the new money, rather than the initial injection, they end up even poorer than before in effective purchasing power terms. The wealthy, by contrast, had the opportunity to grow their wealth, if only temporarily. And they also had the option, while the boom was underway, of taking profits by cashing out and moving into gold, as some of them chose to do early in 1720.

---

6 James Narron and David Skeie, "Crisis Chronicles: The Mississippi Bubble of 1720 and the European Debt Crisis," New York Federal Reserve, 10 January 2014.

When the smoke cleared from the economic rubble, a handful of wealthy people had become wealthier still, a vast number of ordinary people had become impoverished, and a good number of the already impoverished had become even more so. Law, in the meantime, had fled France, in the middle of the night, for fear of his life. He took up gambling with his own money, rather than that of other people, and due to his undoubted intelligence made a modest living. Yet he died in relatively poor circumstances, absent family or friends, in Venice in 1729.

John Law was more than just a colorful character; he was in fact way ahead of his time. Indeed, he conceived in some detail the modern monetary structure most take for granted today: a sole, central bank as money issuer; money backed by debt rather than a tangible commodity; fractionally reserved banking; and the highly flexible, at times aggressive, use of all the above to stimulate an economic boom through financial speculation, with apparent benefits at first, only to be followed by an inevitable market crash and economic bust. While they might not consider things in quite this way, Greenspan, Bernanke, Yellen, and their colleagues and counterparts in the US and abroad are all monetary practitioners in the Law tradition. We have experienced their booms and busts on prior occasions. It is highly likely that, as long as the current monetary policy regime so continues, we will experience them again.

Living as we are in an age of banking and financial crises, Cantillon's monetary insights are worthy of fresh consideration. Moreover, Cantillon's remarkably advanced monetary theories also include a compelling explanation of how monetary policies can contribute, if in mostly subtle, unseen ways, to growing wealth inequality over time. Indeed, a thorough exploration of his insights is essential to understanding contemporary economic developments generally. It is to this we now turn.

Chapter 2: Cantillon and the Austrian Economic School on Money and Financial Crises

> "There is tragedy in the world because men contrive, out of nothing, tragedies that are totally unnecessary—which means that men are frivolous."
>
> —Henry de Montherlant, *La Rose de Sable*

A brief synopsis of the Austrian Economic School (AES)

Beginning in the 1870s with Carl Menger, the "father" of the school if there was one, Austrian School economists determined that market (i.e. free exchange) prices for economic goods were set at the margin where supply and demand met at any given point in time and place, rather than according to their average cost of production or specific cost of labor inputs. Eugen von Boehm-Bauwerk was the first to offer a holistic theory of capital and interest (or rent). Friedrich von Wieser was first to systematically apply the powerful concept of "opportunity cost," or trade-offs, to all areas of economics. The Austrian economist Friedrich von Hayek was the first to offer a comprehensive explanation for business cycles (for which he would eventually be awarded the Nobel prize in economics). Ludwig von Mises was the first major economist to predict and show how central economic planning would eventually fail in the Soviet Union and elsewhere. Joseph Schumpeter was the first to demonstrate the salutary effects of occasional recessions as a means to qualitatively re-order the capital stock so as to incorporate new technologies and more efficient methods of production, a process he termed "creative destruction." Indeed, the Austrian School has a formidable history of innovative thinking and of being proven more or less right, time and again, by major historical events.

Economists of the Austrian Economic School (AES) did not overlook or dismiss William Jevon's view that Cantillon's insights into money were essential to an understanding of how money and monetary policy can affect an economy and potentially exacerbate inequality. Rather, they thoroughly integrated them into their holistic economic framework. This process began with von Boehm-Bauwerk and Knut Wicksell and continued in the work of von Mises and von Hayek.

Austrian economists place central importance on the role of money and monetary conditions on the real economy. They also focus on how monetary conditions can influence asset as well as consumer prices. This is because the Austrians have a theory of capital formation (or destruction) that is intertwined with the prices of assets. As prices are information, entrepreneurs will seek continuously to allocate and reallocate capital based on the real-time flow of asset price information. This real-time, complex process extends over potentially long periods of time, such as those required to develop new technologies and to build the new plant and equipment required to implement them. Indeed, the sheer, mind-boggling complexity of a modern economy is so great that it cannot possibly be understood by any one person or group of persons. Thus, Austrian economists, while acknowledging that there is no such thing as perfection in human affairs or in an economic marketplace, nevertheless believe that the spontaneous market, and the market alone, is the ideal way for information to flow efficiently through the economy in a way that maximizes social benefits.

If you do intervene and interfere, however, with what would otherwise be a natural and self-regulating capital formation and allocation process directed via asset prices, then these actions can distort price signals and result in resource misallocations, including the boom and then bust of financial crises. That said, markets cannot function efficiently if property is in dispute and the rules and regulations regarding how property can be used are constantly changing. Thus, Austrian economists believe that strong private property rights and a clear, stable rule of law are essential to a healthy economy and the sustainable growth thereof. Uncertainty, while a fact of economic life, is minimized when the ownership and use of property are not in dispute and when rules and regulations are few in number, easy to understand and have low compliance costs.[7]

Another important factor that sets the AES apart, among other things, is that unlike the Keynesian or Monetarist schools, it holds that what happens at the "micro" level of the economy necessarily aggregates into the "macro" but also that the same laws must apply consistently at both the micro and macro level, as is the case with Newtonian physics. For example, in the Austrian School there is no "paradox of thrift" in which increased rates of savings can be desirable for individuals but not for an economy as a whole. Unlike Keynesians, Austrians hold that if it is sensible and rational for individual economic agents to increase their rate of savings, then this must also be sensible and rational in the aggregate. Nor is there any guarantee that monetary policies of inflation or money targeting at the macro level will prevent imbalances arising at the micro level, for example in housing, banking, or finance generally. Indeed, economists of the AES were almost alone in predicting that the prolonged period of artificially low and stable US interest rates in the

7 Critics of the Austrian School sometimes suggest that it contradicts itself because it wants the state to stay out of the economy, yet the state is required to enforce property rights. Some modern members of the Austrian School do border on holding Libertarian views of the ideal role of the state, if any. Classical Austrian School economists were far more accepting of the role of the state in enforcing property rights and adjudicating disputes. Indeed, they believed the state's role was absolutely essential. The Constitution of the United States, strictly limiting the role of the federal government in the economy and society, yet giving the Congress the power to regulate commerce, is entirely consistent with such thinking.

period 2002–2006 would eventually lead to a credit bubble and a major financial crisis.

Why did the Austrian School fall out of favor?

The question must thus be asked, given the history above, why has the economic mainstream drifted so far away from the venerable Austrian School of Menger, Mises, and Hayek?

There are several possible reasons. One is what Murray Rothbard termed "the Whig view of the history of economic thought."[8] This is a subset of the better known, general "Whig view of history," perhaps best represented by Scottish Enlightenment philosopher David Hume, that history is the evolution of an ever-more perfect world, of constant if not always understood or appreciated progress. Hence, the dominant school of economic thought today is superior to those that have come before, because it is that of today, not yesterday. No further explanation is required or desired. (It is worth noting here that German late Enlightenment / early Romantic philosopher Georg Wilhelm Friedrich Hegel postulated a more subtle, dialectical process of historical progress. Karl Marx would subsequently adapt this particular strain of teleological thought to demonstrate in his unique way the inevitable replacement of Capitalism by an anarchic form of Communism and the "withering away of the state.")

We know such thinking is flawed. History shows us it is flawed—recessions, financial crises, and depressions, including that in much of the euro-area today, feature with some regularity. Were economic theory and economic and monetary policies truly steadily improving, then 2008 should either not have happened at all, or it should have been relatively short-lived in its effects.

But this demonstrably false sense of steady (or sporadic) progress is nevertheless surprisingly common across all knowledge disciplines,

8 Murray Rothbard, *Classical Economics: An Austrian Perspective on the History of Economic Thought, vol II*, (Edwin Elgar Publishing), 1995.

not only in economic and monetary matters. Indeed, even in the hard sciences, where presumably only hard facts and evidence should matter, there can be tremendous resistance to new ways of thinking.

In support of his argument, Rothbard cited the work of historian of science Thomas Kuhn, who cogently demonstrated this to be the case in his 1962 masterwork, *The Structure of Scientific Revolutions.* According to Kuhn, even in hard science, it is not the facts that matter. Rather, it is the "paradigm," as Kuhn chose to call it. Facts that clearly do not fit the existing paradigm are either conveniently ignored, or those proffering them are persecuted outright, such as with Galileo's observations of Jupiter's moons. He explains thus:

> Normal science, the activity in which most scientists inevitably spend almost all their time, is predicated on the assumption that the scientific community knows what the world is like. Much of the success of the enterprise derives from the community's willingness to defend that assumption, if necessary at considerable cost. Normal science, for example, often suppresses fundamental novelties because they are necessarily subversive of its basic commitments. Nevertheless, so long as those commitments retain an element of the arbitrary, the very nature of normal research ensures that novelty shall not be suppressed for very long. Sometimes a normal problem, one that ought to be solvable by known rules and procedures, resists the reiterated onslaught of the ablest members of the group within whose competence it falls. On other occasions a piece of equipment designed and constructed for the purpose of normal research fails to perform in the anticipated manner, revealing an anomaly that cannot, despite repeated effort, be aligned with professional expectation. In these and other ways

> besides, normal science repeatedly goes astray. And when it does—when, that is, the profession can no longer evade anomalies that subvert the existing tradition of scientific practice—then begin the extraordinary investigations that lead the profession at last to a new set of commitments, a new basis for the practice of science. The extraordinary episodes in which that shift of professional commitments occurs are the ones known in this essay as scientific revolutions. They are the tradition-shattering complements to the tradition-bound activity of normal science.[9]

Given the relative subjectivity of the social sciences, including economics, one should wholly expect that the power of the presiding paradigm to misconstrue, ridicule, or simply ignore inconvenient facts and their associated theories would be all the more powerful in stifling real understanding, productive debate and progress.

Kuhn also noted that one reason why paradigms were so hard to break down once established was that those in highest regard within the discipline—akin to the high priests of a hierarchical church—had so much to lose if challenged by unorthodox thinking. We laugh at the Papal persecution of Galileo today, but to them it was no laughing matter. His observations, plain to see as they were through a telescope, directly contradicted the venerable, geo-centric or Ptolemaic paradigm of the day, thus threatening the very foundations of Church power.

Today we generally pat ourselves on the back that, whether atheists or not, we tend to treat science as wholly distinct from religion. And yet quasi-faith-based paradigmatic thinking nevertheless still infects science to a great if underappreciated degree. Take the "Big Bang" Theory, for example, which has stood for decades but is still mere theory. This is due

9 Thomas Kuhn, *The Structure of Scientific Revolutions*, (Chicago: University of Chicago Press) 1970.

in part to the fact that, notwithstanding huge investments in research into the origins of the universe, there is still no convincing data to confirm it. Although I am hardly an authority on this matter, I do note that, in my youth, astrophysicists believed strongly that, due in large part to the Big Bang framework, a Grand Unified Theory of the universe was within reach. All they needed for confirmation was a powerful enough supercollider. Today, some thirty years later, against these optimistic expectations, they are nearing exasperation. All the observational and computing power of which they could only have dreamed a generation ago is today at their disposal, yet they haven't got qualitatively farther than did Einstein a century ago with math, chalk, and slate? Could it be that astrophysics has become stuck in a paradigm that has outlived its usefulness and is now retarding rather than facilitating progress? I don't have the answer but no doubt Kuhn would agree the question is clearly worth asking.

I would argue that there is another, somewhat less-subtle process whereby economics drifted away from the powerful tenets of the Austrian School. This can be observed in the process of formally dismissing the Austrian approach which began with Irving Fisher and John Maynard Keynes, who strongly disagreed with the Austrians in the 1930s about certain (although hardly not all) causes of the unfolding Great Depression and even more strongly about the potential cures. Keynes and Hayek in particular engaged in a fierce, ongoing debate. Economic historians claim that Keynes eventually won the debate *de facto*, because economic policy moved in the direction he prescribed, namely a vast increase in and expansion of government fiscal support for aggregate demand at times of weak private demand and a rising propensity to save.

Thus, it can and should be argued that when it comes to actual policy, the Keynesian viewpoint can be seen as a self-serving one. Government officials and bureaucrats of all stripes naturally endorse that which justifies their existence and their innate desire to extend their power and control, something that was in vogue in the 1930s not just in the United States but around the world, as one government after another sought to arrogate more power to itself, in several cases with highly unfortunate consequences.

These consequences were studied somewhat systematically by Nobel laureate James Buchanan, who did not characterize himself as an Austrian School economist but did admit to strong leanings in that direction. As with many economists of his generation, he served in the US military during the Second World War, in his case on the staff of Admiral Chester W. Nimitz. Although identifying at the time as leaning socialist in economic and political matters, following the war he completed a PhD at the generally free-market-oriented University of Chicago. While there, studying under Frank Knight of early Monetarist fame, he came to focus on comparisons and contrasts between the incentive systems obtaining in the public and private economic spheres. He is today considered to be the father of the Public Choice (or Virginia) school of economics, which to this day retains a strong relationship with the AES.[10]

As Buchanan argued in much of his work, most bureaucratic impulses to regulate and control may seem benign in principle but in practice they can cause much damage due to the skewed incentives at play, which can result in bad policies and resource misallocations. While the debate rages to the present day, many prominent economists, including the Monetarists, hold that there are few if any things the public sector can do better or more efficiently than the private and that the latter should, therefore, be left to itself, with the authorities getting involved only when necessary to help sort out financial crises. (Central banking is a key exception, where Monetarists consider it essential to maintaining financial and thus economic stability.) But what, then, is the cause of financial crises, which clearly do happen with sufficient frequency to merit proper consideration? As it happens, the AES takes

10 Ronald Coase, a contemporary of Buchanan and also a Nobel laureate, had Austrian leanings in some of his views and much of his work can be understood as at least a partial affirmation if not confirmation that the Austrian framework has much to offer the economics profession more generally.

a quite different view on the causes of crises than that of the economic mainstream. It is thus to a more detailed discussion of the financial crises that we now turn.

Mainstream economists on the causes and consequences of financial crisis

Many economists and economic historians have studied financial crises, including the Great Depression. Irving Fisher, Hyman Minsky, Charles Kindleberger, and the non-Austrian observers of financial crises generally ascribe severe ones to some form of "market failure," in which one or more major private sector actors, such as a large bank, say, take excessive financial risks and that when some exogenous shock hits what has become a fragile institution and system, a crisis ensues. But this sort of thinking assumes that the financial markets exist in a vacuum essentially uninfluenced by government economic policies or the policy regime itself. Central banking, as has normally been practiced ever since the First World War and in some specific instances prior, injects an element of moral hazard into the banking system as central banks, in practice, have been able and usually willing time and again, not only in 2008, to rescue so-called too-big-to-fail institutions with artificially low interest rates or even explicit bailouts. They have also facilitated the financing of large government debts through "financial repression," a euphemistic term for using economic and monetary policy to appropriate the private wealth of savers in order to use it for government debt service without the need for explicit and politically unpopular tax increases.

A comparison between the English and Scottish banking systems during the nineteenth century is highly instructive in this regard. George Selgin, an Austrian monetary economist, has done extensive work in this area. Whereas English chartered banks were regulated by the Bank of England, which had a mandate to provide liquidity to banks that overextended credit and got into trouble, the Scottish chartered banks had no such recourse to any form of emergency liquidity. Indeed, Scottish banks operated in a self-regulating way such that, if one bank was perceived by other banks to be extending too much credit and taking excessive risks, they would begin to lose access to the interbank lending market and face higher interest rates on their incremental borrowings. They would then have to make a choice: find a way to pass these rate increases on to clients, thereby losing market share, or simply curtail further lending until such time as their access to incremental credit fell back in line with their peers.

In either case, the brakes would be placed on further credit expansion beyond what was generally perceived by participants in the money market to be a sustainable rate of money and credit growth. No central bank was required to maintain what economic historians agree was a stable and resilient Scottish banking system. Moreover, this system provided the financing for the Scottish Industrial Revolution, which at times experienced economic growth rates of as much as 10 percent per annum, such as when Glasgow was the world's largest shipyard. The idea that a central bank is a necessary part of a stable banking system and rapidly growing economy is hogwash.

By contrast, south of the border, where the Industrial Revolution was also in full swing, banking crises became increasingly common. The Bank of England found it was drawn into liquidity crises nearly every time there was a material economic slowdown. Walter Bagehot, arguably the most famous financial journalist of his era, disparaged this moral hazard and wrote of it frequently. In his private papers, he expressed his desire to get rid of the Bank entirely. In public, he was more restrained in his rhetoric, instead suggesting that the best way to reduce the growing moral hazard problem was to restrict the crisis-activities of the Bank to merely "lend freely, at penalty rates of interest, against good collateral," which became known as Bagehot's Dictum.

The Austrian School On Financial Crises

Bagehot was hardly the only prominent nineteenth-century voice against the moral hazard implicit in the central banking policy regime of the time. There was a raging debate for years between those like Bagehot, Cobden, and members of the so-called banking school on the one hand, and those of the so-called currency school over this topic. The former argued for a competitive banking system along Scottish lines; the latter for a central bank to control credit expansion through bank regulation.

For the economists of the AES, central bank monetary policy is not just one but indeed the *primary* cause of economic instability and systemic disequilibrium. This view was first put forward in robust form by von Mises and von Hayek in the early twentieth century. While this is heresy to the economic mainstream, the Austrians have much evidence to support this view.

Take the Great Depression of the 1930s, by far the most studied financial crisis of all time. The mainstream view of the Depression was that it was at first a particularly severe banking panic, along the same lines as those of 1907 and 1921, but due to its sheer scale it shifted the economy so far from equilibrium that banks began to fail in large numbers, and so many workers were displaced that unemployment became chronic and initiated a nasty feedback loop of weaker demand, leading to less supply leading to a collapse of industrial production and even of agriculture.

There is an extensive literature on the causes of the Great Depression, how policymakers responded, and why, eventually, the Depression ended. There is, however, significant disagreement about all of the above. The conventional wisdom, as represented by the bulk of the contemporary economic mainstream, is that the Depression was caused in large part by the US Federal Reserve, which failed to respond adequately to a sharp contraction in the domestic money supply that resulted from a severe drop in interbank lending.

Milton Friedman and Anna Schwarz put forward this thesis in detail in their monumental work, *A Monetary History of the United States*. They contend that, had the Fed done its job correctly by preventing a large contraction of the domestic money supply, the United States would have experienced only a severe recession, not a prolonged depression.

Austrians, however, see the Great Depression very differently. They trace its roots back to the aftermath of the First World War, when European governments, including that of Great Britain, tried all manner of artificial means to restart their devastated economies. Beginning in 1927, even the United States got in on the game, by easing credit conditions at the request of the Bank of England, to help stimulate demand for British exports. This was a major monetary contributing factor to the stock market bubble, which was driving share prices to record highs. But as with all bubbles, it eventually burst in late 1929.

The monetary factors cited above, while no doubt important, are only part of the story, however. While most closely associated with the presidency of Franklin Delano Roosevelt (FDR), in fact it was already under Herbert Hoover that the government initiated a range of unprecedented steps, beginning in 1930, to intervene in the economy in various ways and artificially support aggregate demand. That Hoover did so largely over the famous public objections of his more traditional, laissez-faire Treasury Secretary Andrew Mellon, should not diminish the importance of his actions. For example, Hoover worked with his mentor and friend, Henry Ford, to prevent any reduction in industrial wages, as declining wages were perceived as potentially negative for aggregate demand and hence growth. This was just one of a number of such initiatives which began under the Hoover administration.

Hoover's support of interventionist measures became increasingly explicit as he campaigned for reelection in 1932. In one major speech he boasted:

> [W]e might have done nothing. That would have been utter ruin. Instead we met the situation with proposals to private business and to Congress of the most gigantic program of economic defense and counterattack ever

> evolved in the history of the Republic. We put it into action. No government in Washington has hitherto considered that it held so broad a responsibility for leadership in such times. For the first time in the history of depression, dividends, profits, and the cost of living, have been reduced before wages have suffered. They were maintained until the cost of living had decreased and the profits had practically vanished. They are now the highest real wages in the world.[11]

While high wages sound nice in principle, they can have a downside, that is, amid weak demand, artificially high wages can result in high rates of unemployment. Indeed, by 1932, unemployment had soared to unprecedented heights. Moreover, it remained stubbornly, persistently high when compared to past recessions, during which wages had normally, naturally declined to reflect the temporarily lower demand for labor.

Taking the international context into account further helps to illustrate the point. Great Britain devalued the pound sterling by some 24 percent in 1931, making its exports to the US much more competitive. Much of continental Europe had already devalued during the 1920s, a lingering consequence of the First World War's destruction of capital and productivity in the most conflict-affected areas. This left the US looking relatively prosperous but increasingly uncompetitive vis-à-vis Europe.

Evidence of this loss of competitiveness began to have political repercussions by the late 1920s, as protectionist pressures grew. By 1929, Congressmen Smoot and Hawley were succeeding in advancing their co-sponsored tariff legislation through the Congress. Suspecting there might be strongly negative consequences for global trade and hence economic growth and corporate profitability generally, Wall Street was spooked. Indeed, some economic historians believe that the proximate trigger for

11 Murray Rothbard, *America's Great Depression*, fifth edition (Auburn, AL, Ludwig von Mises Institute), p. 187.

the great stock market crash of October 1929 were reports of a major compromise in the US Senate making it highly likely that the proposed, highly protectionist Smoot-Hawley Tariff Act would pass. When combined with mounting background evidence of a decline in industrial production having begun earlier in the year, this finally provided enough straw to break the great Roaring 20s stock bull market's back.

The stock market crash began on October 29, subsequently named "Black Tuesday." It would not run its full course until 1934, when FDR finally took action to effectively reverse Hoover's rigid wage policies by devaluing the dollar by some 40 percent by executive order. This action restored US labor competitiveness in one massive stroke, albeit at the one-off cost of also devaluing Americans' savings by some 40 percent versus gold. While the Great Depression would take over another decade and a world war to play itself out entirely, the deflationary part had ended. Mild price inflation became the norm thereafter, posing a puzzle for those economic historians who trend to treat deflation as a major contributing if not only cause of the Depression. This gently rising-price environment would remain the case under the post-WWII Bretton–Woods system.

If the causes of the Depression are somewhat misunderstood in key respects, what of the cures? The conventional wisdom is that FDR's Keynesian "New Deal" programs, including fiscal stimulus intended to create jobs, are of central importance. Yet when one understands that the persistently high unemployment of the Depression was in large part the result of government policies to support real wages, which otherwise would have declined more quickly to market-clearing levels, then alternative explanations become rather more plausible.

Once FDR took over, he took expansionary actions on both the fiscal and monetary fronts, including the large dollar devaluation. But growth remained weak, and unemployment remained high throughout the 1930s, notwithstanding (or, perhaps, due to) a huge expansion of government in many sectors of the economy. By the early 1940s, the

United States was at war and, as the Keynesians celebrate to this day, government deficit spending soared to unprecedented heights.

Many within the modern economic mainstream cite this as the primary reason why the Depression finally ended. But guess what? As part of the war effort, workers were forced to accept sharply lower wages. Also overlooked is that the US private savings rate soared in the 1940s as businesses and households paid down debt and rebuilt savings. Of course, many households were more able to save as they now had two incomes, with the work-force expanding dramatically as women entered it *en masse* for the first time in US history. In this revisionist view, it was not war spending that ended the Depression; rather, it was a dramatic reduction in wages to more competitive levels and a large increase in the savings rate, the very developments that were strongly opposed by Presidents Hoover and FDR from 1930 to 1939!

The Austrian School thus has a strong claim to the best explanation of what causes financial crises generally, including that in which we remain mired, now a full business cycle on from the spectacular monetary responses to 2008. In this explanation also lies the ability to forecast future crises in terms of their rough scale, although not with any precise measure of timing. However, the Austrian School also offers a comprehensive view on how economies function generally in all aspects, crisis or no.

We should, therefore, give due consideration to the highly developed, sophisticated Austrian viewpoint that monetary policy can at the very least be a source, if not necessarily the only cause of economic crises. This is particularly true in the event that monetary policy is highly activist in nature, manipulating the money supply aggressively in a futile attempt to smooth business cycles or to support economic growth generally, as central banks routinely do today.

The insidious effects of an activist monetary regime, however, go beyond the causes of misallocations, imbalances, and the associated economic instability. They are also an important source of economic inequality, as they distort the information used to determine efficient allocations not only of capital, but of labor. Attempts to prop up asset (capital) values with expansionary monetary policies, including quantitative easing, thus over time siphon off the labor share of income in favor of capital. The economic mainstream generally fail to see this, as did Smith and the Monetarists, as they are viewing the economic through a flawed paradigm including a critically flawed assumption of "neutral" money. And so it is to an exploration of the monetary sources of inequality that we now turn.

Chapter 3:
The Sources of Economic "Inequality"

> "Why have labor market institutions and social norms related to inequality changed at about the same time that skill bias of technology accelerated? This may be a coincidence, or the overall changes in inequality may be the result of changing labor market institutions and social norms, and less the product of technology."
>
> —Daren Acemoglu, writing for the NBER
> (National Bureau of Economic Research)

DOES ECONOMIC INEQUALITY MATTER? THIS provocative question tends to evoke a visceral, emotional response by many, and even during what are considered to be relative prosperous economic times. In times of economic difficulty, such as our present age of high rates of un- or underemployment, in particular for the relatively young and unskilled, and stagnating (or even outright declining) real median household incomes, it becomes the basis of political campaigns, as demonstrated recently in the US, UK, and a handful of continental European countries. (Of course, inequality is a perennial focus of political campaigns in much of the developing world, in particular in Latin America.)

While beyond the scope of this book, I do believe that inequality matters and that it can threaten the modern, liberal, democratic traditions that most Europeans and North Americans have come to take for granted. Extreme inequality begins to resemble slavery, in that the choices of the poor are so restricted relative to those wealthy few that the poor are essentially faced with a Hobson's choice of doing one of a handful of menial jobs with little if any hope for economic advancement, or doing no job at all and living, if not in poverty, then in dependency. Extreme inequality is also associated with political instability, vicious economic cycles, and social stagnation.

This chapter will explore primarily the monetary sources of inequality, with specific reference to the monetary theories of Cantillon and the Austrian Economic School, as described in the previous chapter. However, let's begin with what we might call the "natural" sources of economic inequality, and review some of the more popular historical and recent literature on the topic.

On "natural" inequality

Few would deny that there is not such a thing as "natural" inequality. Although the processes involved are not known in specific detail, it is widely believed that Mother Nature does not bestow her physical, mental, and perhaps even emotional gifts in equal measure across the population. Yes, the "nature vs. nurture" debate has raged in some form almost since the dawn of philosophy, yet while the advances of modern science have certainly made some additional progress in our understanding, it remains unclear to just what extent nature matters. We know, however, that it does. And that it matters at all implies that there is naturally some degree of inequality in society.

This holds true, no doubt, whether a given society is characterized as primarily capitalist or socialist in structure. Even in highly socialistic societies there are those individuals who, for whatever reason, rise to the top of the social structure and enjoy the associated benefits in some degree. Yes, there are the clever and charismatic "Gandhis" among us who might eschew material things voluntarily, but we should have no doubt that, were they to turn their formidable abilities to amassing even a small amount of wealth, that they would most probably meet with somewhat greater success than the average individual.

The inequality debate, therefore, requires one to determine whether inequality is somehow simply natural, flowing from nature in some way, or unnatural, as in caused by the organization of society itself in a way that is unfair and could, through social reform, be made fairer. Thus, the inequality debate is perhaps better understood as one of "fairness," which in modern times has always held a prominent place in the political lexicon, if not always in the economic one.

There are many who hold that a capitalistic system of strong private property rights is in itself unfair. One of the earliest, most cogent and thorough critics of capitalism—indeed, the man who gave it the name—was Karl Marx. *Das Kapital* remains a classic work of social economics, if one that has lain outside the Western liberal mainstream. It was, in its time, the foremost critique of that burgeoning mainstream, and it inspired several generations of anti-capitalist reformists and revolutionaries. (The Austrian School would arise some decades later as critics not only of Marx but also of the German mercantilists or "historicists" as they were known at the time.)

While it is beyond the scope of this book to refute Marx in general, it is instructive to refute his specific view that, over time, capitalist societies would naturally tend toward inequality. Indeed, according to economic and social historians, inequality generally *declined* in the developed world during most of the twentieth century, including in the United States, at least up until the 1970s. (Please keep that decade in mind.)

Let's look at the crux of Marx's inequality theory in more detail. What Marx is arguing, and what is subsequently updated by neo-Marxist Thomas Piketty in his best-selling book *Capital in the 21st Century*, is that labor has a certain value and that the capitalists who own the means of production exploit their workers such that they are not fairly and fully compensated for their labor. Hence the "class-conflict" concept for which Marx is particularly famous. This exploitation is made possible because the workers have only little to no bargaining power vis-à-vis the owners of the capital goods. As productivity increases, as it tends to do in capitalist societies due to innovation, technology, etc., the benefits thus accrue disproportionately to the owners of capital. Over time, therefore, as an economy becomes ever more productive, the capitalists grow ever richer while the typical laborer is left behind.

Sounds plausible, right? Perhaps, but here again the evidence suggests otherwise, as historical periods associated with higher productivity growth are as if not more frequently associated with declining rather than increasing inequality. Let's now return to the 1970s, the decade in which the long twentieth century trend toward less inequality begins to reverse and productivity growth also slows down. What happened? What changed?

Well, arguably the single most important economic development of the 1970s, and one of the most important of the entire twentieth century for that matter, was President Nixon's unilateral, probably unconstitutional and supposedly "temporary" August 1971 decision to end of the official conversion of dollars into gold at any price and, from 1973, to allow the dollar to free-float versus other currencies.

What followed thereafter were sharply higher prices for oil and other imports. Rather than maintain a stable money supply, the Federal Reserve accommodated the so-called oil-shock to keep growth going, but this would lead, in time, to asset and consumer price inflation and, no surprise, to a trend of rising inequality. Since US interest rates peaked in the early 1980s, bondholders have ridden the inflation gravy train, which has been remarkably steady. Shareholders have also benefited, although the ride has been rougher. But best of all has been the ride for those owning prime property and fine art, who have done the best of all. The "wealth" supposedly created by inflationism is really wealth redistribution in disguise, for one of the mostly unseen and misunderstood effects of monetary inflation is that the gains in worker productivity accrue disproportionately to the owners of capital.

Figure 3.1: The growing disconnect between productivity and typical worker's compensation, 1948–2013

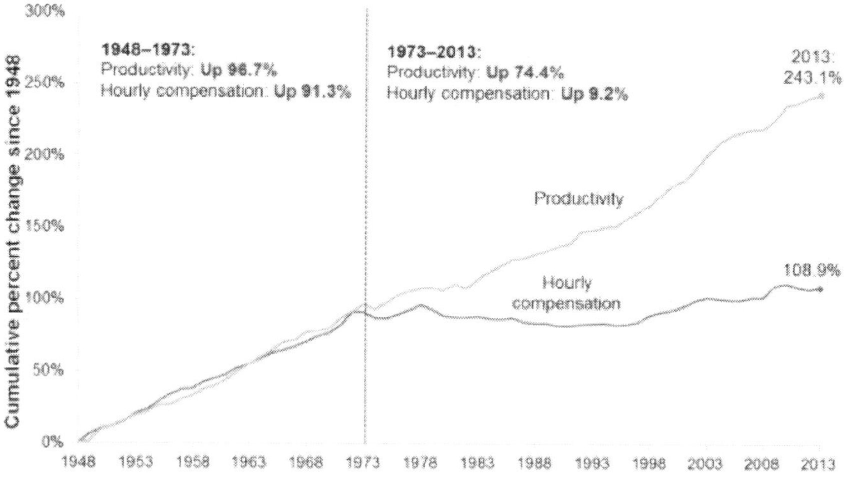

Source: Economic Policy Institute (EPI); US Bureau of Labor Statistics

Figure 3.2: Household income of the broad middle class, actual and projected assuming no growth in inequality, 1979–2011

Source: Economic Policy Institute (EPI); US census data

No, this is not "fair." It is also not natural to capitalism. Under a properly capitalist system, in which each participant can freely exchange their labor, accumulated capital, or ingenuity, then as workers become more productive they will be able to command higher real wages. That there has been essentially complete stagnation for nearly half a century notwithstanding positive labor productivity growth is clear evidence that inflationism fuels "unnatural" inequality which favors the owners of capital over labor.

There are, however, those who argue that technological innovation also fuels inequality. This is difficult to dispute in its entirety and certainly those highly productive, innovative individuals and businesses that find ways to build a better mousetrap, or for less cost, will find that they become wealthy as a result. But wait, if their wealth is thus derived from a free and fair exchange with their customers, what on earth is "unfair" about that? What can possibly be unfair about making people's lives better by producing things they want at prices they can afford? Yes, there are those like Karl Marx and his contemporary disciple Thomas Piketty who take the other side of this argument but ultimately their ideas rest on two assumptions, which in turn reduce to the same:

1. That laborers are unable to make free and reasonable decisions regarding what available work they wish to do and how much they require to be compensated for it (i.e. the "Labor Theory of Value")
2. That consumers are unable to make free and reasonable decisions regarding what they wish to consume and how much to pay for it

As we live in an age of choice, when we expect to be able to choose our lifestyles and the products we consume, there aren't many who would embrace assumption 2). But do you see how assumption 1) is essentially the same? The workers are the consumers. They are ultimately exchanging their labor and consumption goods with each other. Yes, the owners of capital sit in the middle as it were, and extract forms of "rent" from their accumulated assets, but the historical data strongly imply that this "rent" does not have a natural tendency to increase over time; rather, any such tendency is not endemic to capitalism at all but rather is an insidious aspect of inflationism.

There is another, simpler way to explain why technological innovation is not the primary cause of inequality but quite possibly the reverse: arguably the greatest single invention of the great Industrial Revolution is mechanized agriculture. Without it, most people would still be agricultural laborers. Standards of living would be far, far lower. Most would-be "capitalists" would just be skilled artisans, unable to source mass labor to work in a factory of some kind, thereby more efficiently mixing economically scalable labor and capital goods.

So-called Luddites were those who rebelled in the eighteenth to nineteenth centuries against mechanized agriculture because they argued that it displaced farm workers. Yes, of course it did. You don't need as many farmhands working the fields if you have a tractor. But is anyone today really prepared to argue that, to reduce inequality, we should get rid of tractors or other agricultural machinery? There was far more economic inequality back in the day of the great landed estates, when many farm laborers couldn't support a family at even subsistence level, yet the lord of the manor didn't work at all if he chose not to, lived the high life, probably also maintained a city residence for social purposes, and shot deer and game for "fun," rather than because this was necessary for survival. Indeed, for anyone to shoot deer or game on the estate without strict permission, including one of the laborers, the penalties could be severe, including imprisonment or even death. Is anyone in this modern age of choice really prepared to go there and defend the view that technological innovation is necessarily a force for exploitation, inequality, and just plain evil?

Yes, technology can displace workers. However, history shows that this tends to be temporary. Displaced workers normally if not always find other employment, although they may have to accept low wages while learning new skills. That can be complicated if minimum-wage laws are in force, preventing workers from temporarily acquiring new skills on the job in exchange for reduced wages. Consider that labor market flexibility was part and parcel of the Industrial Revolution. Minimum wage laws were essentially nonexistent.

Yes, workers would occasionally organize and strike for higher wages, and often they would succeed. I, for one, do not see anything wrong with workers voluntarily organizing to press for higher wages, or for employers to make a nursery or school available for their children, or perhaps a medical center, or any one of the many facilities that had become relatively common in and around factories by the middle of the Industrial Revolution. But for workers to organize violent action to damage capital goods or render them inoperable even by those workers who would prefer to work instead is a different matter. That intrudes on private property rights. Worse still is when the government actively seeks to promote and support such action by taking sides to garner votes. (Recall that the "Soviets" that would form into the USSR in the 1920s originated as local labor unions.) Imagine had property rights not been secure during the nineteenth century and capitalists—call them Robber Barons if you prefer—had been unable to secure their plant, property, and equipment. Can anyone honestly believe that the Industrial Revolution would nevertheless have succeeded in quintupling the average family's real income over the course of just a few generations?

To return to an essential point from earlier, the AES absolutely and emphatically does not advocate economic anarchy. There must be social institutions in place that can recognize, protect, and enforce property rights. There must be recourse to economic fraud. There must be a robust legal system for adjudicating disputes. Friedrich Hayek perhaps put it best when he explained how governments are essential for setting the rules of the game, but they should not participate in it. Like a football match, or any exciting, competitive sport, if the rules are unclear, everyone just keeps arguing with or, worse, buying off the referee rather than trying to play their best. Frequently changed or arbitrarily enforced rules and regulations encourage rent-seeking behavior, erode commercial ethics, and undermine what could otherwise be healthy economic progress.

In this regard, it is important to recognize that money manipulation is a particularly insidious form of arbitrary and sometimes frequently changing regulation. It results in all the deleterious effects noted above and, as we explore in some detail in the following chapter, also fuels inequality of the unnatural, immoral sort.

Chapter 4: The Non-Neutrality of Money and "Cantillon Effects"

> "Every change in the money relation alters...the conditions of the individual members of society. Some become richer, some poorer. Each change in the money relation takes its own course and produces its own particular effects..."
>
> —Ludwig von Mises, *Human Action*

WHILE WE HAVE DISCUSSED HOW a capitalistic system, in of itself, certainly allows for a degree of "natural" economic inequality—that arising from voluntary exchange mixed with varying rates of productivity and the resulting evolution of the distribution of capital—we have also showed how even major technological innovations may temporarily but don't necessarily exacerbate this natural inequality. They can in fact reduce it. There arises confusion, however, when an economic system is not purely capitalist but contains within it elements that artificially distort the otherwise voluntary exchange of labor and capital, and thus the natural distribution of wealth and income. Depending on how it is conducted, one of these can be monetary policy. Nearly all contemporary Austrian economists, including those associated with the Mises Institute at the University of Auburn in Alabama, believe strongly that modern monetary policies, in particular those of the US Federal Reserve, are fueling economic inequality due to the associated "Cantillon effects." Indeed, many Austrian economists specifically predicted that the bank bailouts and unconventional monetary policies initiated in 2008–09 and subsequently continued long thereafter would exacerbate inequality and, so far at least, they appear to have been precisely right. (This should give the mainstream critics of the AES some pause, especially those who have argued otherwise, including those who implemented the policies in the first place.)

Cantillon effects are the distortions created by artificial money injections into the economy. Unlike today's economic mainstream, which generally dismisses that which it cannot purport to model precisely, Cantillon's work on monetary economics focused on the highly complex "non-neutrality" of money, that is, that new money does not enter the economy simultaneously and proportionately in all sectors or at all stages of production, trade, and consumption. Rather, money tends to impact only one or several economic sectors at first, where it raises capital goods (i.e. asset) prices, and/or the price level for closely associated goods and services. Only later, as that money circulates into the broader economy, does it begin to affect the price level in other areas, including consumption goods, eventually permeating the economy as a whole, thereby finally raising the general price level that is the primary—in some cases only—focus of today's economic mainstream. By that time, however, the damage is done. Inequality has increased and economic calculation has been distorted, perhaps dangerously so. Malinvestments have been made. Indeed, trying to steer the economy while looking only at the one, very last aspect of what money creation does to the economy is akin to driving while looking through the rear-view mirror. It is reckless and yet it is precisely what modern, activist central banking is all about.

Now, it might be presumed that, once the permeation is complete, that all prices will have adjusted uniformly higher, as the Monetarists are wont to assume would occur with the mythological "helicopter drop" of money popularized by Milton Friedman. According to Austrian School economists, however, this is far from the case in actual practice. Ludwig von Mises describes the potential for Cantillon effects to affect the distribution of incomes and wealth thus:

Is it possible to think of a state of affairs in which changes in the purchasing power of money occur at the same time and to the same extent with regard to all commodities and services and in proportion to the changes effected in either the demand for or the supply of money? In other words, is it possible to think of neutral money within the frame of an economic system which does not correspond to the imaginary construction of an evenly rotating economy? Is it possible to answer [this question] categorically in the negative?

The answer…must obviously be in the negative. He who wants to answer it in the positive must assume that a deus ex machina approaches every individual at the same instant, increases or decreases his cash holding by multiplying it by n, and tells him henceforth he must multiply by n all price data which he employs in his appraisements and calculations. This cannot happen without a miracle.

Every change in the money relation alters…the conditions of the individual members of society. Some become richer, some poorer. Each change in the money relation takes its own course and produces its own particular effects…

With the real universe of action and unceasing change, with the economic system which cannot be rigid, neither neutrality of money nor stability of its purchasing power are compatible. A world of the kind which the necessary requirements of neutral and stable money presuppose would be a world without action.

All plans to render money neutral and stable are contradictory. Money is an element of action and

> **consequently of change.** Changes in the money relation, i.e. in the relation of the demand for and the supply of money, affect the exchange ratio between money on the one hand and [goods and services] on the other hand. These changes do not affect at the same time and to the same extent the prices of the various commodities and services. They consequently affect the wealth of the various members of society in a different way. [Emphasis added][12]

Let's now look in more detail at the compelling evidence that in the US, measures of inequality (e.g. the Gini coefficient) ceased their multidecade decline in the 1970s, following the depegging of the dollar to gold, and began a clear multidecade increase beginning in that decade.

A Gini coefficient is a ratio that measures the dispersion in income (i.e. inequality) relative to a perfectly equal distribution. It does so by calculating the incremental, cumulative share of income earned by the population as a whole, from the bottom on up. A perfectly equal distribution would result in a 45-degree line. In practice, due to inequality, the line is in fact curved and lies beneath the diagonal, as illustrated below:

Figure 4.1: Gini Coefficient Diagram

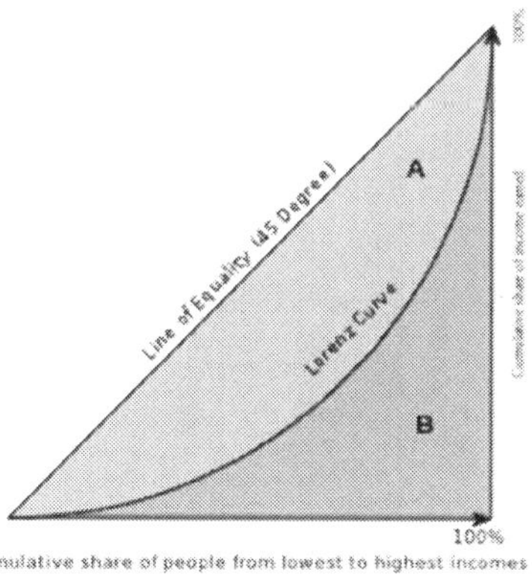

12 Ludwig von Mises, *Human Action* (Indianapolis: The Liberty Fund) 2007, p. 416–7.

Specifically, the Gini coefficient measures the ratio of area B to areas B+A. As inequality declines, B rises toward "1"—the "line of equality." As inequality increases, B falls towards zero. By implication, the more convex (curved) the line, the more unequal the distribution of income.

In the chart below, we plot the history of the Gini coefficient for the US and several other countries. Note the gentle decline in the US coefficient into the 1970s and subsequent reversal. Note also how most countries on this chart do not simply follow a similar pattern.

Figure 4.2: Historical Gini coefficients across countries

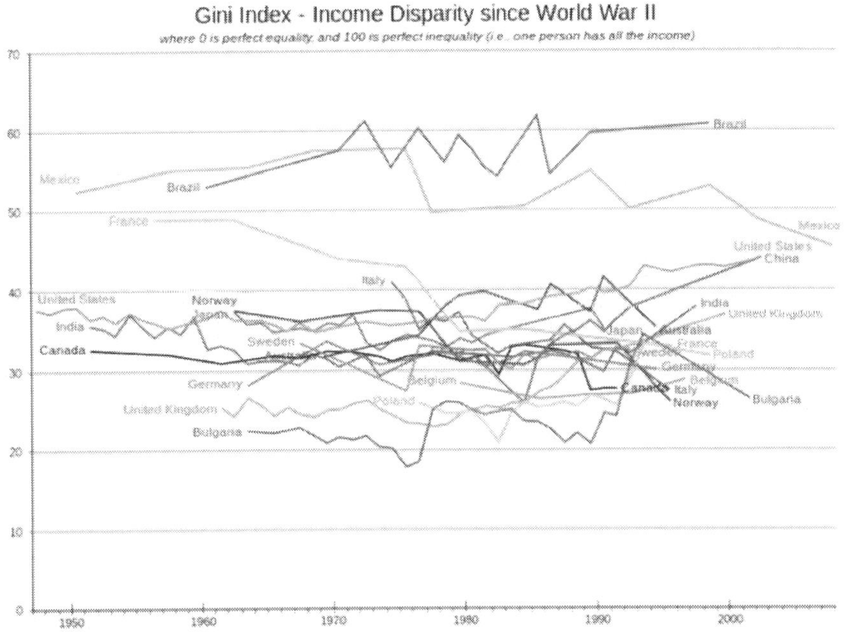

Source: CreativeCommons; license to reproduce: http://creativecommons.org/licenses/by-sa/3.0/

Let's now look specifically at the US, including the more recent history, as provided by US Census data:

US Gini Coefficient: 1967–present

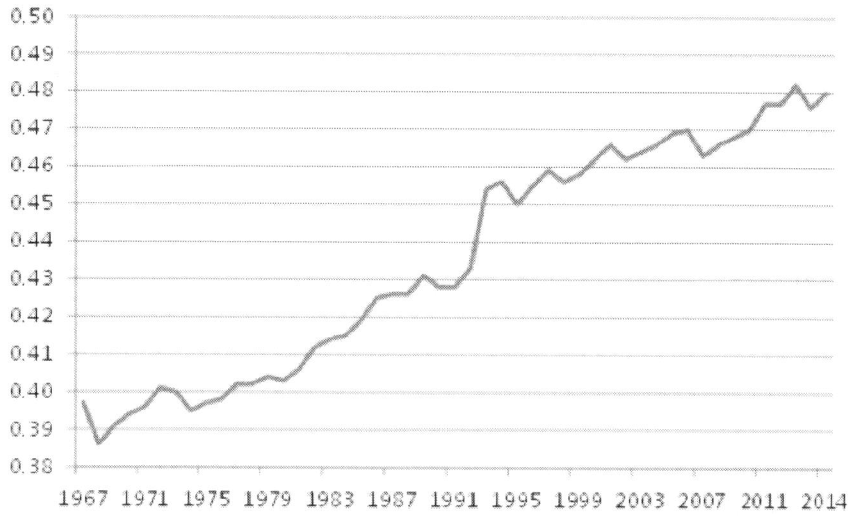

Source: US Census Bureau historical income tables. See here: https://www.census.gov/hhes/www/income/data/historical/inequality/

Note that while the trend reversal was not obvious at first, it subsequently accelerated in the early 1980s and, with the notable exception of a blip higher in the early 1990s, it has continued to rise at a relatively steady rate thereafter. The brief declines in the coefficient in 1973–4, 1995, and 2008 were due primarily to sharp declines in the stock markets, affecting primarily the top five percent of households.

The evidence presented above is circumstantial, to be sure. There is just no scientific way to isolate the monetary from the other variables in the complex system of a modern economy and determine with certainty whether and to what extent the rise of activist, inflationist monetary policies have contributed to growing economic inequality. But that there is a link has become increasingly evident post-2008 and is thus becoming rather difficult to ignore, even by those mainstream economists who, for the most part, have always denied the Cantillon–Austrian contention that money was not essentially neutral and thus that activist monetary policy would in practice favor the relatively wealthy holders of capital assets rather than the rank and file workers of a modern economy.

The money/inequality debate enters the mainstream

Although the possible role of Federal Reserve monetary policies in contributing to inequality remains a fringe topic within the economics profession to be sure, it has not gone entirely unnoticed by the mainstream. William Cohan, a former Wall Street executive who has written several books on investing, holds that the Fed's quantitative easing:

> [A]dds to the problem of income inequality by making the rich richer and the poor poorer. By intentionally driving down interest rates to low levels, it allows people who can get access to cheap money on a regular basis to benefit in extraordinary ways.[13]

Even a former Federal Reserve governor, Kevin Warsh, has expressed this opinion on multiple occasions, in one instance characterizing modern Federal Reserve policy as "reverse Robin Hood…making the well to do even more well to do."[14]

Mr. Warsh also participated in a symposium hosted by the influential Washington, DC, think tank, the Brookings Institution, to debate "Did the Fed's quantitative easing make inequality worse?" Papers presented included "Gauging the impact of the Fed on inequality during the

13 "How Quantitative Easing Added to the Nation's Inequality Problem," *New York Times*, 22 October 2014. Link here: http://dealbook.nytimes.com/2014/10/22/how-quantitative-easing-contributed-to-the-nations-inequality-problem/?_r=1

14 This statement was made in an interview on CNBC television, linked here: http://video.cnbc.com/gallery/?video=3000287822

Great Recession"; "Regional heterogeneity and monetary policy"; and "Distributional effects of monetary policy."[15]

One of the co-authors of a paper above, Andreas Huster, is on the research staff of the New York Federal Reserve. In November 2015, the New York Fed published his paper exploring how the policy of quantitative easing affected regions within the United States. Among other things it observed that "recent unconventional monetary policy had less of a beneficial effect for the areas of the country that were doing relatively poorly at the time the policy was announced."[16] The paper stops short of concluding that this is necessarily a problem—regional wealth differences are entirely normal in a large country such as the United States—but the plain observation is nevertheless that Fed policies have exacerbated rather than mitigated these regional differences in recent years. (That the NY Fed would publish a paper on this rather controversial topic was noticed by the influential World Economic Forum (WEF), which holds an eponymous annual conference in Davos in Switzerland and is considered by many to be one of the most influential annual gatherings of the global economic policy elite.)[17]

Nor is the US the only country to present increasingly compelling evidence that money injections can exacerbate inequality. The Bank of Japan, for example, has observed that, following a prolonged period of a stable Gini coefficient for that country, there has been an increase during the past fifteen years or so during which monetary policy has been

15 A link to this event is here: http://www.brookings.edu/events/2015/06/01-inequality-and-monetary-policy

16 "Did Quantitative Easing Interact with Regional Inequality?" Federal Reserve Bank of New York, 2 November 2015. Link here: http://libertystreeteconomics.newyorkfed.org/2015/11/how-did-quantitative-easing-interact-with-regional-inequality.html#.VkMGRbfhDIW

17 "Are Central Banks Making Inequality Worse?" *World Economic Forum Agenda*, 9 November 2015.

characterized by aggressive quantitative easing and other unconventional monetary policy measures.[18]

Most recently, in late 2016, even the prime minister of the UK, Theresa May, claimed that the Bank of England's policy of quantitative easing was exacerbating inequality and that perhaps the Bank should no longer be fully independent of the government. Her chancellor, Phillip Hammond, subsequently made similar remarks. Prominent MP and member of the Treasury Select Committee, Steve Baker, has been banging the drum for monetary reform for some time and even co-sponsored a Commons debate on the topic earlier in 2016.

One doesn't tend to find much evidence of anything, however compelling, if one is trained not to look. That the debate on whether monetary policies can have distributional effects is now entering the mainstream is highly significant. This strongly suggests that the evidence, previously overlooked, is increasingly widespread and thus difficult to ignore. For those mainstream economists who have been trained within a paradigm that regards monetary effects on the economy to be essentially neutral, this is a loud wake-up call.

Central banker denials

Under pressure from the shifting terms of debate above and now increasingly on the defensive, current and former central bankers are being forced to respond to the criticism. Among others, former Federal Reserve chairman Ben Bernanke, now scholar-in-residence at the Brookings Institution, has weighed in on the topic. Recall that as discussed above the Brookings Institution recently hosted a forum on the possible monetary policy effects on inequality, although Mr. Bernanke was not in attendance. In his blog entry on the topic, Mr. Bernanke

18 "Bank of Japan Survey Data Reveals Signs of Growing Inequality in Japan," *Bloomberg News*, 5 November 2015. Link here: http://www.bloomberg.com/news/articles/2015-11-05/boj-survey-data-reveals-signs-of-growing-inequality-in-japan

offers several reasons why we should not believe that monetary policy is a material source of inequality. The first reason is that:

> [W]idening inequality is a very long-term trend, one that has been decades in the making. The degree of inequality we see today is primarily the result of deep structural changes in our economy that have taken place over many years, including globalization, technological progress, demographic trends, and institutional change in the labor market and elsewhere. By comparison to the influence of these long-term factors, the effects of monetary policy on inequality are almost certainly modest and transient.[19]

As we have observed above, widening inequality is indeed a "very long-term trend," one that got going in the 1970s, once President Nixon untethered Federal Reserve monetary policy from the constraints of the gold-backed Bretton-Woods system. Mr. Bernanke chooses to ignore completely this highly relevant historical coincidence rather than attempt to dismiss it. It could be he is not even aware of it, although I find that possibility unlikely. He does, however, cite a range of factors that he claims are primarily responsible, such as technological progress and globalization.

Of course, technological progress and globalization did not only begin even a few decades ago. They have been part and parcel of economic progress for many generations, including the astonishingly rapid progress of the Industrial Revolution and rise of the middle-class discussed earlier. How then does Mr. Bernanke explain that, as we also observed above, the Gini coefficients for many countries were stable or even falling during the decades leading up to the 1970s, when notable technologies such as telecommunications, chemicals, air transport, and

19 "Monetary policy and inequality," Brookings Institution blog, 1 June 2015.

huge advances in health care took place? When global trade expanded rapidly? How can he be so "certain" he is correct when the data do not, at first glance, support his "very long-term" claim but in fact contradict it?

Mr. Bernanke's second major point in his blog post is that:

> [M]onetary policy, if properly managed, promotes greater economic stability and prosperity for the economy as a whole, by mitigating the effects of recessions on the labor market and keeping inflation low and stable. Even if it were true that the aggregate economic gains from effective monetary policies are unequally distributed, that would not be a reason to forego such policies. Rather, the right response is to rely on other types of policies to address distributional concerns directly, such as fiscal policy (taxes and government spending programs) and policies aimed at improving workers' skills. Policies designed to affect the distribution of wealth and income are, appropriately, the province of elected officials, not the Fed. Alternatively, if fiscal policymakers took more of the responsibility for promoting economic recovery and job creation, monetary policy could be less aggressive.[20]

Having first presented a historical argument without supportive and with possibly outright contradictory evidence, Mr. Bernanke now makes an even bolder claim that monetary policy promotes economic stability. As we observed in previous chapters, with reference to the Great Depression and, more recently, 2008, the evidence suggests the opposite is true. The Federal Reserve has made major mistakes in the past and, having apparently not learned the correct lessons, might well be repeating these again while you read this book. Zero interest rates and quantitative easing have created huge asset bubbles and imbalances,

20 IBID.

which more and more observers are concerned threaten the financial system with yet another major crisis in the future.

Rather than consider for one moment that Federal Reserve policy might be complicit in these crises of the past and quite probably the future, Mr. Bernanke then proceeds to conveniently pass the buck to those directly responsible for fiscal policy, namely politicians. For example, he implies that redistributional (e.g. progressive) taxation might be able to address inequality.

Progressive taxation might indeed have an impact, but has Mr. Bernanke considered why that should even be necessary in the first place? If the rising asset prices associated with inflationary monetary policies weren't exacerbating inequality in the first instance, why would fiscal policy need to be involved at all? Indeed, without inflationary monetary policies—a *de facto* form of regressive taxation falling primarily on the poor and working class via Cantillon effects—perhaps the overall tax burden on the economy could be lower, something that many economists would argue would support growth in general. And if growth in general were supported in this way, then there would be less of a case to make that monetary policy need be expansionary or activist at all.

Bernanke's argument here thus reduces to something of a logical tautology that can be shown as such when viewed in reverse order. In any case, by offering it up in the way he does, he is engaging in a conveniently self-serving pass-the-buck exercise, that monetary policy is probably irrelevant to rising inequality and only fiscal policy can have any meaningful impact in addressing it.

Mr. Bernanke makes some additional, highly erroneous claims, for example that debtors in the economy tend to be poorer than creditors and so should benefit disproportionately more from low interest rates. But as we well know, the poor have only limited access to credit, frequently at punitive interest rates. The profits on such lending accrue to leveraged financial institutions, huge borrowers in their own right, yet ones that borrow at a fraction of the cost of their indebted customers. Rather than showing us a case for the relative neutrality of monetary policy, Bernanke has here inadvertently identified a precise mechanism whereby artificially low interest rates and quantitative easing indeed exacerbate inequality.

Mr. Bernanke has thus laid out a case for the relative irrelevance of monetary policy in the inequality debate. In doing so, he makes several bold, associated claims, but, for whatever reason, he chooses not to support them with appropriate, compelling evidence. Why not is left to the reader to ponder. On other points, he inadvertently undermines his own argument. One is left with the impression that his treatment of the issue is merely an impulsive, haphazard response to mounting criticism, not only from the fringes but increasingly from the economic policy mainstream, hence the reason why he felt it necessary to respond at all. His response, as it happened, generated some prominent responses of its own. For example, the prestigious free-market think tank the CATO Institute published a somewhat academic paper debunking Bernanke's arguments, which included the following:

> This view of QE rests on shaky theoretical foundations. It requires us to accept an understanding of the term structure of interest rates that has been widely discredited in the economic literature and to make several implausible assumptions about the behavior of investors.
>
> The theory underlying the program is also difficult to justify empirically; in fact, there is virtually no credible evidence that QE led to persistent reductions in long-term yields via the channels identified by the Fed. The fact that QE was not accompanied by any substantial increase in bank lending further undermines the possibility that it stimulated economic activity.
>
> Quantitative easing did have unintended consequences, however. Income was redistributed away from people on fixed incomes and toward better-off investors, while

> pension funds were forced to hold securities with greater default risk. Other problems may yet materialize: the distorted markets and excessive risk-taking encouraged by QE could lead to renewed economic instability, and the huge increase in the monetary base that QE entailed could cause inflation if the Fed loses control of excess bank reserves.[21]

Bernanke's article also illustrates that Marx was almost certainly right about certain things if wrong about the natural tendency of capitalism toward inequality. Marx was a pioneering sociologist, describing in great detail how the social "superstructure" of higher education and media would be used by the capitalists to mask or to justify rising inequality, thereby keeping the workers docile, not prone to rebel. He also introduced the concept of a "petty bourgeoisie"—the middle class, if you will—being carefully won over by the capitalists because the more capable and harder working of them would be able to enjoy in more prosaic form some elements of the capitalist lifestyle. But whereas for Marx the capitalist needn't work at all to enjoy the high life—merely collect rent on capital goods and property—the middle class had to work hard all right and perhaps save for years before being able to enjoy some high living during weekends or while on vacation or in retirement. Nevertheless, according to Marx, this was enough to get the "petty bourgeoisie" to buy into a system that was fundamentally stacked against them and their higher socioeconomic aspirations. Bernanke's self-serving defenses and justifications for helping to perpetuate the myth that monetary policy is neutral is a highly apposite example of a co-opted intelligentsia unwittingly reinforcing this nefarious social dynamic.

As a result of Bernanke's and other central bankers' rampant inflationism in monetary policy since the 1970s and especially post-2008,

21 CATO Institute, *Policy Analysis*, no. 783 by David Thornton, http://object.cato.org/sites/cato.org/files/pubs/pdf/pa783.pdf

the "petty bourgeoisie" needs to borrow more and more to keep up with the elite, for example to purchase a home. The only way to maintain a middle-class lifestyle is to go into debt and hope that asset prices just keep on rising. But this is the basis for neither a stable economy nor society. Asset boom and bust isn't just economically destructive. It is socially destructive too. When only the most reckless, lucky speculators able to time the boom and bust correctly can keep up with the economic elite, something is deeply wrong. Hard work, savings, and thrift make for a far more robust society, or anti-fragile one, as investor, academic, and author Nassim Nicholas Taleb argues in his book of that name. Instead, we now observe arguably the most fragile social and political fabric since the mid-nineteenth century, when empires began to crumble in Europe and the Civil War erupted in the US. While hardly a prediction, sadly I would not be at all surprised if the inflationism-fueled trend toward rising inequality led to rising social disorder over the coming years. This represents the darkest phase of the monetary cycle of history but, as with all such cycles, the restoration of sound money provides the basis for a restoration of social order generally and, eventually, renewed economic and social advancement.

Chapter 5: The "Reserve Currency Curse" and the International Aspects of Cantillon Effects

> "The fact that many countries as a matter of principle accept dollars to offset the US balance-of-payments deficits leads to a situation wherein the United States is heavily in debt without having to pay. Indeed, what the United States owes to foreign countries it pays—at least in part—with dollars that it can simply issue if it chooses to. It does so instead of paying fully with gold, whose value is real, which one owns only because one has earned it, and which cannot be transferred to other countries without any danger or any sacrifice. This unilateral facility that is available to the United States contributes to the gradual disappearance of the idea that the dollar is an impartial and international trade medium, whereas it is in fact a credit instrument reserved for one state only."
>
> —French President Charles De Gaulle, February 1965

HAVING SHOWN THAT MONETARY CANTILLON effects can have a material impact on economic inequality within an economy, it remains to consider how these effects can also spill over internationally. As the issuer of the primary global reserve currency, the US Federal Reserve may be the source of significant international Cantillon effects. Indeed, I believe that these effects are in certain respects easier to identify than those observed domestically. There have also been some major studies supporting this view. First, let us consider the important role played by a reserve currency in the international monetary system.

What, exactly, is a reserve currency? It is one that is used to pay for imports from abroad and is then subsequently held in "reserve" by the exporting country, as it does not have legal tender status outside of its country of issuance. In the simple case of two countries trading with one another, with one being a net importer and one a net exporter, over time these currency "reserves" will accumulate in the net-exporting country. In practice, as reserves accumulate, they are initially held as bank deposits but are subsequently invested in some way, for example, in government bonds issued by the importing country or perhaps purchases of corporate securities. In this way, the currency reserves earn some interest and possibly realize some capital gains, rather than just sit as paper scrip in a vault.

Beyond a certain point, however, accumulated reserves will be perceived as excessive by large holders in the exporting country, in which case they can either reverse the net trade position and start paying for net imports with the accumulated reserves, or alternatively they can exchange a portion of their reserves with another country or entity at some foreign-exchange rate. For this reason, other factors equal, as the supply of reserves accumulate, but with demand constant, the reserve currency will depreciate in value.

As time goes on, trade imbalances and reserve balances grow in tandem, as does the natural downward pressure on the value of the reserve currency as described above. This leads to what Belgian economist Robert Triffin called a "dilemma": for trade to expand, the supply of reserves must increase. Yet this implies a weaker reserve currency over time, something that can lead to price inflation. Indeed, under the Bretton Woods system of fixed exchange rates, the supply of dollar reserves grew and grew, price inflation increased, and, eventually, as one European central bank after another sought to exchange its "excess" dollar balances for gold, this led to a run on the remaining US gold stock and the demise of that particular monetary regime.

While hailed as an important insight at the time, Triffin was pointing out something rather intuitive: printing a reserve currency to pay for net imports is akin to owning an international "printing press," the use of which causes net global monetary inflation and, by association, some degree of eventual, realized price inflation.

From Triffin back to Cantillon

Now let's combine Triffin's insight with that of Cantillon. As discussed in previous chapters, money enters the economy by being spent. But the first to spend it do so before it begins to lose purchasing power as it expands the existing money supply. The money then gradually permeates the entire economy, driving up the overall price level. Those last in line for the new money, primarily everyday savers and consumers, eventually find that, by being last in line for the new money, their accumulated savings are being de facto "diluted" and the purchasing power of their wages diminished. Increased inequality is the result.

Extrapolated to the global level, this non-neutrality of money implies that an issuer of a reserve currency is the primary beneficiary of the international Cantillon effects. First in line for the new international money you have the owners of capital in the reserve-issuing countries, who use the new money to accumulate more global assets, and on the other you have workers the world over who receive the new money last, after it has placed general upward pressure on prices. Growing global wealth disparity is the inevitable result.

Another way to think about the benefits of issuing the reserve currency is that it generates global seignorage income. Federal Reserve notes pay no interest. However, they can be used to purchase assets that do bear interest. No wonder the Fed always turns a profit; it issues dollars at zero interest and collects seignorage income on the assets it accumulates in return. But in a globalized economy, with the US a large net importer and issuer of the dominant reserve currency, this seignorage income is largely if indirectly sourced from abroad, via the external accounts.

This becomes particularly notable in the event that domestic credit growth is weak relative to that abroad. The Fed may print and print to stimulate domestic credit growth, but if that printing does not get traction at home, it will instead stimulate credit growth abroad and, eventually, contribute to higher asset and consumer price inflation around the world.

Over time, this will impact the relative competitiveness of other economies, where wage growth is likely to accelerate, eventually making US labor relatively more competitive. That may sound like good news, but all that is really happening here is that US wages end up converging on those elsewhere, something that should happen in any case, over time, between trading partners as their economies become more highly integrated. But as mentioned above, to the extent that this wage convergence process is driven by artificial global monetary inflation, rather than natural, noninflationary economic integration, the Cantillon effects discussed earlier result in real wages converging downward rather than upward, implying a global wealth transfer from "owners" of labor—workers—to owners of capital.

So-called anti-globalists disparaging of free trade and economic interaction are thus not necessarily barking mad—well, perhaps some are—but they are barking up the wrong tree. The problem is not free trade; the problem is trade distorted by monetary inflation. If you want workers around the world to get fairer compensation for their labor, shut down the reserve currency printing press. And if you also want them to have access to the largest possible range of consumer goods at the lowest possible cost, remove trade restrictions, don't raise them.

On reserve currencies, backed and unbacked

As it happens, prior to the First World War, the bulk of the world was on the classical gold standard. Although the British pound sterling was the dominant reserve currency, it was not possible to print an endless amount to pay for endless imports, as external reserve currency balances were regularly settled in gold. The British pound thus held its value over time, as did other currencies on the gold standard, and there was no "Triffin Dilemma" resulting in growing, unsustainable trade imbalances. Moreover, absent monetary inflation, there were no insidious Cantillon effects taking place. Industrial wages were generally stable through these decades, which were characterized by mild consumer price deflation. This implied an increase in workers' purchasing power and standards of living. So while there are certain parallels between sterling's previous, gold-backed role as a reserve currency and that of the unbacked, fiat dollar today, there are even greater differences. (For those curious how such a stable and successful international economic order could break down so completely in such a short period of time, please turn to the extensive literature on the causes and consequences of WWI, arguably the greatest tragedy ever to befall Western civilization.)

Returning to the present, countries that have been exporting to the US and accumulating dollars in return are increasingly getting the joke, but they aren't laughing. In recent years, senior officials in a number of countries, including those rich in natural resources or with competitive labor costs, have criticized US monetary policy while suggesting that gold should play a greater role in international monetary affairs. The BRICS (Brazil, Russia, India, China, now joined by South Africa), individually and together, have already made numerous official, public statements to this effect. One can only imagine what is being discussed in private, behind closed doors.

In 2012, the BRICS' monetary concerns were shared openly by the prime minister of Turkey, historically a "swing state" in its global orientation, yet currently a member of NATO and thus at least a nominal US ally. PM Erdogan, who may be somewhat controversial in the opinion of Western leaders, yet is more popular with the electorate in his country than most of his counterparts are in theirs, had this to say in criticism of the International Monetary Fund (IMF):

> The IMF extends aid on a who, where, how and on what conditions bases. For example, if the IMF is under the influence of any single currency then what, are they going rule the world based on the exchange rates of that particular currency?
>
> Why do we not switch then to a monetary unit such as gold, which is at the very least an international constant and indicator which has maintained its honor throughout history. This is something to think about.[22]

Historians will note that once upon a time, France was also a full member of NATO, but following President De Gaulle's decision to challenge the dollar-centric Bretton Woods system in the mid-1960s, there erupted a series of dollar crises that culminated in the collapse of the Bretton Woods regime in the early 1970s. Is history about to repeat? (Incidentally, history has already nearly repeated at least once before, in 1979–80. While the mainstream historical economic narrative about this period is that the Fed resorted to putatively high interest rates to fight the high rate of domestic price inflation, one look at the behavior of the dollar in 1979 and 1980 tells a different story, that the air of crisis at the time had an important international dimension. FOMC meeting transcripts also reinforce this arguably "revisionist" historical view that the dollar's international role was at risk.)

Clearly there is growing dissatisfaction with the current set of global monetary arrangements, which allow the US to print the global reserve currency to pay for imports, an "exorbitant privilege" as it was termed by another French president, Valery Giscard d'Estaing. Under the Bretton Woods system, France or any participating country for that matter could

22 "Erdogan suggests shift from dollar to gold," *Daily Shabah*, 10 November 2012.

choose to exchange its accumulated dollars for gold. As predicted well in advance by French economist Jacques Rueff, a contemporary of Robert Triffin, the exercise of this choice to exchange dollars for gold by not only France but a handful of other countries led to a run on the US gold stock in 1971 and an end to the dollar's gold convertibility.

Is reserve currency status a curse in disguise?

Let's now change tack in this discussion. Is reserve currency status a blessing or a curse? The answer may seem obvious. After all, isn't it nice to hold the power of the global printing press? To enjoy relatively lower borrowing costs and greater purchasing power? To possess the "exorbitant privilege," as it were? On the surface yes, but what lies beneath?

As Lord Acton is purported to have said, power tends to corrupt. By corollary, absolute power corrupts absolutely. And to the extent that a power that is held nationally is exercised internationally, then the corruption thereof has a deleterious international economic impact.

In the case of a reserve currency, the benefits of lower borrowing costs and cheap imports accruing to the issuing country appear to result in overborrowing and overconsumption relative to the rest of the world, eroding the domestic manufacturing base over time and widening the rich-poor gap to levels that are socially destabilizing. Trade wars, currency wars, or other forms of economic conflict are the inevitable result. In some cases, actual wars follow. In others, they don't. But in all cases, the reserve currency curse is recognized only too late, when an economy begins consuming its own capital in a desperate and unsustainable attempt to maintain its previous standard of living. Austrian economist Ludwig von Mises described capital consumption as akin to "burning the furniture to heat the home." Sure, it might work for a time, but what comes next? The walls? The floorboards? The roof?

Returning to the economy, both creating and maintaining a capital stock requires savings. Now what happens if there IS no savings? What if, for example, the financial assets, which are claims on the present and future productive value of the capital stock—net of depreciation of course—rise in value to the point that the holders thereof feel themselves "richer" and neglect to save? What if, for whatever reason, the central bank holds interest rates artificially low, such that there is little incentive to save? What if, in response to an unusually prolonged slump in economic activity, the central bank starts directly and artificially propping up asset prices by buying securities, thereby making it even less attractive to save?

Well, guess what? Amidst artificial disincentives to save and asset price distortions that make people feel "richer," what, exactly, is going to happen to the capital stock? Rather than grow, or even be properly maintained, it is going to depreciate, lowering the potential future growth rate. Capital consumption is just about the worst thing that can happen to an economy, and it is particularly tragic if it is not caused by some external shock such as a war or natural disaster but rather is self-inflicted as a result of failing to save enough to maintain the capital stock.

Don't be surprised when you look around and see crumbling infrastructure, whether public or private, in the US and certain other supposedly well-developed, mature modern economies. With asset prices artificially high, discouraging investment, and the return on savings artificially low, discouraging savings, there is naturally little in the way of incentives and resources available to maintain the existing capital stock, much less expand it. And don't be fooled into thinking that somehow higher taxes would help. Is the private sector going to save more, or less, if the tax burden rises? The answer to that is obvious. No, there are only two ways in which the existing capital stock can be properly maintained: with either a higher private savings rate, presumably a result of higher after-tax interest rates or, alternatively, for the government to redirect existing entitlement spending—consumption—toward infrastructure instead.

There is also another important implication. The currencies of countries that experience capital consumption tend to lose value over time. This is most often because, in response to the implied weaker growth, the authorities tend to get more aggressive in their attempts to compensate with monetary policy. This chronic currency weakness naturally leads to international investors being unwilling to hold the currency and perhaps unwilling to invest in the country at all. But what if we are talking about the country issuing the reserve currency? What if we are talking about the US today? If international investors are unwilling to hold it, well then beyond a certain point, it will cease to serve as the reserve currency. Without sufficient acceptance, it will be replaced by something else. What I believe that something else is—gold—and how the transition will quite possibly come about, comprise the core topics of the following two sections of this book. But first, some additional monetary history is in order, to bring us fully up to date in international monetary affairs.

Section II:
Why the Days of the Fiat Dollar Are Numbered

> "[T]hree-hundred and seventy-one grains of four sixteenth parts of pure, or four hundred and sixteen grains of standard silver."
>
> —Original definition of a US dollar, 1792 US Coinage Act

> "This note is legal tender for all debts, public or private."
>
> —Current definition of a US dollar, as stated on each Federal Reserve note.

When one thinks of a reserve currency, one doesn't think of one that is exploding in supply, pays a zero rate of interest, is backed by a central bank that apparently will stop at nothing to prevent an overleveraged economy from saving, is issued by a government running soaring budget deficits used to finance prolonged wars and open-ended welfare policies, is the legal tender for an opaque and quite possibly insolvent or even fraudulent financial system (e.g., the relentless stream of banking litigation and settlements for wrongdoing), and has been steadily losing purchasing power for decades. No, a reserve currency is naturally expected to be not only a reasonably stable store of value but also, arguably, the most stable store of value for the world at large; the anchor for all other currencies, be they officially pegged or allowed to float; and the universal, benchmark unit of account for measuring wealth generally.

Of course, for most of the dollar's existence as the world's primary reserve currency, things looked rather different. In 1944, the United States was by far the largest, most dynamic economy in the world, with an industrial base bigger than the rest of the world put together. (Of course, much of the European and Japanese industrial base had been destroyed by 1944.) Victory in World War II was within sight, and the United States was emerging as the clear winner. Although Britain, France, and the Soviet Unions were on the winning side as allies, their countries had suffered far more in terms of casualties, both military and civilian, and in terms of destroyed or damaged infrastructure. All were essentially bankrupt and, without considerable US assistance, Britain and France were at risk of losing control over their long-held overseas empires (which they, in fact, did give up during the subsequent two decades).

The United States took advantage of this overwhelmingly dominant position and, in that year, negotiated the Bretton Woods arrangements (named after the New Hampshire town where the conference was held) between the victorious powers, with the notable exception of the Communist Soviet Union. Following a multidecade period of global monetary mayhem, the ultimate cause of which was the economically devastating World War I, the United States took it upon itself to try to restore some degree of global monetary stability, in a way suited to US interests, of course. It was generally accepted that a return to some form of gold standard was desirable, as it was believed responsible for the monetary stability that underpinned generally healthy global economic growth in the decades leading up to World War I, a period economic historians refer to as that of the classical gold standard. As such, the cornerstone of the Bretton Woods arrangements was that the dollar would become the global reserve currency, fixed to gold at $35 per troy ounce, and that other currencies would then be fixed to the dollar. It was a nice arrangement for the United States in that member countries' central banks were effectively forced to hold dollar reserves. This had the effect of lowering US borrowing costs, a tremendous economic benefit not only for the US government but for US borrowers generally.[23]

23 A study by consulting firm McKinsey in 2009 estimated that US borrowing costs were some 0.5 to 0.6 percent lower because of the dollar's reserve currency status. See "An Exorbitant Privilege? Implications of Reserve Currencies for Competitiveness," McKinsey Discussion Paper, December 2009.

There was, however, a hitch, which was that by pegging the dollar to gold, in the event that other countries ran persistent trade surpluses with the United States—exporting more than they imported—then they would accumulate ever-growing dollar reserves. At some point, they might desire to exchange some of these dollars for gold at the official rate of $35 per ounce. Indeed, already in the 1950s, there was concern in France and, to a lesser extent, Germany, that the rate of dollar reserve accumulation was undesirable and unsustainable. But with the French franc and German mark fixed to the dollar, their persistent trade surpluses required rising dollar reserve balances.

It was Charles de Gaulle, under the influence of legendary French economist Jacques Rueff, who eventually decided to begin exchanging some of the accumulated French dollar reserves for gold. At this time, the United States held a substantial portion of the world's gold reserves, and making occasional gold transfers was not considered problematic. But as the years went by and the transfers grew, observers began to wonder whether the Bretton Woods arrangements were sustainable longer term. The United States held only so much gold. At some point, it might start to run out. What then?

A brief digression: why exactly was the US economy chronically losing gold to Europe? Well, by the 1960s, the United States was running chronic government deficits to finance a rapidly growing welfare state at home and wars, hot and cold, abroad. These deficits needed to be financed. Private domestic savings were insufficient to cover these public deficits, so the savings needed to come from elsewhere, namely, Europe and, later on, also Japan. With foreigners supplying an ever-growing portion of the savings to the United States, their dollar reserve balances rose and rose.

Eventually, observers no longer needed to wonder where this was going. The market price of gold in London began to rise above $35 as global investors began to lose trust in the willingness of the United States to keep the dollar pegged there indefinitely. Gold was thus being hoarded into private savings as a way to protect wealth from the growing risk of a future dollar devaluation. There were coordinated attempts by central banks and governments in the late 1960s to hold the gold price down to $35 per ounce, under London "gold-pool" conventions, but they failed under the growing demand for wealth protection. Finally, in 1971, the situation became untenable, and President Nixon made an executive decision to renege "temporarily" on the Bretton Woods arrangements and allow the dollar to float, that is, to decline theoretically without limit versus the market price of gold and, by corollary, versus any currency that chose to remain fixed to gold at the previous fixed rate. The unbacked fiat dollar as we know it today was born.

As for the future of the fiat dollar, to properly understand where we are going it is necessary to place contemporary events in the context of the monetary cycle of history introduced in Section I. Under Bretton Woods and for the entirety of its history, the US dollar was explicitly linked to gold in some way. While there is no specific reference to such a link in the Constitution of the United States—other than the link implied by giving the Congress the power to "coin" rather than "print" money—it was wholly unnecessary, as the circulating money of the time was overwhelmingly silver or gold coin, in particular the Spanish-milled silver dollar.[24]

24 The history of the dollar long predates that of the Congressional definition in the 1792 Coinage Act. Indeed, the dollar was originally known as the *thaler* or *Joachimsthaler,* which translates into English as "from the Joachim Valley," which is in Bohemia, today part of the Czech Republic. Count Hieronymous Schlick, a Bohemian prince, minted the thalers in the sixteenth century. They were considered such a superior coinage that they became the standard by which other European coins were measured. The greatest coin minters in European history, the Spaniards, who brought back the bulk of the silver and gold bullion from the New World in the sixteenth to eighteenth centuries, named their benchmark coins *dollars,* after the fabled thaler. The term *pieces of eight* is also related to the thaler in that it refers to the fact that the Spanish dollar, when introduced, was worth eight Spanish reales, the previous standard Spanish coin.

The Coinage Act of 1792 is the first instance of the US Congress exercising its Constitutional monetary power by specifying an exact definition of a dollar as a fixed weight of silver. The act also specified the value of the dollar as a fixed weight of gold by setting an official gold-to-silver ratio at 15 to 1, thus making bimetallism official federal policy. The act stipulated that the dollar would henceforth serve as the official unit of account for the federal government, as it does to this day.

Yet the definition of a dollar has changed radically since. In the 180 years following the Coinage Act, as a result of one crisis or another, the dollar's explicit link to silver and gold was gradually weakened. President Lincoln temporarily went off the bimetallic standard, issuing greenbacks to finance the Civil War. President Franklin D. Roosevelt nationalized gold holdings in 1933 and then devalued the dollar versus gold from $26.12 to $35 per ounce in 1934 in an unsuccessful attempt to end the Great Depression. It would be left to President Nixon, however, to sever the link to gold entirely, which he did abruptly at first in August 1971, then more formally in 1973, inaugurating the era of the unbacked, floating fiat dollar, with no official link to gold, which exists to the present day.

This section explores the reasons behind Nixon's decision to close the gold window and the subsequent history of the fiat dollar, which, as we shall see, has been one of a steady series of crises, each progressively larger than that which came before it, and which collectively leave the US and global economies on the weakest monetary foundation in history, with only a tiny portion of currencies meaningfully backed by official gold holdings.[25] In any reasonable long-term economic comparison, such as reference to average growth rates, or per-capita real income growth, the fiat dollar has been an economic disaster that continues to unfold before our eyes. Fortunately, the days of the fiat dollar are numbered. As we discuss in this section, the monetary cycle of history

25 Today, at current gold prices, only about 2% of the US money supply is backed by gold.

has entered a transitional phase in which the dollar, which has become a "bad" money, is in process of being displaced and, in time, replaced by gold. Let us first begin with a little history and then introduce some game theory. As we shall see, only gold can provide the game-theoretical international monetary equilibrium for an increasingly multipolar world highly dependent on trade.

Chapter 6: The Window Closes

> "In the past seven years, there has been an average of one international monetary crisis every year. Now who gains from these crises? Not the workingman; not the investor; not the real producers of wealth. The gainers are the international money speculators. Because they thrive on crises, they help to create them."
>
> —President Richard M. Nixon, August 15, 1971, speech suspending the dollar's gold convertibility

Treasury Secretary Connally was on vacation in Texas at the beginning of August 1971 when Treasury Undersecretary Paul Volcker requested his urgent return to Washington. A major global monetary crisis had been brewing for months, as one country after another sought to exchange some portion of its dollar reserves for gold, as was allowed under the Bretton Woods system of fixed exchange rates that had been in place since 1944. By July 1971, the US gold reserve had fallen sharply, to under $10 billion, and at the rate things were going, it would be exhausted in months.

Secretary Connally coordinated economic, trade, and currency policy. Nixon thus tasked him with organizing an emergency weekend meeting of his various economic and domestic policy advisers. At 2:30 p.m. on August 13, they gathered in secret at Camp David to decide how to respond to the incipient run on the dollar.

With the various attendees seated in the President's Lounge of Aspen Cabin, the president initiated the proceedings with a request that Volcker provide an update on recent events. The air of crisis grew thick as Volcker reported one country after another requesting to exchange dollar reserves for gold. Indeed, that very morning, the British had placed a request to exchange $3 billion in dollar reserves for gold. Something had to be done. Fast.

It quickly became clear that nearly all participants, including both Connally and Volcker, were in favor of suspending gold convertibility and floating the dollar versus other currencies. The primary dissenter was Arthur Burns, chairman of the Federal Reserve, who felt that almost any other action was preferable to abandoning the venerable gold standard that had provided the monetary foundation for more than a century of astonishing global economic development, including, of course, that of the United States. He also felt that suspending convertibility would send an obvious signal of US economic weakness around the world, although, of course, this was precisely why there was an accelerating run on the dollar in the first place.

Rather, Burns favored dramatic policy action on the domestic front to restore global confidence in the dollar, including sharply higher interest rates if necessary. But everyone in the room knew that, were interest rates to spike higher, this would most probably cause a sharp recession, implying that Nixon was unlikely to be reelected the following year.[26]

In a final, desperate appeal to the emotions of those in the room who appeared to already have made up their minds, Burns suggested that "*Pravda* will headline this as a sign of the collapse of capitalism." Yet his objections, however passionate, were overruled by the other participants. The next day, notwithstanding a further consultation with Burns, the president made his decision to close the gold window, effectively ending the Bretton Woods era of fixed exchange rates by executive order.

26 Burns's specific recommendations at Camp David may have been rejected, but the key aspects of his plan to restore confidence in the dollar, including sharply higher interest rates, anticipated the series of steps that future Fed Chairman Paul Volcker would take in 1979–1981, when another run on the dollar ensued.

On Monday, he announced the end of dollar convertibility as one of several bold measures—collectively termed the Nixon Shock—intended to shore up a deteriorating US economy. In doing so, he blamed the "international money speculators" for causing the series of monetary crises and claimed that, by suspending convertibility, the speculators would be "defeated."[27]

Contemporary observers of the time and historians to this day consider this speech to have been a major political success. Not only did it create the impression that the president was in charge of the situation but also it created a villain that no American could help but love to hate: the international money speculator. But as with so many political speeches, it had little in common with the truth, as we shall see.

"Exorbitant Privilege": The real reason Why Bretton Woods collapsed

The dollar has been a floating, fiat currency ever since Nixon's August 15 executive order closing the gold window. But while Nixon chose to blame speculators for the gold-backed dollar's demise, the truth is rather different. Bretton Woods did not collapse because of speculation—after all, it was foreign governments, not only speculators, that were draining the US gold reserve—but because of unsustainable US monetary and fiscal policies that had been in place since the early 1960s.

Beginning in 1961, Jacques Rueff, French economist and informal policy adviser to President Charles de Gaulle, published a series of papers predicting that a steadily deteriorating US balance of payments position would eventually lead to a collapse of the Bretton Woods system of gold convertibility and fixed exchange rates to the dollar. As such, he recommended that the system be converted back into something more

27 This account of the events immediately preceding Nixon's infamous suspension of convertibility on August 15, 1971, is provided with permission by Joanne Gowa, author of *Closing the Gold Window* (Ithaca, NY: Cornell University Press, 1983).

along the lines of the classical gold standard, in operation from 1880 to 1914, under which balance of payments deficits between countries were regularly settled in gold itself, rather than in the currency of any one country in particular.[28]

As Rueff explained it, the rapidly growing, export-oriented European economy of the late 1950s and early 1960s was accumulating dollar reserves at a rate that would invariably cause economically destabilizing money and credit growth, leading to inflation. The solution to this situation under the classical gold standard would have been straightforward: countries running chronic trade surpluses would steadily accumulate foreign currency, which they would then periodically exchange for gold, thereby maintaining stable exchange rates and limiting domestic money and credit growth. Countries running chronic trade deficits, however, would have to provide the gold. In the event that gold reserves ran low, a country would be forced to raise interest rates to stem the outflow. By increasing the domestic savings rate and weakening domestic demand, the trade balance would swing from deficit into surplus, and, in time, the gold reserve would be replenished.

Under Bretton Woods, however, the balance of payments was not regularly settled in gold but rather in dollars. This allowed the United States, in theory, to create as many dollars as required to purchase as many imports as desired, as these would be absorbed by the central banks of the exporting nations as reserves. As exchange rates were fixed, countries did not have the option of allowing their currencies to rise versus the dollar as a way to slow or reduce the growth of dollar reserves. Reserves would thus grow indefinitely. For the United States, this was akin to being given an unlimited line of credit by its trading partners.

French Finance Minister (and, later, president) Valéry Giscard d'Estaing famously described this theoretical ability to print unlimited dollars for unlimited imports as an "exorbitant privilege." Of course, just

28 Jacques Rueff compiled his essays into two major books on the topic of Bretton Woods: *The Age of Inflation* (1964) and *The Monetary Sin of the West* (1972).

because one has such a privilege does not mean that one will abuse it, but beginning in the 1960s, the US began to do just that. Among other things, in the early 1960s, the US:

- was in process of building the interstate highway system, the world's largest construction project in history to that time
- entered and subsequently escalated a war in Southeast Asia, fought primarily in Vietnam
- dramatically increased domestic social welfare spending as part of President Lyndon Johnson's "Great Society" programs

Although perhaps not so egregious by the modern standards of US government budget deficits, taken together these "guns and butter" projects led to a massive increase in the federal budget, which, in turn, stimulated global economic activity generally and contributed to a large swing in the US external trade position from surplus to deficit.

Figure 6.1: The US merchandise trade balance in the 1960s (USDbn)

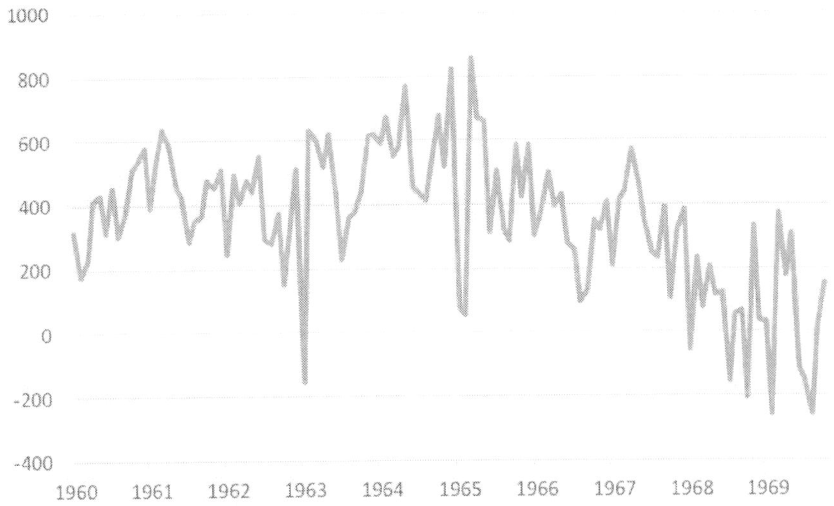

Source: Federal Reserve.

As a direct result, dollar reserve balances around the world began to grow at an accelerating rate. Giscard d'Estaing was only one of many European government officials who expressed a sense of unfairness regarding the Bretton Woods system, not only in theory but also, increasingly, in practice. Indeed, even de Gaulle himself weighed in on the matter in a press conference in early February 1965 in which he stated that, "Any workable and acceptable international monetary system must not bear the stamp or control of any one country in particular."[29]

De Gaulle then pointed out that the only standard that fits this description is that of gold, which "has no nationality" and which, of course, has historically been regarded as the pre-eminent global currency. With the dropping of this bombshell, the formal European assault on Bretton Woods began. As *Time* magazine noted, "Perhaps never before had a chief of state launched such an open assault on the monetary power of a friendly nation."[30]

This article was written more than six years prior to the proximate crisis that led Nixon to close the gold window. It is obvious that speculators were not behind d'Estaing's or de Gaulle's comments. Nor were they behind the following actions, as detailed in the same *Time* article:

- France converted $150 million into gold in January 1965 and announced plans for convert another $150 million.
- Although done quietly, rather than to the fanfare coming from France, Spain exchanged $60 million of its dollar reserves for gold.[31]

President Johnson responded to the accelerating drain of the US gold reserve by easing the requirement that the Federal Reserve System hold a 25 percent gold backing for dollar deposits. While this no doubt bought some time, the die had been cast. Following de Gaulle's opening barrage, the demise of Bretton Woods and of the gold-backed dollar was probably

29 As quoted in, "Money: De Gaulle v. the Dollar," *Time,* February 12, 1965.

30 "Money: De Gaulle v. the Dollar," *Time,* February 12, 1965.

31 IBID.

inevitable. Perhaps, had US politicians been willing or able to make some tough fiscal choices in the late 1960s, things might have been different. But Johnson, Nixon, and the dictates of domestic US political expediency determined otherwise. In the end, as Nixon himself put it, it would take seven years and seven crises to finally sever of the gold-dollar link.

It is an interesting historical curiosity that, notwithstanding Rueff's prescience and de Gaulle's pontification, it was, in fact, West Germany that *de facto* torpedoed Bretton Woods with a decision to allow the mark to float on May 11, 1971 (although it should be noted that this was done in consultation with France and other European Community member nations). In doing so, West Germany signaled in no uncertain terms to all countries around the world that the mark would henceforth be an alternative to the dollar as a reserve currency, and one with a highly competitive, rapidly growing economy behind it. The "gold-laden truckloads" as also noted in the *Time* article above had been rolling for years. But it was not speculators at the wheel in summer 1971; rather, European governments had finally lost patience with inflationary, unsustainable US fiscal and monetary policies and were voting with their vast reserves of accumulated dollars, and with their gold.

Closing the Gold Window as an Example of Global Monetary Regime Change

One theme of this book that reappears from time to time is monetary regime change, an important part of the monetary cycle of history described in the Introduction. Nixon's closing of the gold window is an example of regime change. The dollar remained the world's reserve currency, but convertibility to gold was suspended. The definition of the dollar changed.

In this case, regime change became necessary because US domestic political objectives came into conflict with its international obligations under the Bretton-Woods arrangements. The United States was unwilling to implement the more restrictive fiscal and monetary policies that would be required to stem the outflow of gold. Arthur Burns strongly preferred that course of action, believing it was in the long-term US interest to maintain convertibility, but he was quite clearly outnumbered by Nixon's other advisers.

In her classic study on this episode, *Closing the Gold Window*, economic historian Joanne Gowa traces the origins of the debate that occurred and decisions that were taken in August 1971 at Camp David. What she finds is that there was a clear, long-held bias within the Nixon administration favoring domestic economic freedom of action over any international monetary constraints. When the two came into conflict, as they did when the gold reserves neared exhaustion, the former naturally won out over the latter.

As she explains in her book:

> [T]he single most important factor explaining the breakdown of Bretton Woods was the...nationalist outlook on the appropriate relationship between the United States and the international monetary system... As a consequence, the monetary system would be supported only as long as it did not infringe more than marginally on US autonomy.
>
> That the two did not collide irreconcilably before 1971 was a result partly of the noninflationary course US domestic macroeconomic policy adhered to until the mid-1960s, partly of the vigorous demand for dollars abroad in the early years of the Bretton Woods system, and partly of the more recent series of ad hoc arrangements concluded between the United States and other governments to insulate the monetary system from the effects of a long series of US payments deficits.[32]

32 Joanne Gowa, *Closing the Gold Window* (Ithaca, NY: Cornell University Press, 1983), p. 103–107.

In other words, the Bretton Woods regime was doomed to fail, as it was not compatible with domestic US economic policy objectives which, from the mid-1960s onward, were increasingly inflationary. There is a clear parallel with today. The dollar remains the preeminent global reserve currency. The United States is also once again following highly inflationary policies in an attempt to support the domestic economy following a massive, housing-related credit bust. Meanwhile, in recent years, numerous economies, including the BRICS (Brazil, Russia, India, China, South Africa), have experienced relatively high rates of domestic price inflation as a direct consequence of US economic policy, shifting their incentives away from a further accumulation of dollar reserves.

As in the late 1960s, US domestic economic objectives are taking precedence over global monetary arrangements, that is, the dollar's position as the preeminent reserve currency. It is only a matter of time before either US policy must change or, alternatively, other countries must act to reduce their accumulated, inflationary US dollar holdings. Today's regime has thus become unstable, although the monetary shoe is on the other foot this time around. It is other countries' domestic policy objectives—in particular their desire to maintain domestic economic and financial stability and contain inflation—that are in conflict with the current global monetary regime.

Chapter 7: Stagnation, Stagflation, and the Rise of "Darth" Volcker

> "When I look at the past year or two I am impressed myself by an intangible: the degree to which inflationary psychology has really changed. It's not that we didn't have it before, but I think people are acting on that expectation [of continued high inflation] much more firmly than they used to. That's important to us because it does produce, potentially and actually, paradoxical reactions to policy."
>
> —Fed Chairman Paul Volcker,
> August 1979 FOMC meeting minutes

1979 WAS NOT AN EASY year in which to be the president of the United States. On the domestic front, although economic growth had been relatively weak on average for years, inflation seemed to trend steadily upward nonetheless. The OPEC member nations had, for the second time in a decade, demanded higher prices, contributing to that unfortunate (and, to Neo-Keynesian economists, perplexing) set of conditions now termed *stagflation.* New economic indicators were invented to help measure the malaise, most notably the Misery Index which simply added up the headline unemployment rate and the consumer price inflation

(CPI) rate.[33] Having risen into mid-double digits by the mid-1970s, it was now rapidly approaching the 20s.[34]

On the foreign front, fifty-three Americans were taken hostage at the former US Embassy in Tehran in November 1979, following the successful revolution of Ayatollah Khomeini and his clerical associates against the Shah, Reza Pahlavi (and the foreign powers thought to be behind him), in February. In Asia, there were occasional reports of sightings of American prisoners of war (POWs) in Vietnam, yet there seemed little the United States could do about it. Following its withdrawal some years earlier, the US army had returned home, demoralized and, in the view of some, disgraced.

It must have seemed so unfair. Jimmy Carter, the 39th president, had inherited an economic mess. Exactly who was to blame was unclear, although as discussed in Chapter 1, the United States spent and borrowed its way into an economic crisis in the late 1960s and early 1970s, and, taking the easy way out, President Nixon famously closed the gold window at the Federal Reserve in August 1971. Without the protection of the Bretton Woods system of fixed exchange rates, the dollar was now in full free float, and occasionally free fall, versus other major currencies.

Yet the dollar's weakness was not limited to currencies. The OPEC oil producing countries, previously selling oil at fixed prices, revolted against this devaluation of the dollar by organizing supply and pricing

33 Economist Arthur Okun created the Misery Index—originally using wage growth rather than consumer price inflation—as a simple means to measure overall economic performance from the perspective of the average worker. It peaked at just under 22 percent in mid-1980, as Carter was running for reelection.

34 The calculation basis for the Misery Index has necessarily changed through the years as the methodologies for calculating the CPI and the unemployment rate have both changed substantially. Were one to calculate the CPI and unemployment rate today as they were in the 1970s, the Misery Index today would be far higher. For more detail on how this adjustment could be made, see economist John Williams's Internet site, *Shadow Government Statistics*, www.shadowstats.com.

conventions, forcing the price dramatically higher in the process. When Nixon told the American people on August 15, 1971, that allowing the dollar to devalue versus other currencies and gold would not be inflationary, he neglected to mention the obvious but unpleasant fact that US trading partners in general, including the oil producers, would almost certainly raise their selling prices in response.

Almost overnight, OPEC became nearly as big a villain in American eyes as the Soviet Union. In was mooted in certain circles how the US military, home from Vietnam, might be redeployed to deal with those Arabs—in so doing displaying traditional American geographical ignorance. Among major OPEC members, Iran is a Persian and Libya a North African country; both are Muslim but neither is Arab. And Venezuela and Indonesia are neither in the Middle East nor North Africa, as those few Americans who did bother to look at a map might have noticed.

The demise of the gold-backed dollar and subsequent policy actions and reactions both at home and abroad all contributed to the harshest set of economic conditions the United States had faced since the 1930s. Sure, the United States was now an immensely wealthier country, with interstate highways striping the landscape from coast to coast and (to paraphrase Herbert Hoover) not just one, but two or more automobiles in every garage.

Indeed, America was now so wealthy that a majority of young Americans were not merely graduating from high school but receiving some form of further education. Americans celebrated their wealth by consuming all sorts of goods and gadgets that had not even existed in any form but a generation earlier, such as televisions and all manner of home appliances. Leisure activities once reserved for the upper classes were now thoroughly middle-class pastimes, such as golf, tennis, sailing, and skiing.

Although the dollar had weakened since being allowed to float in 1971, it was still strong in purchasing power terms versus the rest of the world. Combined with the arrival of long-range, relatively cost-efficient jet travel, middle-class families could now contemplate foreign vacations, and those who did were amazed that they could eat fine French cuisine for the cost of an ordinary restaurant meal at home or stay in a grand hotel in many Old World cities for the cost of the local Holiday Inn.

The problem, however, as psychologists have learned, is that it is not the level but rather the change in our standard of living that matters when people consider whether they are satisfied with the economic state of affairs. We are wired to expect either stability or improvement—any sense of outright economic decline, even from a lofty level, can raise dissatisfaction quickly, with obvious consequences for politicians.

Boldly optimistic on assuming office in 1977, Carter believed that he could use his salt-of-the-earth charm—he had been a successful peanut farmer before entering politics—to reach out to ordinary (voting) Americans and not just palliate their concerns but reinvigorate their spirit and shake America out of its national funk. In the epitome of this style, he began broadcasting regular fireside chats, in which he would wear a cardigan sweater in front of a modest, slow-burning fire, implicit signals to Americans that there were simple, commonsense ways to deal with higher energy prices. Once seated comfortably, he would inform his audience of what was going well, what could be improved, and how lucky they were to be citizens of such a fine country.

But perhaps like all peoples, Americans might enjoy listening to promises and platitudes, but what they really want are results. They were promised victory in Vietnam. They got defeat. They were promised a Great Society. They got civil strife and deficits. They were promised wage-and-price controls. They got a weaker dollar and inflation. They were promised the American dream. And they felt they were slipping into a nightmare. It might not have been Carter's fault, but the consequences were showing up on his watch.

As the economy continued to get worse, Carter found that he had an unusually short honeymoon period with the electorate. But optimism gave way not to pessimism but to determination. He seized the opportunity to mediate peace talks between Egypt and Israel, eventually presiding over the Camp David accords, which would contribute to the decision to award him the Nobel Peace Prize in 2002. He embraced efforts to deregulate certain industries, such as railroads, airlines, and communications. He even made a push to provide comprehensive health care for all Americans but failed to convince Congress to go along.

Perhaps most important of all, Carter faced down the financial markets and set about repairing the economic damage unleashed in the aftermath of the breakdown of the Bretton Woods system.

The rise of "Darth" Volcker

In the summer of 1979, as he approached the end of his first term and began campaigning for his second, Carter had a choice to make, certainly one of the most difficult decisions he would ever make. Inflation was rising. The dollar was falling. Unemployment was high, and it looked like the economy was beginning to weaken. The choice in question was whom Carter was going to appoint to be the new chairman of the Federal Reserve when the seat was abruptly vacated by Bill Miller, who left to head up the Treasury. The candidates included David Rockefeller, arguably the most powerful banker on Wall Street. But he declined, citing his prominent position and the public image problems it might create for the president. In his place, he recommended his onetime colleague and friend, Paul Volcker, who, incidentally, had been a key player in President Nixon's economic policy team and in the policy debates that culminated in the August 1971 Camp David meeting at which it was decided to end the dollar's convertibility into gold.

Notwithstanding Volcker's long tenure in various economic policy roles, the problem with Volcker, according to some of Carter's senior advisers, was that he was perhaps too independent; in other words, he was a noted hard money advocate who would not cave to pressure from the president or anyone else. He might not be enough of a team player.

But Carter overrode his advisers, sensing that the best way to deal with an economic crisis was to bring in a tough guy with market credibility who, hopefully, would shore up White House economic credentials generally.

Carter could have done like some presidents before him, including Nixon, and deliberately given the economy a jolt of stimulus heading into the reelection campaign, boosting job prospects and carrying him through to a second term, but instead he did what he thought was best for the country, which was to tackle the problems before him right there and then, although he knew it could cost him the election. He overruled his advisors and appointed Volcker. And he lost to Reagan in a landslide.[35]

Paul Volcker was not just known as perhaps the tallest man on Wall Street. He had a solid reputation both as a banker and as a public servant. Notwithstanding a stellar career at the Chase Manhattan Bank, at the Treasury, and at the Federal Reserve Bank of New York, he was not particularly wealthy by Wall Street standards. He eschewed luxury. As one example, he commuted on foot, briefcase in hand, from a relatively modest apartment to his New York Fed office in Maiden Lane. Yet his legendary support for tight monetary policy would soon earn him the nickname "Darth" Volcker.

Following his appointment, Volcker didn't waste any time. At his first Federal Reserve Board meeting as chairman in August 1979, Volcker asked around the room for comments on the current state of the

35 It has been claimed, based on Carter's initial press conference following Volcker's appointment, that the president was not particularly aware of what Volcker planned to do at the Fed and appointed him in the expectation that he would provide continuity rather than an abrupt change in policy. While this is possible, it seems not plausible that a president clearly in the midst of an economic crisis, who has just announced a major cabinet reshuffle, would prefer continuity over change, rhetoric notwithstanding. In Volcker's own account, he stressed the need for tighter policy and strict Fed independence in his meetings with Carter prior to his appointment. For a thorough account of how Carter came to appoint Volcker to the chairmanship, see Joseph B. Treaster, *Paul Volcker: The Making of a Financial Legend* (Hoboken, NJ: John Wiley & Sons, 2004).

economy, what the Fed should be watching, and whether a change in policy was appropriate.

His board of governors, colleagues, and a handful of senior staff subsequently chimed in with a great deal of comment on the state of industrial production, inventories, employment, exports and imports, and all manner of economic activity. The general message was that the economy appeared to have entered a recession, although to what extent and for what duration was, naturally, unclear. But in keeping with the conundrum of those times, there was also reference to stubbornly high inflation regardless of economic weakness.

Once the discussion had completed an initial circuit around the room in this fashion, Volcker weighed in, invoking a dramatic change in subject and tone. Rather than talk about economic activity in any detail or anything remotely quantifiable, he focused on the more basic, qualitative issues of confidence, credibility, psychology, and symbolism:

> **This is a meeting that is perhaps of more than usual symbolic importance if nothing else.** And sometimes symbols are important.
>
> In general, I don't think I have to go into all the dilemmas and difficulties we face for economic policy. It looks as though we're in a recession; I suppose we have to consider that the recession could be worse than the staff's projections suggest at this time…
>
> **When I look at the past year or two I am impressed myself by an intangible: the degree to which inflationary psychology has really changed.** It's not that we didn't have it before, but I think people are acting on that expectation [of continued high inflation] much more firmly than they used to. That's important to us because it does produce, potentially and actually, paradoxical reactions to policy.

Put those two things together and **I think we are in something of a box—a box that says that the ordinary response one expects to easing actions may not work, although there would be differences of judgment on that. They won't work if they're interpreted as inflationary;** and much of the stimulus will come out in prices rather than activity…

I think there is some evidence, for instance—if a tightening action is interpreted as a responsible action and if one thinks long-term interest rates are important—that long-term rates tend to move favorably. **The dollar externally obviously adds to the dilemma and makes it kind of a "trilemma." Nobody knows what is going to happen to the dollar but I do think it's fair to say that the psychology is extremely tender… I'm not terrified over the idea of some decline in the average weighted exchange rate of the dollar or some similar measure. The danger is, however, that once the market begins moving, it tends to move in a cumulative way and feeds back on psychology and we will get a kind of cascading decline,** which I don't think is helpful. In fact, it's decidedly unhelpful to both our inflation prospects and business prospects…

In terms of our own policy and our approach, I do have the feeling—I don't know whether other people share it or not—that economic policy in general has a kind of crisis of credibility, and we're not entirely exempt from that. There is a similar question or a feeling of uncertainty about our own credentials. So when I think of strategy, I do believe that we have to give some attention to whether we have the capability, within the narrow limits perhaps in which we can operate, of turning expectations and sentiment…

Specifically, that suggests that we may have to be particularly sensitive to some of the things that are looked at in the short run, such as the [monetary] aggregates and the external value of the dollar. When we're sensitive to those things, there's certainly a perceived risk of aggravating the recession… it would be very nice if in some sense we could restore our own credentials and [the credibility] of economic policy in general on the inflation issue.

To the extent we can achieve that, I do think we will buy some flexibility in the future… If we're going to be in a recession, by all traditional standards the money supply does tend to be a little weak and interest rates go down. I suspect that's a pretty manageable proposition for us if long-term expectations are not upset at the time by any decline in interest rates—an action we might actually have to take to or want to take to support the money supply. But **I don't think that approach will be a very happy one unless people are pretty confident about our long-term intentions. That's the credibility problem…**

I don't know what the chances are of changing these perceptions in a limited period of time. But as I look at it, I don't know that we have any alternative other than to try…

In saying all that, I don't think that monetary policy is the only instrument we have either. I might say that my own bias is, while I certainly think in the particular situation we find ourselves it's premature to be arguing for a big fiscal policy move, that such a move might be

> necessary. If it is necessary, it ought to be through the tax side and it ought to be through a tax program that not only deals with the short-run situation but fits into the long-term objectives... Ordinarily I tend to think that we ought to keep our ammunition reserved as much as possible for more of a crisis situation where we have a rather clear public backing for whatever drastic action we take. But I'm also fairly persuaded at the moment that some gesture, in a framework in which we don't have a lot of room, might be a very useful prophylactic—if I can put it that way—and would save us a lot of grief later. **If we can achieve a little credibility both in the exchange markets and with respect to the [monetary] aggregates now, we can buy the flexibility later.**
>
> So, in a tactical sense, that leads me to the feeling that some small move now...together with a relatively restrained [monetary] aggregate specification might be desirable...
>
> I might only say that I'm somewhat allergic to the use of the discount [rate] as pure symbol—in other words move the discount rate and do nothing else because I think there's already some flavor of that in market thinking. We do that about once and that means the symbol is pretty much destroyed for the future.[36] (Emphasis added)

This meeting represents a turning point in US monetary policy. In subsequent meetings, Volcker worked toward building a consensus around the idea, initially laid out in these remarks, that the Fed needed to communicate in a fundamentally different way with the financial markets. Given that the stagflationary 1970s had seriously undermined

36 FOMC meeting transcript, August 1979, pp. 20–23.

the Keynesian economic concept of the Phillips curve,[37] in which there was a quantifiable and manageable trade-off between unemployment and inflation, Volcker aimed for a clean break, and in short order he got it. To anchor inflation expectations, Fed policy itself needed an anchor. In October 1979, the Fed announced that, going forward, it would target growth rates in monetary aggregates believed to be consistent with low and stable inflation. The Phillips curve was out. Unemployment had been relegated *de facto* to a second-order priority. But the financial markets were not convinced. They would first have to test the Fed's new regime to see just how credible it was.

Their opportunity was not long in coming. In early 1980, notwithstanding a weakening economy, money growth remained surprisingly strong. The Fed, in line with its new policy, pushed interest rates higher and higher. The economy now began to weaken dramatically. Unemployment soared.[38] But Volcker was relentless. His priority, to restore credibility in the Fed and the dollar specifically and, by implication, in the US economy generally, remained unchanged. The money supply continued to grow above target and so the Volcker Fed continued to raise interest rates. Recession be damned; the Fed kept on tightening. At the peak, interest rates reached over 20 percent (Figure 7.1).

37 Although associated with Keynesian theory, economist William Phillips did not publish his paper claiming that there was a quantifiable trade-off between wages and unemployment until 1958. Although discredited during the 1970s, several modified, Neo-Keynesian versions of the concept live on today, including the NAIRU, or non-accelerating inflation rate of unemployment, and Gordon's triangle model.

38 Those who follow US economic statistics closely are aware that the Bureau of Labor Statistics changed the definition of the so-called headline unemployment figure in 1994, from what is known today as U5 to U3, removing "discouraged workers" from the calculation. On either measure, unemployment today is comparable in magnitude to the peak reached in 1982.

Figure 7.1: US Money Growth and Fed Funds 1976 to 1982

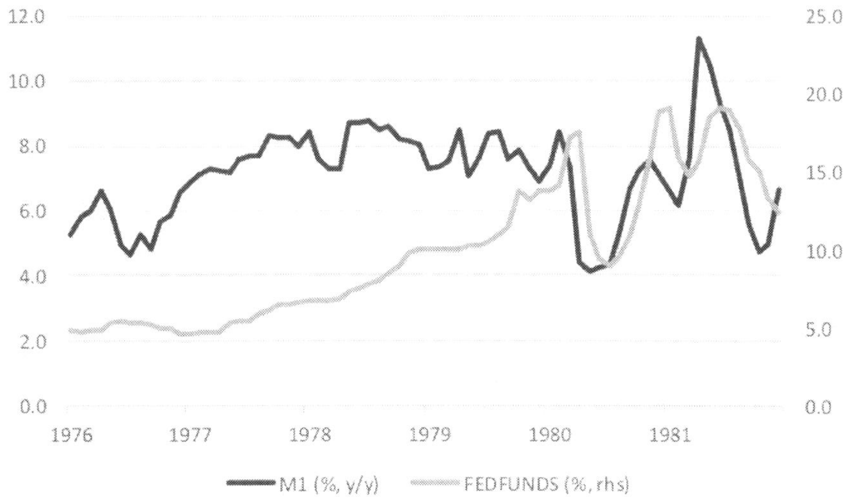

Source: Federal Reserve.

The reaction on Capitol Hill was predictable. In one instance in the summer of 1981, when Volcker was answering questions before a Congressional committee, he explained that, notwithstanding the recession, rates were going to remain high as long as money growth failed to slow. Vitriol followed:

> The Congressmen literally shrieked. Frank Annunzio, a Democrat from Illinois, shouted and pounded his desk. "Your course of action is wrong," he yelled, his voice breaking with emotion. "It must be wrong. There isn't anybody who says you're right." Volcker's high interest rates were "destroying the small businessman," decried George Hansen, a Republican from Idaho. "We're destroying Middle America," Representative Hansen said. "We're destroying the American Dream." Representative Henry B. Gonzalez, a Democrat from Texas, called for Volcker's impeachment, saying he had permitted big

> banks to be "predatory dinosaurs that suck up billions of dollars in resources" to support mergers while doing little to help neighborhood stores and workshops and the average American consumer.[39]

Volcker, however, refused to back down. The Fed's credibility was at greater stake than at any time since the 1930s. Unemployment continued to rise. Several large banks were distressed. Auto manufacturer Chrysler was on the verge of bankruptcy. It was at this time of greatest stress that Volcker hosted his former colleague and friend, John Exter, for a visit at his office at the Federal Reserve Board in Washington.

Exter was regarded by Volcker and his counterparts around the world as the central banker's central banker. Part retired since the early 1970s, he had been active in banking in the US and abroad since the 1940s, and had served as vice president of the New York Federal Reserve, senior vice president of the First National City Bank (Citibank) and the first governor of the Central Bank of Sri Lanka (Ceylon), founded in 1950 following the independence of Ceylon from India a few years earlier. He was also an active investor. In the 1960s, he not only warned against the policies that he believed would lead to a dramatic devaluation of the dollar and rise in the price of gold but, witnessing that his advice was going unheeded by those in greatest power and influence, positioned his investments so as to profit from them. And he did so, handsomely.

Following his retirement from Citibank in 1971, he went into private consulting work and managed his by-then substantial fortune. He specialized in gold and gold mining investments and sat on the board of ASA Ltd. His clients included wealthy investors in the US and around the world.

No other US banker of the time had such extensive domestic and international private and public banking experience. None had had his

39 Joseph B. Treaster, *Paul Volcker: The Making of a Financial Legend* (Hoboken, NJ: Wiley & Sons, 2004), p. 5.

degree of foresight to invest their savings as John had, accumulating a large holding of gold and gold mining shares. He had literally seen it all, and had predicted much of what he eventually saw, including what was unfolding in the US in the spring of 1981.

That day, Exter was astonished to discover that against the walls of Volcker's office were stacked piles of one-foot planks of lumber, sent by unemployed construction workers in protest at the many building projects cancelled because of record high interest rates. Some of the 2x4s were even personalized. On one was written, "Because of your high interest rates, Mr. Volcker, I've lost my job, my wife has divorced me, and I'm losing my teeth and hair, you no good SOB." Volcker was clearly in need of some reassuring advice from those he respected most, and Exter was as high on that list as anyone.

Retired or not, Exter never shied away from offering helpful if potentially harsh advice when asked. So when a desperate friend asked for John's help, he was only too pleased to provide it. That said, John could have responded with an entirely justified degree of schadenfreude. After all, Volcker had been active in US policy circles since the 1960s and was among those who had not always heeded John's advice. But schadenfreude was not in John's character. Rather, he went straight to offering his friend his best, honest economic advice. He suggested to Volcker that, in his view, he had already restored the Fed's credibility as an inflation fighter; that money supply growth would soon begin to trend lower; that the battle, as it were, had now been won; and that it was time for the Fed to start easing interest rates to stabilize the economy.

Volcker found it hard to believe what he was hearing. He had expected Exter to recommend more of the same, to stay the course. Even higher interest rates perhaps, or tighter bank reserve requirements, some form of tough economic love, whatever was required to break the back of the rampant inflation. Yet Exter argued that this had now been accomplished, that Volcker could begin to ease off the monetary brakes. How could he know that?

Perhaps it takes a true monetary hawk to know when policy is convincing and credible and when it is not. John was a highly accomplished and experienced economist, and had an extensive analytical toolbox from which he could draw. In any case, Volcker appears to have followed Exter's advice and began to ease interest rates within weeks of their meeting. Not long thereafter, money supply growth indeed began to slow, as did the rate of price inflation. By 1982, the inflation rate had fallen to under 3 percent, yet the economy was beginning to recover sharply. The stock market rallied. Growth soon picked up. Unemployment declined. And yet inflation remained low. The dollar grew stronger. Not only was the recession over but the battle against the dreaded "stagflation" had been won. John Exter had been proven right. Volcker's credibility grew. The dollar reemerged as a strong, stable currency.

In 1984, basking in this pronounced economic success, President Reagan was reelected in a landslide. In that same year, he publicly gave Volcker tremendous credit for his achievements and reappointed him to a second term at the helm of the Federal Reserve. Yet little did Reagan know how things could have turned out differently. Had the Fed continued pressing on the monetary brakes for too long the economy would have failed to recover meaningfully prior to 1984, and Reagan might well have lost his bid for a second term. Volcker might not have received a reappointment. The economy might have spiraled downward into a deep financial crisis. The US dollar might have lost global investors' confidence and continued to lose value, leading right back into the stagflation Volcker had long sought to end.

US economic and monetary policy might be made by institutions such as the Federal Reserve and the Treasury but all policies are the product of real decisions by real people, receiving real advice that they can either heed or ignore. John Exter's advice was at times heeded, at times not during his long career and retirement. In 1981, it was heeded, Volcker succeeded, Reagan celebrated, and the country experienced what was rightly described during Reagan's reelection campaign as "Morning in America." That the dawn came as it did, as soon as it did, was quite possibly due to the sage advice of John Exter.

There was another interesting topic of discussion late that spring afternoon: gold. Volcker knew that Exter was an expert in gold and gold investments, and he asked him what he thought of the outlook. John explained why he believed that gold served as an insurance policy against financial calamity. But then he went further. He predicted how someday, perhaps when it was least expected, there would be a sudden debt crisis, investors would rush into gold, and the entire banking system would be at risk of collapse. Volcker removed his glasses, rubbed his eyes, and said, "John, I hope you are wrong, but I respect you too much to rule out your predictions."

John Exter died in 2006, aged ninety-five. He may not have lived to see the global financial crisis of 2008 unfold, but as with most major economic developments of his time, he predicted it. He was more than just an ordinary banker. He was a banker for all seasons, and a monetary theorist of the first order.[40]

"Darth" Volcker's legacy

Although Volcker's policies no doubt contributed directly to the most severe recession since World War II, he achieved his goals. Inflation plummeted from double digits to less than 3 percent by the mid-1980s. The dollar not only stabilized but also, by 1984, had recovered its entire 1970s decline (as measured in trade-weighted terms versus other major currencies). The United States reemerged as a productive, dynamic economy. Yet when the going got tough again in the late 1980s and the dollar was once again in sharp decline, Volcker had left the stage, replaced by Alan Greenspan. The rest is an instructive episode of economic and

40 This account of John Exter's meeting with Volcker in spring 1981 is based on a series of the author's interviews with Exter's son-in-law, Barry Downs, who retains custody over John Exter's personal papers.

monetary policy history, a history of asset bubbles and financial bailouts. It is to that we now turn.

A Brief Introduction to Neo- and New-Keynesian Economics

This book makes occasional reference to Neo- or New-Keynesian economics, the dominant schools of thought represented by the economic mainstream today and those that inform the implementation of monetary policy all major developed economy central banks. The vast bulk of tenured economics professors and central bank research staff are members of these schools, which trace their roots back to John Maynard Keynes, who postulated that government deficit spending was an essential policy tool that could be used to moderate economic downturns, in particular those associated with weak or insolvent financial systems, in which the normal channels of money and credit creation were disrupted.

By the late 1940s, basic Keynesian theory had fallen out of favor. Among other prominent economists, Paul Samuelson and James Tobin set about making it more robust and incorporating some of the elements of classical economics, introducing what became known as Neo-Keynesian economics. In particular, Neo-Keynesian economics made much use of quantitative time-series analysis, something which by the 1940s had become much easier to perform due to new mathematical techniques and to the greater availability of robust historical economic data.

Due to an inability to properly predict or model the stagflationary 1970s, and increasingly challenged by Rational Expectations Theory (RET), Monetarism, and the economists of the so-called Chicago School, including Milton Friedman, Neo-Keynesianism eventually incorporated some of the key tenets of RET and Monetarism. This synthesis led to the creation of New Keynesian Economics.

In general, New Keynesian economists believe that while government deficit spending is an essential policy tool at certain times, monetary policy is generally more appropriate for managing "normal" business cycles in which there is little credit impairment evident. Even in the case of severe credit impairment, central banks can do much in terms of unconventional monetary policy to help moderate downturns and mitigate financial crises. Ideally, monetary and fiscal policies should be coordinated to achieve the desired macroeconomic results.

This book is highly critical of Neo- or New Keynesian Economics, and therefore of the current economic mainstream, for a variety of reasons that will become evident over the course of the text. But it is intellectually dishonest and simply unfair to attack an idea without first presenting it, at least in cursory form, as I have done here.

Chapter 8:
Of Bubbles and Bailouts

> "Surely difficult challenges lie ahead for the Fed, some undoubtedly of our own making."
>
> —Fed Chairman Alan Greenspan, August 27, 2005

THINGS WERE LOOKING RATHER GRIM for the US economy in mid-1987, soon after Paul Volcker left his job at the helm of the Federal Reserve. The dollar was falling, fast. Inflation and inflation expectations were rising. It was clear that the Fed was going to need to start raising interest rates soon, perhaps sharply. Having successfully broken the relentless uptrend in consumer price inflation and supported the dollar in the early 1980s with explicit monetary targeting, double-digit interest rates, and the most severe post–World War II recession to date, financial markets were naturally increasingly fearful that the Fed might follow a similar if less severe script again. While the exact trigger will perhaps never be known, this was the fundamental economic backdrop that led to the great stock market crash of October 19, 1987, when the Dow Jones Industrial Average declined by 23 percent (Figure 8.1).[41]

41 Several triggers for Black Monday have been proposed in a number of papers. One relatively recent study was prepared by Federal Reserve staff and listed rising global interest rates, a weaker dollar, and a rising US trade deficit as potential fundamental, macroeconomic causes and a proposed corporate tax change, listed options expiry, and large redemptions from a prominent mutual fund group as potential immediate triggers. See Mark Carlson *A Brief History of the 1987 Stock Market Crash with a Discussion of the Federal Reserve Response*, Federal Reserve Board of Governors Finance and Economic Discussion Series, 2006.

Figure 8.1: The falling dollar was a key part of the fundamental background of the 1987 crash

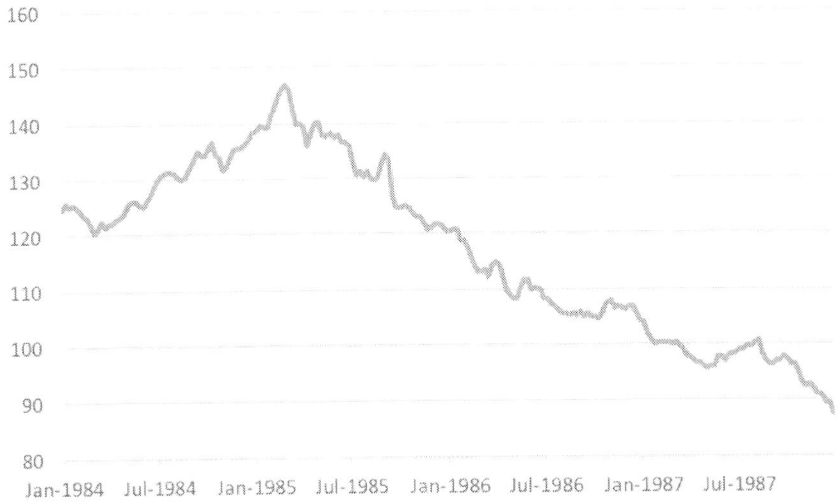

Source: Federal Reserve.

Alan Greenspan, a veteran of US economic policy-making circles but a neophyte at the Fed, sensed correctly that an emergency easing of interest rates and other liquidity-enhancing measures would help to restore confidence in the equity market, financial system, and economy generally and prevent a possible recession. Sure enough, equity markets bounced sharply in the following days and continued to climb steadily in the following months, recovering all losses with what seemed little effort.

This episode was most certainly a baptism by fire for Greenspan and one that, no doubt, taught him at least one important lesson: if done quickly and communicated properly to the financial markets, emergency Fed policy actions can provide swift and dramatic support for asset prices. But at what cost?

Although Greenspan might consider this his first major crisis-management success, was the Fed's policy reaction to the 1987 crash proportionate or even appropriate? Was it an equal but opposite reaction that merely temporarily stabilized financial markets or did it, in fact, implicitly expand the Fed's regulatory role to managing equity prices? Indeed, one could argue that this intervention was merely the first of a series of progressively larger Greenspan "'puts"—to use the financial market jargon for providing monetary support—that the Fed would offer to the financial markets during the eighteen years that the so-called Maestro was in charge of monetary policy and, let's not forget, bank regulation.

Having received a shot in the arm from the abrupt easing of monetary conditions in late 1987, as well as the lagged effects of a much weaker dollar, the US Consumer Price Index rose more than 5 percent year over year in early 1989, and the Fed raised rates in response, eventually tipping the economy into a recession. One aspect of the 1990–1993 recession that received much comment and analysis was the "double dip" aspect to it. Whereas the initial phase of the recession looked like a fairly typical business investment and inventory cycle, the second phase was characterized by a general credit crunch that constrained growth in most areas of the economy. What was the primary cause of this credit crunch? Why, the long-forgotten savings and loan (S&L) crisis.

The forgotten US housing bubble

The American dream of home ownership is normally associated with the US economy's capitalist traditions. However, according to many politicians, it is something that simply cannot be achieved without ever-growing government regulation and subsidies. Politicians just love finding ways to assist their constituents with home purchases. In some cases, there is so much government help available that homeowners end up owning homes they can't afford. In the 1980s, Congress decided that, to make housing more affordable, it would ease certain regulations previously restricting the lending activities of savings and loans (S&Ls). Credit would thereby become more widely available to a range of borrowers who previously might not have qualified. Importantly, this also included risky commercial lending.[42]

Seeking higher returns, some S&Ls broadened their lending activities, expanded their balance sheets, and focused more and more on the riskiest, most lucrative opportunities. As S&Ls were financed primarily by deposits, they needed to offer more attractive deposit rates to expand. But because all deposits were insured in equal measure by the Federal Savings and Loan Insurance Corporation (FSLIC, the S&L equivalent of the FDIC, the Federal Deposit Insurance Corporation), depositors would shop around, seeking out the best rates. Deposits therefore flowed from the more conservative to the riskiest institutions offering the highest rates on deposits—fully insured, of course. Some of the most aggressive S&Ls went on a shopping spree, snapping up their more conservative counterparts and deploying their newly acquired deposits into the latest, greatest, high-risk, high-return ventures.

The results were predictable. By the late 1980s, a huge portion of the S&L industry was insolvent. The recession of 1990–1991 made a bad situation worse. The FSLIC funds were rapidly depleted. But a federal guarantee is supposed to be just that, a guarantee, so Congress put together a bailout package for the industry. A new federal agency, the Resolution Trust Corporation (RTC), issued bonds fully backed by the US Treasury and used the proceeds to make insolvent S&L depositors whole.

All of this took time, however, and as the bad assets of the S&Ls were worked off, the economy entered part two of the double dip, and the credit crunch intensified. The Fed, however, knew what to do. By taking the Fed funds rate all the way down to 3 percent, real interest rates were effectively zero for the first time since the 1970s (Figure 8.2). The Fed then held them there for nearly two years, finally raising them in early 1994, when it was absolutely clear that the economy was recovering strongly and the credit crunch was over.

42 A reasonably complete timeline of the key events leading up to the S&L crisis is provided by the FDIC at www.fdic.gov/bank/historical/s&l/.

Figure 8.2: US Real Interest Rates Were Effectively Zero in 1992–1993

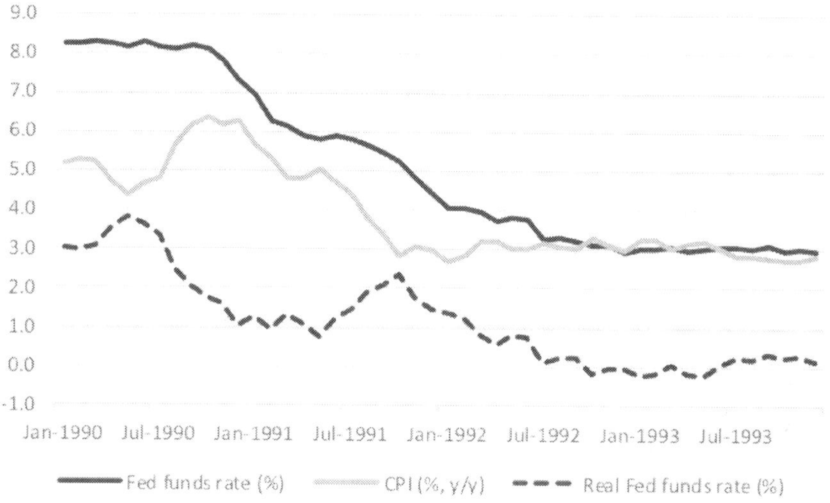

Source: Federal Reserve.

Fast-forward a decade. We all know that the origins of the most recent boom and bust in US housing and credit can generally be traced back to the highly accommodative Fed policy implemented in the wake of the dot-com bust in 2001–2003. By late 2003, there was clear evidence that the US housing market was surging, and homeowners were extracting record amounts of equity from their homes, thereby stimulating the broader economy. However, amid relatively low consumer price inflation, the Fed determined—incorrectly, we now know—that interest rates should rise only slowly, notwithstanding the surge in asset prices.

With the Fed moving slowly and predictably, risk premia for essentially all assets plummeted. In a Fed policy speech in the mid-2000s, Greenspan referred to the "conundrum" of low-term premia for US Treasury bonds. But low credit spreads for corporate bonds and low implied volatilities for nearly all assets were clear evidence of inappropriately loose Fed policy all the way into early 2007.

By the time the subprime mortgage crisis hit in mid-2007, the economic damage had been done. There had been vast overconsumption at home and overinvestment around the world, resulting collectively in perhaps the most monumental misallocation of resources, outside of wartime, in world history. There was no avoiding the subsequent, inevitable crash; the new challenge quickly became how to prevent a complete collapse of the financial system. At this point, the crisis acquired an overt political dimension as US and some other countries' taxpayers were asked, in various direct and indirect ways, to bail out those institutions at risk of insolvency and default.

In retrospect, the entire US S&L debacle, from its origins in regulatory changes and government guarantees, through the risky lending boom, bust, credit crunch, and fiscal and monetary bailout can be seen as a precursor to the far larger global credit bubble and bust of 2003 to the present. Just replace the S&Ls with Fannie and Freddie and the international "shadow banking system." But there is no need to change the massive moral hazard perpetrated by government regulators, including, of course, the Fed, and the reckless and greedy financial firms that played essentially the same role in both episodes.

Those surprised by the post-2008 efforts by the Fed and other regulatory bodies to expand their power over the financial system and the economy in general have not been paying attention to history: for every market action, there is a disproportionate regulatory and monetary policy reaction that increases the moral hazard of the system, laying the foundations for an even greater crisis in future. History may not repeat, but it certainly rhymes, as we explore in some detail in the following chapter.

Chapter 9: Why Financial Genius Fails, or, a Forensic Study of the 2008–2009 Global Credit Crisis

> "The US economy is in danger of a recession that will prove unusually severe and long… The great question is what will happen to the variety of financial asset bubbles in the United States when the housing bubble bursts and the economy slumps."
>
> —Kurt Richebaecher,
> former Chief Economist of Dresdner Bank, 2006

MUCH EXCELLENT ANALYSIS HAS ALREADY been written regarding the origins and key events of the 2008–2009 global credit crisis. In this chapter, I am not going to flog a dead horse. I am, however, going to explore some of the subtler ways in which the moral hazard created by US economic policy in the period 1987–2006 contributed to the near-collapse of the financial system in late 2008.

The key lesson is that the US regulatory regime does not promote financial stability but, in fact, undermines it. As such, the US financial system is inherently unstable and fundamentally at odds with the current fiat dollar reserve currency standard, on which I will elaborate on later.

A BRIEF HISTORY OF FAILED FINANCIAL GENIUS

The dustbin of financial history is littered with examples of failed genius, in which extraordinarily bright, determined, hugely successful financiers or traders encounter a set of circumstances that take even them by surprise, and, lo and behold, they go suddenly, sometimes spectacularly, bankrupt. Long-Term Capital Management (LTCM), a large hedge fund that employed several Nobel Prize winners yet failed in 1998, threatening the entire US financial system, is a high-profile example, but there are many more. No doubt there were also clever folks involved in running the Knickerbocker Trust (failed 1907), Austrian Kreditanstalt (1931), Continental Illinois National Bank (1984), more than 1,000 US savings and loans (1986–1991), Barings UK (1995), and, of course, Bear Stearns, Lehman Brothers, Merrill Lynch, Washington Mutual, and Wachovia (2008).

No doubt equally clever people were running the myriad hedge funds and funds of funds that have been forced, for one reason or another, to close their doors. As we know, in recent years, huge numbers of math, science, and engineering graduates and PhDs from the world's best universities entered the financial industry and went to work building subprime collateralized debt obligations (CDOs), among other toxic securities, that have lost most or, in some cases, all of their value. There was certainly plenty of genius to go around—too much, perhaps.

Perhaps hiring geniuses doesn't guarantee that your firm won't go bankrupt or that it won't threaten the broader financial system. But what if it made it even more likely? What if some of the very geniuses who have been involved with financial failures in the past and are now the authorities on what exactly went wrong and what needs to be done, or avoided, to prevent future crises are, in fact, drawing wrong, potentially dangerous conclusions?

Let's focus this discussion on the observations of a gentleman getting much press of late, Jim Rickards, author of the recently published book *Currency Wars* and former general counsel to LTCM. In a 2009 interview, he explained what he believes are perhaps the key reasons why the financial industry so badly miscalculated the risks it was taking going into the recent crisis:

> As general counsel of LTCM, I negotiated the bailout, which averted an even greater disaster at that point. What strikes me now, looking back, is how nothing was changed; no lessons were applied. Even though the lessons were obvious, in 1998. LTCM used fatally flawed VAR risk models. LTCM used too much leverage.[43]

These value at risk (VAR) risk models to which Rickards refers are models that assume that financial asset price movements are normally distributed; that is, they follow a bell-shaped curve under which one standard deviation from the mean encompasses roughly two-thirds of all potential outcomes, and by the time you have moved three standard deviations away, you capture some 99 percent of all outcomes. That leaves the 1 percent, which is known in the industry as a once-in-a-century event—so unlikely that, for practical business purposes, there is little if any reason to worry about it.

The critical importance of the assumption that financial variables are normally distributed should not be underestimated. It is central to essentially all aspects of modern finance, ranging from how assets are to be valued, to how much capital traders, funds, or banks should hold against leveraged positions. As a prominent example, the original Black-Scholes option pricing model, developed in the 1970s and for which the Nobel Prize in Economics was awarded in 1997, assumes a normal distribution. Although subsequently modified in various ways, option pricing models in use today still explicitly assume the normality—bell-curve distribution—of returns.

Rickards is quite right that VAR is a fatally flawed concept. There is overwhelming evidence that financial price returns are not normally

43 This quote, and all subsequent quotes from Rickards in this chapter, are taken from a fascinating interview by Kathryn Welling in *Welling@Weeden* 12, no. 4 (2010). We take this opportunity to thank *Welling@Weeden* for permission to use these quotes.

distributed but rather follow what is known in physics as a power curve distribution. Rickards describes this as:

> . . . a different kind of degree distribution. Any degree distribution is simply a plotting of the frequency of an event relative to the severity of the event. . . . A power curve, one of the most common degree distributions in nature, which accurately describes many phenomena, has fewer low impact events than the bell curve but has far more high impact events. . . .
>
> A power curve says that events of any size can happen and that extreme events happen more frequently than the bell curve suggests. This corresponds to the market behavior we have seen in such extreme events as the crash of 1987, LTCM's collapse, the dot.com bubble's bursting in 2000, the housing collapse in 2007—you get the idea. Statistically, these events should happen once every 1,000 years or so in a bell curve distribution—but are expected much more frequently in a power curve distribution. In short, a power curve describes market reality, while a bell curve does not. . . .
>
> Bell curve distributions in this context describe continuous phenomena and power laws describe discontinuous but regular phenomena.

Now we notice here two things. First, Rickards is a seriously intelligent fellow with significant direct market experience and superior statistical knowledge. Second, and far subtler but hugely important, we see that the financial industry as a whole has chosen to embrace VAR models, notwithstanding overwhelming historical evidence that they dramatically underestimate risk. If the financial world is populated by geniuses, what possible explanation could there be for that? Well, he has an explanation:

> [T]he history of science is filled with false paradigms that gained followers to the detriment of better science. People really did believe the sun revolved around the earth for 2,000 years and mathematicians had the equations to prove it. . . . In effect, once an intellectual concept attracts a critical mass of supporters, it becomes entrenched. . . .
>
> I don't know whether it was denial or inertia or because people got so wedded to the elegance of the mathematics they'd done that they hated to leave all that work behind. . . . In other words, Wall Street decided that the wrong map is better than no map at all—as long as the maths are elegant. And that led to calling extreme events a sort of special case, a "fat tail," which just meant they were happening more frequently than a bell curve would indicate.

Perhaps that's it. But no, that's not all. Rickards goes one step further, which, given the huge rise in proprietary trading activities in recent decades, rings true:

> [A]nother reason the Street was loath to throw out the whole notion of normally distributed risk, and tried to salvage it instead by putting a fat tail on it, is that the alternative, a power curve, just didn't look that palatable to most practitioners and so comparatively little work has been done in applying power curves to financial markets. . . .
>
> The thing is, power curves don't have a lot of predictive value. Since most financial researchers approach the field

> precisely to gain a trading edge, once they discover power curves aren't much use there, they move on. . . .

Good insight. Probably spot on. The consequences, as we know, have been devastating. Rickards uses the severity yet unpredictability of earthquakes as an excellent analogy for financial crises and for what he believes should be done to avoid them in future:

> We know that 8.0 earthquakes are possible and we build cities accordingly, even if we cannot know when the big one will strike. Likewise, we can use power curve analysis to make our financial system more robust even if we cannot predict financial earthquakes. And one of its lessons is that as you increase the scale of the system, the risk of a mega-earthquake goes up exponentially. . . .

Unfortunately, this is not something that Wall Street or its various regulators currently comprehend. After all, the institutions that were too big to fail back in 2008 are even larger now, posing a greater systemic threat.

But I'm not so easily convinced of Wall Street's ignorance in this matter. I will explain why in a moment. First, allow Rickards to continue with his explanation:

> I've always thought the problem was that, although Wall Street was very active in hiring a lot of PhDs—astrophysicists, applied mathematicians and others with very good quantitative theoretical skills, it didn't let them use their heads. What happened was that their Wall Street managers said, "Look, here's how the financial world works and we want you to model it and code it and develop it and write these equations and programs." And so they did. . . . [I]nstead of telling them what to do, they should have listened.

Now, why is that, do you think? As mentioned earlier, I have an idea. Those Wall Street managers telling their quants what techniques to use were clever enough to understand that, were they to employ models based on power curve distributions, it would not make proprietary trading any more profitable, as such models lack predictive power. But it would dramatically increase their cost of capital, as their capital bases would need to be large enough to ensure against power-curve-implied earthquakes. Capital would need to increase, and balance sheet leverage decrease exponentially, alongside any growth in proprietary trading operations. How convenient and coincidental that Wall Street executives collectively created a VAR-based risk management culture at every single major trading firm, without exception, notwithstanding the overwhelming historical evidence that VAR is fatally flawed!

Perhaps Rickards is just being polite. I have no such compunctions when it comes to entertaining ideas of possible conflicts of interest between Wall Street executives and their firms' shareholders. The evidence may be circumstantial, but it is clear. It was never in Wall Street's interest to seriously consider replacing VAR-based with power-curve-based risk management because it would have raised the cost of capital, thereby curtailing profits, salaries, and bonuses.

But wait a minute. Am I implying that Wall Street executives were willing to risk the bankruptcy of their own firms and even the collapse of the entire financial system by deliberately employing far too much leverage? Yes, I am. As a managing director at multiple major global financial institutions in the period 2000–2008, I had ample opportunity to observe the prevailing attitudes toward risk at the highest levels, and how key decisions were made. There was a consistent, clear bias in favor of risk taking, with risk management playing only a supporting, enabling role. Those taking the greatest risks generally received the greatest rewards, including, importantly, rapid promotion. The executive committees of the major firms were thus comprised overwhelmingly of those most successful at pushing risk taking to its practical limit, which included placating (or, in some instances, bullying) those in risk management.

Remember, these Wall Street executives are smart guys. Perhaps as smart as Newton. Perhaps as smart as Rickards. Perhaps smarter still. So smart that they took a good look back at post–World War II financial market history and saw that *in every single instance in which the threat of systemic failure arose, policymakers intervened with progressively greater assistance.* And in every instance, the policy reaction has proven, in hindsight, to be disproportionate to the crisis, and the moral hazard implicit in the system has grown. Indeed, it could be argued that the regulators have made the financial world safe for fundamentally flawed, VAR-based risk models. If the power curve distribution does indeed obtain, and the 2008–2009 crisis provides crystal clear evidence that it does, then given that the too-big-to-fail firms are now even larger than they were prior to the Lehman Brothers bailout, an even larger financial crisis, with an even larger bailout price tag, lurks in the not-so-distant future. (At the time of this writing, a crisis an order of magnitude greater than that sparked by the Lehman Brothers failure appears to be brewing in the euro-area banking system, which has a huge net exposure to the heavily overindebted nations of Greece, Ireland, Portugal, Spain, and even Italy, which has the third-largest government debt in the entire world. The ECB has responded by purchasing incremental portions of these countries' debts and by providing unprecedented three-year financing to euro-area banks. While such actions do buy time, they don't in any way address the underlying causes of the crisis, that is, the excessive debt and leverage in the system.)

A REGULATORY SILVER BULLET?

Regardless of whether Rickards believes that Wall Street executives deliberately chose to ignore the implications of the power curve distribution or were simply blissfully unaware, he has specific recommendations for how to avoid another major financial crisis:

> [O]nce we understand the structure and vulnerability of the financial system in this way, some solutions and policy recommendations become obvious. . . .
>
> They fall into three categories: limiting scale, controlling cascades and securing informational advantage. . . .
>
> I certainly would favor the Volcker Rule and I would favor bringing back something like Glass-Steagall. And I'd favor imposing stricter capital ratios on banks and brokers.

What these recommendations collectively would do is give substantially greater power to regulators to determine how Wall Street is run. But stop right there. Is this realistic? Who, exactly, is going to determine how to limit scale? How can we have any confidence that such decisions will not be highly politicized? By controlling cascades, are regulators not providing an implicit subsidy for excessive risk taking? Rickards might counter that his proposed stricter capital ratios would limit such risk taking, but once again, can we be at all confident that such capital ratios will be set in a sensible, objective, nonpoliticized way, given the history of chronic failures on the part of regulators to effectively carry out their mandates? (The most recent such example of regulatory failure appears to be the MF Global bankruptcy, where client funds, thought to be segregated, were in fact used as collateral for proprietary positions. If true, this demonstrates at a minimum persistent regulatory incompetence or, alternatively, regulatory complicity in fraudulent practices at the highest levels of the US financial system.)

My concerns with a purely regulatory-based solution to serial financial crises come down to the following: Is Rickards really prepared to place his faith in the regulators who enabled the S&Ls to embark on their fateful 1980s lending binge, who failed to see the dot-com bubble but then wasted no time slashing rates when the market crashed, who denied that there was a housing bubble even as they were claiming that the nascent subprime crisis was contained, who were supposedly overseeing

Fannie and Freddie in the years prior to bailing them out completely, who repeatedly missed (or chose not to hear) the warnings about Bernie Madoff, who glossed over Lehman's category-105 repo transactions, and who bailed out AIG Credit Default Swaps CDS at par even though such contracts were trading at a huge discount in the market?

To be fair, Rickards is in good company. There are numerous policy makers and financial commentators who appear not to have learned the lesson that the US financial regulatory regime not only repeatedly fails but also fails so completely, consistently, and predictably that Wall Street has made a highly profitable business out of being bailed out. As Sir Isaac Newton might ask, have these folks fumbling about for a regulatory-based solution to Wall Street excess thought to apply the scientific method properly, isolating key assumptions and controlling for all factors? If they did, they might see the disturbingly consistent pattern right before their eyes and draw the obvious conclusion.

I agree wholeheartedly with Rickards that VAR is a flawed concept and that a power curve approach to risk management would be a welcome step in the right direction. But with all due respect, I am horrified at the prospect that the dysfunctional US financial regulatory system would be tasked with such an important initiative.

If more such misregulation is not the answer, then what is? My proposed solution is as simple as it gets: throw Wall Street and the City of London to the wolves. The US Congress and UK Parliament should pass laws making it illegal for their respective governments or any agencies thereof, including their central banks, to provide any form of direct financial assistance whatsoever, under any circumstances, to the nondepositor (e.g., wholesale, interbank) sources of funding for the financial system.

How would financial markets respond? Presumably, absent any explicit or implied guarantees, the share prices of weak financial firms would decline, perhaps to levels implying a high risk of insolvency. The weakest institutions would probably also find that their bonds were trading at a large discount and would find it difficult, if not impossible, to refinance at attractive rates. They would be forced to shrink their balance sheets—if not immediately, then gradually over time. Larger (uninsured) depositors would begin to withdraw funds from those institutions deemed at growing risk of failure and place them in stronger institutions. They would also most probably spread deposits around, seeking greater diversification of risk. In general, capital would flow from weak to strong financial institutions, exactly what is needed to avoid a repeat of 2008.[44]

Shareholders, now aware that assistance would not be forthcoming in a crisis, would demand that financial executives not only increase their respective firms' capital cushions but also devote more resources to and provide greater transparency of risk management. For institutions taking material proprietary risk in trading or investment banking, a general move back to a partnership model, in which executive wealth is tied to the stability and longer-term survival of the firm and in which conflicts of interest with shareholders and bond holders are minimized, would probably take place. Specifically, shareholders would probably demand that risk management replace flawed VAR-based methodologies with those based on a power-curve distribution. What Rickards thinks should be done by chronically incompetent regulators would almost certainly be done in short order by increasingly competent, if imperfect, financial executives, in response to shareholder pressure.

Mistakes would still be made. Geniuses aren't perfect. But absent a homogeneous VAR-based risk-management culture, the risk of systemic failure would be all but eliminated. If any firm grew to the point of

44 There are those who would argue that government-funded deposit insurance itself is a form of moral hazard. Rather than enter such a discussion, I find it simpler to emphasize that were financial shareholders and bond holders to act as if there was no implied bailout for financial firms, they would demand more sensible risk management and far higher capital ratios, quite possibly along the lines of what Rickards recommends. Doing away with the FDIC is probably not necessary in this regard.

posing a systemic risk, the cost of capital for the entire system would rise accordingly, constraining growth and reallocating resources to less risky nonfinancial business sectors.

I believe I know why financial genius fails. The answer is surprisingly simple, really: because failure pays so much better than success. Only when action is taken to ensure that success pays better than failure will financial crises threatening the health of the entire economy become a thing of the past.

2008 CRISIS POST-MORTEM: GLOBAL MONETARY DISORDER

Much has been written on the topic of what caused the 2008–2009 global credit crisis. In some cases the argument is put forth that it was pure accident. I strongly disagree. Yet regardless of whether Wall Street firms or other banks in the US and other countries were aware of the risks they were running, or whether policy makers realized that, through the decades, the degree of moral hazard had grown to system-destabilizing proportions is ultimately moot. However, as a result of the Federal Reserve and certain other central banks resorting to a historically unprecedented general global monetary inflation to try and keep the increasingly fragile system afloat, the global monetary order has entered a state of unstable equilibrium, which makes the situation in 1971—the year President Nixon suspended gold convertibility—look rather tame by comparison. Therefore, we now turn to a discussion of equilibrium dynamics.

Chapter 10:
An Unstable Equilibrium

> "A Nash equilibrium is defined as a strategy combination with the property that every player's strategy is a best reply to the other players' strategies. This of course is true also for Nash equilibria in mixed strategies. But in the latter case, besides his mixed equilibrium strategy, each player will also have infinitely many alternative strategies that are his best replies to the other players' strategies. This will make such equilibria potentially unstable."
> —Economist John Harsanyi at the Nobel Prize Seminar in honor of Mathematician and Economist John Nash, 1994

WHILE AS A SEPARATE SUB-DISCIPLINE within the economics profession, game theory is relatively new, some of the basic tenets have been around for as long as society itself. At its core, game theory is nothing more than the study of how individuals act in social situations in which there is some degree of competition. *Bargaining* and *haggling* are terms that come to mind. But what sets game theory apart is that it attempts to calculate precisely what the outcome of a given bargaining or haggling session is likely to be.

To do so, game theorists need to make certain assumptions, for example:

- What are the true interests of the players?
- What are their alternatives?
- How might the interests and alternatives of one player be taken into account by the other players?

It is this last question that is at the heart of John Nash's concept of an equilibrium that can be applied to a game with a potentially infinite number of participants. A system (game) can be said to be in equilibrium when no player has a better alternative to their existing behavior (strategy), given the interests and alternatives of the other players.

By way of an example, in a scene from the 2002 film *A Beautiful Mind,* the young John Nash is at a bar with several fellow male PhD students, enjoying a few beers, when in walks a stunning, beautiful, young blonde lady, as well as a few of her perhaps slightly less stunning (if hardly unattractive) brunette girlfriends. At once, he and each of his buddies notice heads turning in unison toward the stunning young lady, then back to each other. The unasked question among the group is "Who is going to be first to approach her?"

As they all stand up and begin moving toward the stunning blonde, young Nash realizes there is a potential problem with what he and his friends are about to do. If all of them try simultaneously to engage the stunner in conversation, thereby essentially ignoring her friends, then it is highly unlikely that she is going to want to remain so engaged for long, regardless of how interesting she might find it personally, as she will be in the uncomfortable position of having the attention of several men at once while her friends have none. The obvious risk is that she and her friends are collectively put off to the point of avoiding the entire group of young men or summarily departing the bar entirely. As such, in the game of determining which of Nash and his friends should first engage the blonde in conversation, the solution is . . .

. . . wait for it . . .

None of them!

Why is that? Consider: As it would turn the woman off were all the young men to approach her simultaneously—and as would almost certainly happen in the event that any one of them made a move in that direction—the best solution is for the men to approach her friends instead. This may seem a suboptimal outcome from the isolated perspective of any one of the young men, in that not one of them will have the opportunity of chatting up the stunner, at least not at first. At a minimum, however, they will be chatting up her friends, something they would all agree is a far better alternative to just sitting at their own table and chatting with each other, as on any other normal evening. The strategy that is the best reply to the other players' strategies provides the Nash equilibrium, in this case, the strategy of approaching the stunner's friends and ignoring the stunner entirely.

With that example in mind, we can now apply the concept of a Nash equilibrium to international monetary relations—in particular, the historical regime changes from one reserve currency to another—and consider how recent global economic and financial developments have destabilized the current, fiat-dollar reserve system. Let us begin with the pertinent historical example of the rise of the dollar—backed by gold—as a challenger to sterling's nearly exclusive reserve status in the early twentieth century.

How World War I destabilized the century-old sterling reserve currency standard

Although previously linked to gold, the dollar has been the dominant global reserve currency since the 1920s, when it assumed this role from the pound sterling. Already by the end of the nineteenth century, the US economy had surpassed that of the United Kingdom in both industrial power and agricultural output. The British Empire in its entirety was still much larger; however, the cost of maintaining it was vast and growing, amid regional instability and growing military commitments.

The pound sterling assumed global reserve status following the hard-won victory over Napoleonic France in the early nineteenth century. For decades, it had been rather touch-and-go as to whether Britain or France would emerge victorious on the continent and, hence, have the upper hand when it came to expanding the colonial empires that both countries had acquired over the course of the prior two centuries. With Napoleon vanquished, Britain had a relatively free hand in much of the world, with the notable exceptions of the Americas and central Asia. It was not for want of trying, however. Britain took on the young United States for a second time in 1812, only to be fought, yet again, to a stalemate. And Britain had a go at Russia in Crimea in the mid-1800s, which turned out more of a defeat, as did its occupation of Afghanistan.

By 1907, as a result of a series of crises in which both the British and French began to regard their respective empires as under threat from an increasingly powerful, unified, and assertive Germany, there was a realignment in European geopolitics. Both the British and French allied with Russia to keep Germany contained (or *eingekreist*—encircled, from the German perspective). When Russia and Germany subsequently clashed in August 1914 over how to respond to the assassination of Austrian Archduke (and heir to the throne) Franz Ferdinand, a general European war broke out.

Regardless of who was most responsible for starting it, World War I was hugely expensive and destructive for all European participants and, tragically, killed or severely injured a substantial portion of the young, productive British workforce. By contrast, although the United States entered the war in 1917, it did so from a position of relative strength, with both sides already nearing exhaustion. By late 1918, US troops began heading home. Although Britain won the war, its government finances did not. By the early-1920s, it was increasingly clear that Britain's economy was struggling to grow while shouldering the twin financial burdens of servicing the huge war debt and maintaining the vast overseas empire.

Having abandoned the gold standard and inflated the currency to help finance the war, Britain did attempt to return to gold in 1925 (although this was poorly executed, as it happens, as we discuss at some length later). Yet the writing was on the wall. Also on the gold standard, yet now with a much larger economy and far sounder government finances behind it, the US dollar was used increasingly in international transactions and as a reserve currency for the global banking system. When in 1931 the British retreated from their return to gold and devalued the pound sterling versus the dollar, it was an acknowledgment of what had been occurring beneath the surface of the global economy for years. A new monetary equilibrium had been found with the dollar, not the pound sterling, at the center.

Let's return to Nash and consider how World War I changed the environment in which the game of global monetary relations was being played. One player, Britain, found its economic position severely weakened. Another, the United States, continued to grow rapidly. Not only was the population growing, so was per capita income. As for other countries, most of them now found they were trading relatively more with the larger and more rapidly growing United States and relatively less with the smaller and stagnating Britain.

Table 10.1: Real GDP per capita ratios for selected country pairs

	UK / US	UK / Germany	UK / France
1870	131	174	170
1913	93	135	141
1929	80	136	117

Source: Angus Maddison historical database.

Therefore, it was only natural that more and more trade was not only transacted in dollars but also invoiced and accounted for in dollars. Moreover, with a larger, healthier economy standing behind it, the dollar was now also regarded as a more reliable store of value, less likely to be suddenly devalued (as sterling was in 1914–18 and again in 1931). As such, for managing risk, the dollar was increasingly seen as the natural reference point and reserve to hold against potential loss, the preferred reserve currency.

The dollar reserve standard thus became the new global monetary equilibrium, although, of course, the dollar was backed by gold, at a rate of $20.67 per troy ounce. As the United States became increasingly prosperous in the 1920s—the Roaring 20s—it began to import relatively more and export relatively less to the rest of the world, and the gold reserve began to flow out. In 1926, the United States held an estimated 45 percent of the entire world's official monetary gold supply (excluding Russia). Yet by the early 1930s, this share fell to under 35 percent.

Following World War II, one consequence of which was a huge accumulation of gold by the United States, the share increased briefly to over 60 percent.[45] Yet once again, as the postwar prosperity set in and the United States began to import and consume more and export relatively less, the share declined steadily thereafter, sinking below 50 percent by the late 1950s. By the mid-1960s, US gold holdings were less than its foreign liabilities. It was precisely this development that so worried the French and other Europeans and led Jacques Rueff, among other economists, to predict the imminent demise of the Bretton Woods system.[46]

How the 2008–2009 Global Financial Crisis Destabilized Bretton Woods II, or the Fiat-Dollar Reserve Standard

While World War I and the financial crisis of 2008–2009 are hard to compare in many respects, such as the devastation they wrought or their political consequences, they have certain things in common. Both had a huge impact on the health of economies, including that of the country providing the global reserve currency. Both led to economic policy

45 While the US had already accumulated large official gold holdings following FDRs confiscation of private gold in 1934, WWII provided a historic opportunity to acquire gold from abroad amidst the extra-legal chaos of wartime. While the exact amount will perhaps never be known, and has been the topic of numerous conspiracy theories, it is generally assumed that some portion of possibly never officially disclosed German and Japanese gold hoards were discovered by US forces during or following the war. What happened to those hoards thereafter is open to dispute.

46 For the historical data cited here, see Henry Hazlitt, *What You Should Know about Inflation* (Princeton, NJ: D. Van Nostrand, 1964).

decisions at the national level that were clearly not in the interest of other nations. As such, both destabilized the Nash equilibrium required to maintain a reserve currency standard.

It is not yet generally understood, however, the extent to which the 2008–2009 financial crisis and global economic policy responses to it have already fatally undermined the fiat-dollar standard equilibrium. This is due primarily to a misconception within the economics profession that for most, if not all, of the key players involved, the costs of moving away from the fiat-dollar standard still far exceed the benefits.

This view has been the conventional wisdom for some years. In late 2003, three prominent economists, David Folkerts-Landau, Michael Dooley, and Peter Garber, published a paper making the case that the so-called Bretton Woods II arrangement of fixed or generally managed emerging market exchange rates vis-à-vis the dollar—a system that had been more or less in place following the various Asian currency crises of 1997–1998—was a stable equilibrium for a variety of reasons. The most important reason given was that the emerging markets were undergoing a long-term structural investment boom that could be properly financed only through export-led growth, much as had been the case under the original Bretton Woods arrangements in the 1950s and 1960s, when Western Europe and Japan exported their way to renewed postwar prosperity. As such, notwithstanding a declining share of global economic output and rising fiscal and current account deficits, the fiat dollar was likely to remain the world's preeminent reserve currency for the foreseeable future, indeed, for decades to come.

Here is the abstract to the paper on the NBER website, which originally appeared in the *International Journal of Finance and Economics*:

> The economic emergence of a fixed exchange rate periphery in Asia has reestablished the United States as the center country in the Bretton Woods international monetary system. We argue that the normal evolution of

> the international monetary system involves the emergence of a periphery for which the development strategy is export-led growth supported by undervalued exchange rates, capital controls and official capital outflows in the form of accumulation of reserve asset claims on the center country. The success of this strategy in fostering economic growth allows the periphery to graduate to the center. Financial liberalization, in turn, requires floating exchange rates among the center countries. But there is a line of countries waiting to follow the Europe of the 1950s/60s and Asia today sufficient to keep the system intact for the foreseeable future.[47]

I was not alone at the time in being somewhat skeptical that this was indeed a stable equilibrium. As a result of maintaining fixed or managed exchange rates with the United States, not only were the emerging markets growing much faster than the United States but also accumulating vast dollar reserves that were then reinvested in US assets, thereby pushing down dollar interest rates and pushing up asset valuations, including, of course, house prices, to levels inconsistent with US household income growth. But with consumer price inflation low as a result of cheap manufactured goods from abroad and low rents at home—the flip side of the increasing rate of home ownership, courtesy of low interest rates—the US Federal Reserve saw no need to raise interest rates in response to the domestic credit, housing, and consumption boom, which ultimately originated from the Bretton-Woods II regime.

47 This paper can be accessed at www.nber.org/papers/w9971.pdf.

Figure 10.1: The Fed has stood by, amid low CPI, facilitating the growth of a colossal debt bubble

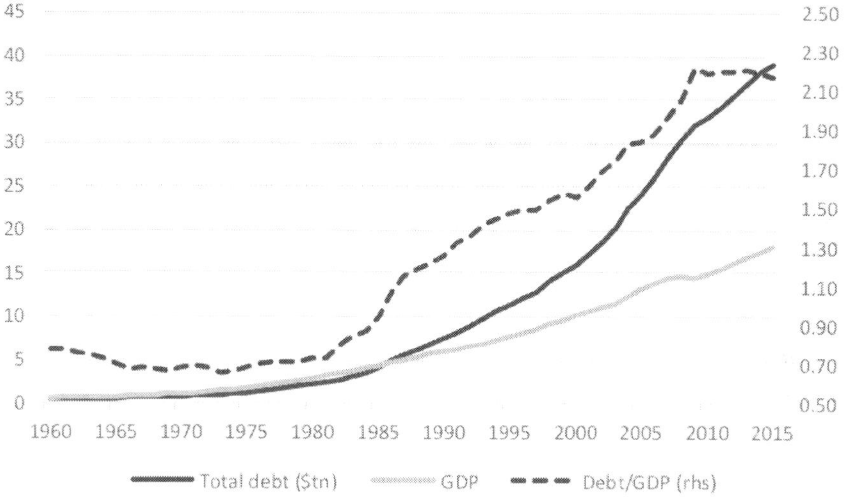

Source: Federal Reserve.

Figure 10.2: The debt bubble is financed in large part by foreign countries accumulating dollar reserve balances

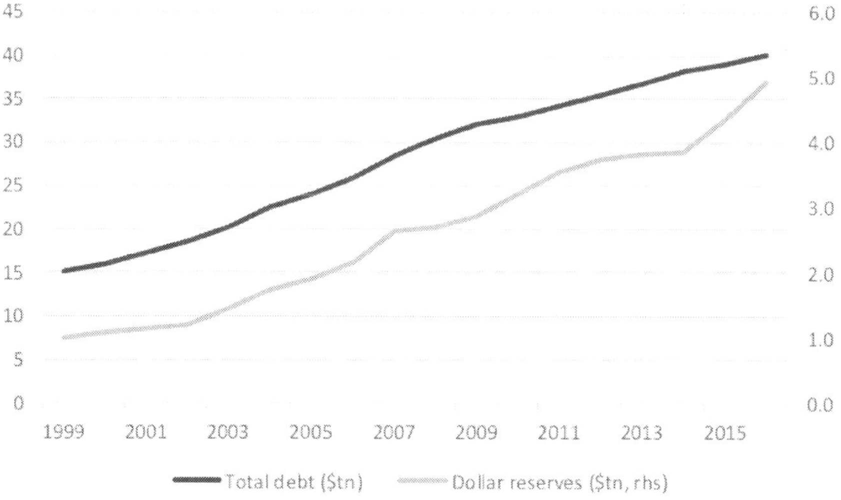

Source: International Monetary Fund.

It is now generally accepted by the economic mainstream that the Fed's decision to hold interest rates low for a sustained period in 2003–2005 was the key contributing cause of the growth of the US housing bubble that burst in 2007, thereby triggering the subsequent global financial crisis. As the bubble was inflating, Fed officials repeatedly claimed that not only was the rise in house prices not a bubble but also that low interest rates had little if anything to do with it. In 2005, Ben Bernanke, who had only recently assumed the Fed chairmanship, claimed that low US borrowing costs were the result of a "global savings glut," in particular in rapidly growing Asian countries, rather than a function of Fed monetary policy.[48] But the global savings glut and Fed policy should never have been separated in this way. The latter directly enabled the former.

By focusing on consumer price inflation only, rather than money and credit growth generally, the Fed completely missed the connection between US interest rates, global savings, investment, and asset prices. It therefore failed to see that its policies were the ultimate cause of the housing bubble and that the global savings glut was just one link in a long money-and-credit chain that had become unanchored. The late great Austrian economist Kurt Richebächer recognized clearly that this was the case. As he wrote in April 2005:

> In earlier studies published by the International Monetary Fund about asset bubbles in general, and Japan's bubble economy in particular, the authors repeatedly asked why policymakers failed to recognize the rising prices in the asset markets as asset inflation. Their general answer was that the absence of conventional inflation in consumer and producer prices confused most people, traditionally accustomed to taking rises in the CPI as the decisive token for inflation.

48 The text of this speech can be found at www.federalreserve.gov/boarddocs/speeches/2005/200503102/.

It seems to us that today this very same confusion is blinding policymakers and citizens in the United States and other bubble economies, like England and Australia, to the unmistakable circumstance of existing rampant housing bubbles in their countries.

Thinking about inflation, it is necessary to separate its cause and its effects or symptoms. There is always one and the same cause, and that is credit creation in excess of current saving leading to demand growth in excess of output. But this common cause may produce an extremely different pattern of effects in the economy and its financial system. This pattern of effects is entirely contingent upon the use of the credit excess—whether it primarily finances consumption, investment, imports or asset purchases.

A credit expansion in the United States of close to $10 trillion—in relation to nominal GDP growth of barely $2 trillion over the last four years since 2000—definitely represents more than the usual dose of inflationary credit excess. This is really hyperinflation in terms of credit creation.

In other words, **there is tremendous inflationary pressure at work, but it has impacted the economy and the price system very unevenly. The credit deluge has three obvious main outlets: imports, housing and the carry trade in bonds. On the other hand, the absence of strong consumer price inflation is taken as evidence that inflationary pressures are generally absent. Everybody feels comfortable with this (mis)judgment.**[49]

---

49 See www.gold-eagle.com/gold_digest_05/richebacher042305.html.

The mistake made by Folkerts-Landau, Dooley, and Garber was that they failed to see back in 2003 that the Fed's easy money policy was fueling rampant money and credit growth that, in time, would lead to a colossal global credit crisis. To be fair, the entire economic mainstream missed it too. But this just begs the question of why. The best explanation is that the modern economics profession focuses primarily on consumer price inflation as a potential source of economic instability, rather than money and credit growth generally. Austrian School economists, such as Richebächer, know better. He was hardly the only Austrian economist to predict the crisis.

The futility of inflation targeting

The fact is, inflation targeting is not a valid way in which to maintain economic stability. Yet the bulk of the developed economies' central banks follow some sort of inflation-targeting policy regarding consumer price inflation. The Fed and the European Central Bank (ECB) both have dual mandates, although these are somewhat different. In the Fed's case, the goal is to maintain low and stable inflation while also achieving full employment. In the ECB's case, the goal is also to maintain low consumer price inflation but also to prevent money growth accelerating to levels that would imply potentially destabilizing credit growth.

The Fed's mandate is in effect a Keynesian one, in that it assumes that there is some theoretical trade-off between inflation and employment and that the central bank can manage this trade-off in practice, thereby maintaining economic stability and achieving a healthy, sustainable rate of economic growth. As we have seen, however, the Fed has failed to do so, primarily because of the serial bubbles and busts that it has engendered by failing to maintain stable money and credit growth and encouraging excessive risk taking with repeated bailouts. As such, the Fed's mandate is misspecified: Not only is there no simple trade-off between inflation and unemployment, as demonstrated by the stagflationary 1970s and are seeing again today, but by the time excessive money and credit growth show up in the consumer price index (CPI), enormous damage may already have been done to the financial system. The CPI is inflation past. Money supply growth is inflation present. And as we shall see later, fiscal deficits are inflation future.

The ECB's mandate, on the other hand, recognizes that there must be some link between money and credit growth, on the one hand, and price stability on the other. It has no set monetary rule but, rather, uses money and credit growth aggregates as an important guide to policy. Thus the ECB's mandate leans a bit in the direction of the Austrian economic tradition.

As it turns out, in sharp contrast to the Fed, the ECB has generally met its inflation target in the decade for which it has been in existence. On multiple occasions, the ECB has raised interest rates, not because growth was particularly strong nor because consumer price inflation had risen significantly, but rather because money and credit growth were strong and accelerating, implying a rising risk of economic instability in future. Yes, the ECB came under much criticism at these times, as money and credit targeting had generally fallen out of favor. But the results speak for themselves. In the years 1999 through 2011, the ECB has done the better job.

Recently, the euro area has been beset by a series of sovereign debt crises that threaten the European monetary union (EMU). However, the ECB is not responsible for the chronic overborrowing of various European governments. These crises are fiscal in origin, rather than monetary. It is true that a number of European banks hold large amounts of sovereign debt that is likely to be restructured in some way and that in some cases the banks lack sufficient capital to take the necessary write-downs and still remain solvent. But here, too, it would be incorrect to blame the ECB, which is not the European banking regulator. Within the EMU, bank regulation remains at the national level.

The relative experience of the Fed and the ECB in recent years demonstrates that central banks' focus on inflation targeting is misplaced.

The focus must instead be on money and credit growth, as the Austrian Economic School has been arguing for the better part of a century.

As can now be seen around the globe, economic instability can take many forms. In some cases it might be associated with consumer price inflation but in others it might not. In all cases, however, it is associated with unstable money and credit growth. With the Federal Reserve at the center of the international monetary system, it is the ultimate source of the international monetary base and, hence, the credit growth, boom, and bust that takes place on top of it.

One by one, various countries are beginning to recognize that the aggressive, unconventional monetary policy of the Federal Reserve may no longer be appropriate for their own economies; yet, as participants in the international monetary system, it would seem they have little alternative. A country refusing to use dollars for trade, for example, risks economic isolation.[50] This helps to explain for example why the BRICS are increasingly cooperating with one another in international economic and monetary affairs, as they have more leverage together than apart. But whether the BRICS or other countries are increasingly dissatisfied, the problem then becomes, if the Fed, the issuer of the world's reserve currency, is not willing to change its ways and follow a mandate that can provide a more acceptable degree of global monetary stability, what is the world to do? Switch to the euro? Unfortunately, the various, escalating euro-area sovereign debt crises obviate that possibility. The yen perhaps? Few would take that possibility seriously, given the chronic quantitative easing and foreign exchange intervention of the Japanese authorities. The

50 This is one reason why the US relies heavily on economic sanctions in its foreign policies, as these can have real teeth. In severe cases, such as with Iran, the US simply forbids other countries to do business with the sanctioned country. As the US authorities can see all US dollar transactions moving through the international banking system, as these must all eventually clear through US banks, they can keep an eye out for countries not honoring the sanctions, and penalize them accordingly. This happened with big French bank BNP back in 2015, which was fined a record $8.9bn for providing financing to Iran, among other sanctioned countries.

Swiss franc? No, the Swiss economy is just too small and its domestic securities markets would not provide sufficient global liquidity to be the dominant global reserve currency.

What of other candidates? Is there any currency out there that both represents a stable economic area and is also managed in a way that would provide sufficient global monetary stability? While there is no national currency that ticks both of those critical boxes, there has been some discussion about turning to the special drawing rights (SDR) unit of account used by the IMF, which could, in theory at least, provide a global fiat reserve currency alternative to the dollar.

The SDR non-solution to global monetary instability

The SDR is a basket of IMF member countries' currencies and is used as a unit of account in the IMF's financing and lending activities. As it stands now, the dollar is the largest part of the SDR basket. However, the basket is reweighted whenever member countries' relative capital contributions to the IMF change, as happened in 2015 when the Chinese renminbi was included in the SDR basket for the first time. Were the BRICS in general to contribute substantial capital to the IMF, then their currencies could be a substantial portion of the SDR basket. As such, so the thinking goes, the SDR is well-suited to accommodate the shifting, global economic and monetary power equilibrium and therefore provide a proper global fiat currency to succeed the fiat dollar.

However, to turn the SDR from a mere unit of account into a true global reserve currency would take a series of steps, some of which would be politically difficult due to the degree of cooperation required. First, the IMF would go from being a supranational bank to supranational central bank, with the authority to print and control the global, SDR-denominated money supply. As was the case with the euro at inception, this would not require that actual printed SDR currency circulates; rather, it could be done by the IMF fixing the exchange rates between all member currencies to the SDR reference basket. Recall that from 1999 to 2002, the euro existed as an electronic currency only, with the printed national legacy currencies providing the circulating notes and coins. But from 1999, the ECB nevertheless controlled the collective money supply and set a single interest rate for the entire euro-area banking system. The same could be the case with the SDR indefinitely. National currencies need never be replaced.

In theory, this solves the dilemma of the current fiat dollar reserve system in that it would no longer be the case that a single national central bank indirectly sets international interest rates and controls the *de facto* global monetary reserve base. Rather, the supranational IMF would set interest rates and grow the money supply in a way that would supposedly serve the broader interests of all IMF member countries. As the IMF describes the proposal in a recent working paper on the topic:

> A limitation of the SDR . . . is that it is not a currency. Both the SDR and SDR-denominated instruments need to be converted eventually to a national currency for most payments or interventions in foreign exchange markets, which adds to cumbersome use in transactions. . . .
>
> A global currency . . . issued by a global central bank would be designed as a stable store of value that is not tied exclusively to the conditions of any particular economy. As trade and finance continue to grow rapidly and global integration increases, the importance of this broader perspective is expected to continue growing. . . .
>
> If [a global currency] were to circulate as a parallel currency but in a dominant role in place of the US dollar, then as in the [system] described above, current account imbalances that reflect today's situation—namely, surplus countries pegging to [the global currency] with deficit countries floating against it—would adjust more symmetrically, and perhaps more automatically, than the current [system]

> since the since the deficit currencies would be expected to depreciate against [the global currency]. . . .[51]

While this sounds nice on paper, consider it in practice, with the experience of the euro area since following the introduction of the single currency as a relevant example. The euro was intended to replace national currencies and to facilitate intra-euro-area balance-of-payments adjustments as described previously. Yet it hasn't worked. One monetary policy has not been suitable for all member countries, notwithstanding a tremendous degree of European economic integration. Yes, the ECB has arguably done a respectable job at balancing the contrasting economic conditions across the euro area and maintaining a relatively high degree of consumer price stability, but it is precisely this apparent operational competence that exposes the systemic flaw for all to see. The fact is that labor and capital have not been mobile enough in the euro area, resulting in local asset bubbles and excessive wage growth in the periphery. Fiscal policy has not been sufficiently uniform and has been too loose in many countries. And as the years have rolled by, the related, cumulative imbalances have grown to the point that the currency union, as currently structured, cannot long continue.[52] Either there must be a far greater degree of economic integration—something you cannot force by policy over any reasonable time horizon—or there must be a formal fiscal and banking union, with automatic transfer payments from wealthy regions

51 "Reserve Accumulation and International Monetary Stability," IMF Policy Paper, prepared by the Strategy, Policy and Review Department, in collaboration with the Finance, Legal, Monetary and Capital Markets, Research, and Statistics Departments and consultation with the Area Departments, April 13, 2010.

52 A good reference point for the growth and scale of intra-euro-area imbalances are the cross-border claims referred to as "Target 2" by the ECB. Among others, prominent German economics professor Hans Werner-Sinn refers to the Target 2 imbalances when making his case that the euro-area, as currently structured, is an unstable and unsustainable currency union. His book, *The Euro Trap* (2014), is a comprehensive treatment of the subject.

to poorer ones and pooled bank deposit insurance underwritten by the stronger economies such as Germany.

Notwithstanding close political ties across borders, few observers believe that the euro area could implement the degree of fiscal and banking integration required to make the currency union sustainable without subverting democracy to a point that would begin to look autocratic and arbitrary and, as such, blatantly incompatible with modern European democratic traditions. The May 2016 decision by the United Kingdom to exit the European Union is but one high-profile example of how, in fact, the trend is European politics is increasingly centripetal. Movements to either leave the EU or fundamentally renegotiate membership terms are large and growing in nearly all EU member states, including the largest and most important, even Germany and France.

Now extrapolate this to the global level. Labor and capital are far less mobile around the world than within the euro area. Fiscal policy is far from uniform. Indeed, there are completely different economic models followed across the world, even if, in general, there has been a trend toward greater liberalization of labor and capital markets in recent decades. Imagine now that a push was made for fiscal and banking union among IMF member countries. It is difficult to believe that democratic countries would choose to move in that direction. As for more autocratic ones, some might and some might not, but few could doubt that such decisions would be driven by raw national interest and not some misplaced hope that what has failed demonstrably at the European level would somehow fare better globally.

In my opinion, the degree of cooperation involved to move the world toward an SDR-based single currency is insurmountable in the current global political, social, and economic context, no matter how much monetary sense it might theoretically make. That said, even on the purely monetary side of the issue, it is highly questionable that even the most qualified central bankers in charge of a hypothetical global central bank could possibly make consistently sensible decisions for how to set global interest rates, grow the money supply, act as a lender of last resort in a crisis, and so on.

Among others, Nobel laureate and so called father of the euro Robert Mundell is highly critical of the possibility that the SDR could somehow replace the fiat dollar as the new primary global monetary reserve asset. As he said in March 2011:

> Today there is no possibility of the SDR or any variant of it becoming a world currency in the sense of a substitute for the role of the dollar in its heyday.[53]

When Mundell refers to the "heyday" of the dollar he is talking about the Bretton-Woods experience, with the dollar not only at the center but backed by gold. The IMF has at no point suggested that an SDR global currency would be gold-backed. But it is understandable that the IMF is making a push to become the issuer of a global currency and serve as the world's central bank. Bureaucrats are naturally drawn to bureaucratic solutions to real-world problems. But as just demonstrated before, a single global fiat currency, based on the SDR or some other arbitrary unit of account, is nothing more than a bureaucratic pipe dream. It is highly unlikely that a global political consensus could be reached for how to construct, share power, and implement policy through a global central bank. And if it were, the large cracks in this highly unstable Nash equilibrium would spread rapidly at the first signs of crisis, with one country after another defecting, and the entire thing would collapse,

53 Presentation to the China G-20 Seminar, Nanjing, China, March 31, 2011. Mundell does, however, see it as possible, and desirable, that the United States, euro area, and China agree to fix their exchange rates, so as to provide a stable, global currency anchor for all others. This, he believes, would be a viable replacement for the fiat dollar. In my opinion, given the demonstrably divergent domestic monetary incentives between the United States, China, and within the euro area itself, it is unrealistic to believe that the actors involved could achieve the degree of agreement and cooperation required to maintain fixed exchange rates for long.

leaving the world no better off than it was under the fiat dollar reserve system, and arguably even worse.

The ever-prescient Jacques Rueff was making precisely these points back in the late 1960s, when the newly created SDR unit of account was already seen as a potential successor to the fiat dollar. In particular, he noted that an SDR reserve system would implicitly reward countries that ran budget and trade deficits and penalize those that did not. This is because SDRs could be created to settle balance-of-payments deficits. Those countries running deficits would be the first to receive the new SDRs. In time, however, these new SDRs, a form of global monetary inflation, would contribute to asset bubbles, resource misallocation, and consumer price inflation. As such, countries exercising restraint in domestic fiscal and monetary policy would bear the costs for others' profligacy. He was particularly concerned about what would happen when a crisis arose:

> Any international monetary crisis, any major outflow of capital...will provide an opportunity for an inflationary issue of SDRs. This in turn will lead to powerful surges of inflation in creditor countries. [54]

An SDR-based system would thus suffer from an inherent moral-hazard problem encouraging deficit spending and domestic inflation, which would periodically spill over into international monetary crises. Under Bretton-Woods, only the United States enjoyed the "exorbitant privilege" of being able to effectively force creditor countries to finance its trade and budget deficits at low interest rates. Under an SDR-based system, any country running trade and budget deficits would have the privilege.

The idea that China, Japan, Russia, oil exporters, or other creditor countries would go along with such a scheme is absurd. Absent a

54 Jacques Rueff, *The Monetary Sin of the West*, (New York: The Macmillan Company, 1970), 171.

hegemon to impose it, the idea that agreement could be reached to enact such as arrangement and sustain it thereafter is far-fetched indeed.

Were Jacques Rueff alive today, he would probably see an SDR-based solution as even more unworkable than in the late 1960s, given the current degree of monetary instability and lack of global cooperation in economic and monetary affairs, both of which are an order of magnitude greater. Fortunately, no fiat currency, national or global, is required to serve as the primary global reserve. History presents the world with an existing, tried, and tested alternative: gold.

The Emergence of the Classical Gold Standard in the 1870s

At this point, it is instructive to consider how the classical gold standard came into existence in the 1870s. Consider that following the various European revolutions of the 1840s and 1850s and the Franco-Prussian war of 1871, the European political landscape had been transformed. A new balance of power had been established on the continent. Economic hardship was giving way to an era of growth, trade, and integration.

There was, however, no dominant economic power, no hegemon to provide a reserve currency for all. The United Kingdom had a global empire and a formidable navy, to be sure, but its ability to project power, economic or otherwise, into the Baltic region or the interior of Eurasia was becoming limited, as demonstrated by the growth of the Prussian-led, central European economic *Zollverein*[55] and, rather more painfully, by the Crimean War.

It was out of this increasingly non-hegemonic political environment, characterized by growing international trade, that the classical gold

55 *Zollverein* translates into English as "customs union." As Prussia grew in size, it began to act as a regional economic hegemon, imposing a form of mercantilism on its neighbors within the Zollverein. Interestingly, it was Prussia, rather than Great Britain, that began to rely more exclusively on gold rather than silver to settle international trade in the years leading up to the classical gold standard.

standard emerged. Rather than being somehow imposed from above by any one country or group of countries, as was the case with the Bretton-Woods system, it arose from the bottom up. Gold provided an objective, universal reference point for cross-border trade between countries that were once and future economic competitors and, at times, military adversaries. Indeed, as one prominent study of the classical gold standard puts it:

> [T]he regime dynamics of the classical gold standard were founded on neither cooperation nor hegemonic leadership. Both the origin and stability of the gold standard, in fact, resulted from much more diffuse or decentralized processes (i.e. not managed at the international level). . . .
>
> Contrary to many visions of the gold standard, the regime dynamics upon which it was founded showed a strongly diffuse character. Moreover, the managerial elements that did show up were quite different from the conventional visions of hegemony and cooperation in the literature on international regimes. The nature of hegemony was much more unintentional and non-state than prevailing theories of hegemonic regimes can account for . . . .
>
> Cooperation, too, fails to explain the origin and stability of the regime. In fact, **it was a failure to cooperate that led to the emergence of the regime in the 1870s**. . . . Moreover, it is not clear that more cooperation would have produced a more stable regime. The lack of cooperative schemes effectively limited the degree to which authorities could allow their macroeconomies to arrive at conditions that would have threatened convertibility (i.e. moral hazard and adverse substitution leading to inflation and fiscal deficits). . . .

> In sum, the gold standard showed very little cooperation among national governments in the process of formal regime building. **The rise of the gold standard can be seen more as a case of a regime emerging from the failure to cooperate.** (emphasis added)[56]

There are, thus, strong parallels between the 1870s and today. The United States began to lose hegemonic status in the 1960s, to which the outflow of gold and the gradual decline in the US share of global economic output attest. The closing of the gold window in 1971 was an important signpost in this regard. More recently, the fiat-dollar standard has demonstrably destabilized the global economy and led to a series of escalating monetary and currency disputes. The global economy is in desperate need of a new, more stable monetary order, yet it must be one that can function absent a hegemon and without an established, institutionalized basis for cooperation.

Back in 1997, over a decade before the 2008–2009 global credit crisis, Nobel laureate Robert Mundell observed that:

> We can look upon the period of the gold standard… as being a period that was unique in history, when **there was a balance among the powers and no single superpower dominated**. [Emphasis added][57]

As it now appears, following decades of relative decline of the US economy and the rise of the BRICS and a handful of other nations, the "balance among the powers" to which Mundell refers may not be so historically unique after all. Indeed, the stage for gold has been set.

---

56 Guilio Gallarotti, *The Anatomy of an International Monetary Regime: The Classical Gold Standard 1880–1914* (New York: Oxford University Press, 1995), 218–227.

57 Robert Mundell, "The International Monetary System in the 21st Century: Could Gold Make a Comeback?" Lecture delivered at St. Vincent College, Letrobe, Pennsylvania, March 12, 1997.

Chapter 11: The Inevitability of Regime Change

> "The seven problems of the present international monetary system... are all related to the change in the role of the dollar."
>
> — Nobel laureate Robert Mundell, presentation to the China G-20 Seminar, March 31, 2011

> "Although textbooks may view gold as the old money, markets are using gold as an alternative monetary asset today."
>
> —World Bank President Robert Zoellick, 2010

THAT WHICH CAN'T GO ON, won't. The fiat dollar standard has destabilized the global economy to such a degree that regime change has become inevitable. With no other viable alternative, absent hegemonic or otherwise stable and established institutional order, gold is going to resume its historical place at the center of the global monetary system. Gold provides the only possible game-theoretic monetary solution to the contemporary, multipolar distribution of global economic power. It is only a matter of time before an event or series of events, possibly another economic crisis, catalyze a historic transition and at least partial remonetization of gold. Indeed, as we will see in Section III, the movement away from the dollar and toward gold has already begun.

A gold standard solves the fundamental global problem of excessive, unsustainable money and credit growth because the supply of reserves becomes essentially finite. You can't print gold, no matter how much a government might wish to, thus gold thereby "disarms" those countries that might otherwise seek to devalue their way through so-called currency wars. Gold is also expensive to produce. You dig more out of the ground only when the price is high enough (or expected returns on financial assets low enough) to justify this diversion of productive economic resources. And what drives the gold price higher or the expected returns on financial assets lower in the first place? Why, excessive money and credit growth. As such, the gold standard is self-regulating. It requires neither a hegemon nor an established institutional order to impose it. Indeed, as we have seen, the classical gold standard arose due to a relative absence of international cooperation in monetary affairs.

Why gold? Why couldn't other commodities provide the basis for international money?

Those not familiar with the classical gold standard and the role of gold as a universal money in general throughout recorded human history frequently wonder why gold, in particular, has been the preferred monetary asset. In fact, as it happens, silver has been more commonly used as money, but for smaller, day-to-day transactions and for intranational rather than international trade. Copper, nickel, and other metals have also been used for everyday transactions and, in many countries, still provide the material for modern coinage. Yet cross-border commerce and balance-of-payments have been dominated by gold. Why should that be so?

First, as mankind has always placed a much higher valuation on gold than on silver, due most probably to its relative scarcity and lack of decay, it is more practical for use in large transactions, which cross-border balance of payments tend to be.

Second, as it is almost perfectly nonreactive, gold has essentially zero industrial uses. Indeed, due to its relatively high malleability, gold has been used in religious art and artifacts or as decorative jewelry more commonly than as bullion, a relatively modern invention by comparison.

Silver and other precious metals have a broad and growing range of practical industrial uses, which greatly affects the available stocks, whereas the world's stock of gold tends to remain relatively constant, growing only slowly over time. This stability of the stock is essential for money. A money with an unstable, unpredictable supply simply can't function as such, as we have already seen in our discussion of why the fiat dollar is losing its preeminent global reserve status.

Third, gold is easily distinguishable from other metals. While platinum is rarer, it can be difficult to distinguish from both palladium and silver. Gold is the only yellow metal.

This combination of gold's unique color, ease of malleability, lack of decay, and relative scarcity is simply not shared by any other metal, nor any commodity substance yet discovered. Gold thus stands alone as the international money standard *par excellence*. There is also the non-trivial matter of historical and cultural precedent which, in certain parts of the world, borders on the religious.

That said, there is a case to be made that for specialized, relatively nondiversified, exporting economies, producing primarily commodities, be they metals, or energy, or agricultural products, the most appropriate money, or valuation benchmark for their exchange rates versus other currencies, could be that which they produce for export. Much work has been done in this area by Jeffrey Frankel of Harvard University.

For the world economy as a whole, however, which is not specialized but rather highly diversified, the only commodity that can credibly claim universal acceptance as money is that which always has, throughout history. Agrarian, artisanal, preindustrial, industrial, and, as demonstrated today, even postindustrial societies have always found gold to possess a unique role as a store of value and, by extension, as a universal money.

The late Roy Jastram opined in his classic work, *The Golden Constant,* that perhaps the most fundamental reasons that gold has held its preeminent monetary place throughout world history ultimately are derived from human emotion. On the one hand, gold is regarded as simply beautiful, perhaps because it is the only metal the color of the sun, the source of all light and life. On the other, even though it provides no physical nourishment, warmth, or shelter, it gives mankind comfort in times of stress or distress. No government-mandated legal tender can possibly replace that which transcends all government, all laws, and, indeed, all things created by man.

Gold provides a solution to the problems associated with modern, activist-centered banking

As for central banking, the problems associated with arbitrary interest rate manipulation and inflation targeting disappear when gold takes center stage. The gold standard cares not what the rate of consumer price inflation is. It cares only about the amount of money and credit circulating in the economy. If too much is circulating relative to the available supply of gold, the time value of money—the interest rate—rises, sucking it back in. If too little, the interest rate declines, releasing more. Yes, a gold standard implies that economic policy makers effectively lose control of the money supply and interest rates, but that is precisely the point. You don't fix a broken global monetary equilibrium by giving policy makers the power to micromanage it to their own arbitrary, nationalistic ends. Rather, you start over, with an objective reference point that restores confidence precisely because it cannot be manipulated by any one country or group of countries to their benefit at the expense of their trading partners. That objective reference point is gold.

This important point has been emphasized by none other than Robert Zoellick, former president of the World Bank. In a provocative editorial published in the *Financial Times* in November 2010, he listed a range of actions that should be taken to help stabilize the global financial system. One of these was to reinstate gold as a universal monetary reference point. Following a discussion of how a number of major currencies, taken together, could form the basis for a new global monetary system, he wrote that:

> The system should also consider employing gold as an international reference point of market expectations about inflation, deflation and future currency values.[58]

In the article, he concluded his discussion of a future role for gold by addressing critics of the idea, pointing out that some may regard gold as "old money" but that the present, stark reality was that gold was clearly now regarded by financial markets as an "alternative monetary asset."

There are other ways in which a return to gold can restore confidence in the international monetary system. Perhaps the simplest is to consider a few recent historical observations: Gold did not cause the great credit crisis of 2008, from which the global economy has yet to properly recover. Gold is not causing the surge in currency volatility and rising price inflation across much of the developing world. Gold did not create the huge imbalances, public and private, foreign and domestic, that built up over the past decades; the fiat dollar did.

For those with a longer historical perspective, it was while on a gold standard in the late nineteenth and early twentieth centuries that the Western world's standard of living effectively quintupled in just a few generations. The idea that a gold standard is incompatible with strong, sustainable economic growth is hogwash; the truth is quite the opposite.

There are those who argue that, had the world still been on a gold standard, the great credit crisis of 2008 would have been even worse, as policy makers' hands would have been tied and they would have been unable to bail-out banks and reliquefy the financial system. But that is getting things backwards. Let's put the horse in front of the cart where it belongs: had policy makers' hands been tied, and the excessive money and credit growth enabled by delinking the dollar to gold thereby restrained, a crisis of systemic proportions would never have materialized in the first place.

58 Robert Zoellick, "The G20 Must Look beyond Bretton Woods II," *Financial Times,* November 7, 2010.

Logic begins from first principles which, when it comes to understanding financial crises, must include a suitable historical starting point. To choose an arbitrary starting point such as October 2008, or the recession of 2001–02, or any recession or financial crisis for that matter is to avoid the need entirely to consider how periods of unanchored money and credit growth might have contributed to those events. While we're talking logic, we can also say that the cure for the crisis cannot be the same as the cause. So why then do some economists claim that the solution to financial crises following on periods of elevated money and credit growth is an even higher rate of money and credit growth? Such nonsense should be recognized for what it is.

As with Bretton Woods, Bretton Woods II was a stable equilibrium only to the extent that the various participants were willing to confer the benefit of lower borrowing costs on the United States in return for perceived global monetary stability and, it was assumed, sustainable rates of healthy, noninflationary economic growth. The global credit crisis has shown this apparently beneficial quid pro quo to have been a mirage. Whereas the last time the world faced a similar situation, in 1971, the United States resolved the issue unilaterally by severing the dollar's link to gold, this time round, the only resolution is for the global economy to sever its link to the fiat dollar reserve standard.

More specifically, Bretton Woods II, like Bretton Woods itself, was unsustainable because of the exorbitant privilege of the US: its ability to print the global reserve currency. Thus, exposed by the Federal Reserve's serial unconventional monetary measures (e.g. QE1, QE2, etc.) for all to see, the major global economic players now have no incentive to perpetuate a demonstrably flawed system, other than to avoid the disruption that would accompany the movement to a new global monetary equilibrium providing a more stable foundation for global trade. But as we shall see, there is a growing body of evidence that, in fact, the groundwork is already being laid behind the scenes for a move away from the fiat dollar standard toward something else. And, as we have also seen, it is gold, and only gold, that solves for the Nash monetary equilibrium in a multipolar world highly dependent on trade. In the next section, we turn to the topic of what the transition back to gold might look like and explore a handful of possible scenarios.

Section III:
Running the Golden Gauntlet:
Transition Scenarios Back to a Gold Standard

> "I now believe that the US will return to some form of a gold standard within the next five years."
>
> —Steve Forbes, April 2011

In Section II, we demonstrated how the fiat dollar standard equilibrium, destabilized by the global credit crisis and subsequent Federal Reserve policy actions, is unsustainable and due a regime change. But the monetary disorder associated with the fiat dollar standard, which became glaringly and painfully obvious to all beginning in 2008, cannot be resolved by moving to just another fiat money standard. There is no currency that can, all at once, replace the dollar with sufficient confidence, objectivity, and trust. While the euro might be the leading candidate, the euro area has increasingly evident underlying economic problems, and many European leaders would not welcome the currency strength that would be necessarily associated with euro reserve currency status. The yen's days as a challenger to the dollar are long gone. The Chinese renminbi, although a potential future candidate, lacks sufficient deep, liquid, and reliable financial markets and, indeed, fundamental legal foundations to take the role.

The special drawing right (SDR), as a basket of currencies, is even more problematic. This is due primarily to the high degree international economic integration and of institutional cooperation and trust required to construct and maintain a global monetary regime that requires the active coordination of a critical mass of its members in both monetary and fiscal matters. As seen in the concluding part of Section II, such cooperation today is unlikely, as US and other major countries' economic priorities so clearly diverge. Those countries running chronic trade deficits and those running surpluses and simply not going to be able to sustainably agree to a system that only grows the current set of large, destabilizing international economic imbalances. As we have also seen in the previous section, the classical gold standard came into existence not because of international cooperation and trust but rather an absence of it, just as we observe today.

While this is perhaps obvious to those who have examined the cycles of economic history and how periods of monetary and credit boom and bust invariably lead back to the stability and credibility of gold, the modern economic mainstream, reared on a fiat currency diet, fails to acknowledge this fundamental economic and historical reality, an integral part of the "monetary cycle of history" introduced at the start of this book. One argument often directed at those advocating or predicting a return to some form of gold standard is that it would simply be too disruptive and destructive to the global economy. But this is like arguing that war, the most disruptive and destructive of all human endeavors, will never happen.

We know such reasoning is superficial and misleading. Wars tend to commence when one or more countries become aggressive, desperate, or some combination of the two. The same is true for major changes to official monetary arrangements. Rising powers seeking to grow their economic clout will do what is necessary to gain access to markets, including establishing credibility for their currency or coinage. Fading powers will resist the loss of such credibility, although they may find that their domestic economic objectives come into conflict with regime maintenance, just as the United States did in 1971. And of course, financial markets will adjust asset prices, interest, and exchange rates as necessary to reflect the ever-shifting risks present in the global economy.

As the twentieth century drew to a close, it was increasingly evident to informed observers, including many economists, historians, and so-called futurists, that US global influence—economic, political, perhaps even military—had begun to fade. The US share of the global economy, nearly 50 percent at the end of World War II, had slipped to less than 25 percent. Moreover, the United States had become a large net debtor to the rest of the world, implying an accelerating transfer of relative wealth and economic power in the future.

Partly as a consequence, US diplomatic influence began to decline in most parts of the world, as regional powers grew gradually more assertive. In Europe, a new, single currency, the euro, challenged the dollar's exclusive reserve currency status. Russia had begun to emerge from a prolonged slump during which obsolete Communist-era industries were restructured and modernized. China had begun to reap the benefits of widespread market-based reforms initiated by Deng Xiaoping more than a decade earlier and was exerting growing influence throughout Asia and around the world. Rival power India was also taking steps in this direction. In South America, the regional giant Brazil finally began to get its economic act together.

Beginning in the mid-2000s, the rising powers of Brazil, Russia, India, and China, more recently South Africa—colloquially known as the BRICS—began to officially recognize their rising power status by holding annual summits to discuss how best to advance their increasingly common interests. In spring 2011, at a summit meeting held on Hainan Island in the South China Sea, to which South Africa, a major gold producer, was also invited, the BRICS made a formal statement that, in key respects, echoed the bombshell comments made by Charles de Gaulle in February 1965:

> Recognizing that the international financial crisis has exposed the inadequacies and deficiencies of the existing international monetary and financial system, we support the reform and improvement of the international monetary system, with a broad-based international reserve currency system providing stability and certainty.[59]

Unlike de Gaulle, who made explicit reference to gold in his famous remarks, the BRICS instead mentioned the potential role of the SDR—the International Monetary Fund currency basket index—in the Sanya

59 This is point 16 of the Sanya Declaration, BRICS Leaders Meeting (with South Africa as a special guest), Sanya, Hainan, China, April 14, 2011.

summit declaration, but the implication was nevertheless clear: the rising economic powers were calling for an alternative to the fiat dollar as the preeminent reserve currency.

And so, the monetary reform genie has been released from the bottle. The global economy, of which the United States has for decades been a declining part, has clearly embarked on the transition away from the fiat dollar reserve standard that has been in place since August 1971.

Lacking both a national fiat currency alternative and the requisite cooperation to move toward the global SDR currency basket standard, as discussed in the previous section, it becomes rather clearer what sort of regime is going to replace the fiat dollar, at least for a period of time during which the global financial system deleverages and heals itself: some form of gold standard.

In this section, we consider what this transition might look like. It could be rather orderly, in particular if the United States decides to take the initiative to return to gold rather than allow itself to be overtaken by events. However, if the monetary cycle of history is any guide, it is unlikely that the United States will have the foresight to initiate a fundamental reform of the global monetary order and ease the transition away from the fiat dollar on its own, thereby relinquishing unilaterally its long-held extraordinary privilege. More likely is an unpredictable, crisis-driven, disorderly, even dangerous process, similar, indeed, to that from which the fiat dollar emerged in the first place.

What kind of a gold standard?

While an important topic to be sure, a detailed discussion of exactly what type of gold standard is likely to succeed the fiat dollar standard is beyond the scope of this book. A key point that will be made in this section is that a gold standard must be credible to be sustainable. Credibility can take any number of specific forms but there must be clear rules regarding how gold is to be exchanged between countries and under what circumstances.

Under Bretton Woods, for example, gold was exchanged periodically, but rather than ship physical gold from country to country, a costly and time-consuming exercise, balance of payment adjustments normally were made by moving bullion from one country's locker to another's in the basement vault below the NY Federal Reserve building in lower Manhattan. France's decision to take physical custody of a sizeable portion of its gold by shipping it back home was the exception, rather than the rule, although it was permitted. Had it not been, Bretton Woods would not have been as credible.

Other factors equal, the fewer the links in the monetary chain between actual transactions, public or private, and the legal and physical transfer of gold, the more credible the regime is likely to be. How much credibility is required is a function of trust. The more countries trust one another, the more tolerant they will be of extraterritorial custody or other conventions of convenience.

Under the classical gold standard in the late nineteenth and early twentieth centuries, there were considerably more frequent transfers of physical gold between countries than under Bretton Woods, in large part because national central banks or even commercial banks were required by domestic law to provide gold on demand in exchange for banknotes. Indeed, banknotes originated as warehouse receipts for stored gold, prior to their adoption for use as money.

Some critics of the gold standard point out how prohibitively cumbersome it would be, in the modern world of electronic banking, to return to a full gold standard under which physical transfers were required. But this argument is specious. There is no difference in principle between electronic banking referencing pieces of paper—as is currently the case—and electronic banking referencing ounces of gold, or fractions thereof. Indeed, the better argument is to point out that modern technology theoretically makes it substantially *less* cumbersome to operate a gold standard and thereby avoid the perennial pitfalls associated with unbacked, fiat currencies. We shall elaborate on this point at the end of this section when we take a look at the purely digital currency bitcoin and blockchain technology more generally.

Chapter 12:
A Golden Bolt Out of the Blue

> "For an enemy that cannot match the US on the land, sea or air, we estimate that the temptation to fight in the financial markets is great. Our financial markets are more vulnerable than ever, the methods for attacking them are easy and inexpensive, and the returns to the enemy in terms of the destruction of wealth and confidence are inestimable. It is imprudent to take this threat lightly or ignore it. There will be no time to prepare once financial warfare commences."
>
> —James G. Rickards,
> author of *Currency Wars* and *The Death of Money*

Imagine if you will the following scenario, set in August 2020:

It was a fine summer evening at Camp David, warm and clear. The president's key cabinet members and policy advisers were assembling in the Presidents Lounge of Aspen Cabin. They had come from all over, not only Washington. The Treasury secretary had been in New York overseeing attempts by the New York Fed to restore confidence in financial markets. The Secretary of State had been in Brazil trying to ease growing trade tensions. The Defense Secretary had been in Taiwan trying to reassure that tiny vulnerable ally that the United States could still defend it against China. And the National Security Adviser had been in London, attending a conference at the Royal Institute for International Affairs.

It had been nearly fifty years since a similar emergency gathering had been hastily arranged, at the request of President Nixon, in that case to discuss policy options for responding to an international run on the US gold stock. This time around, things were both similar yet different. While there was no run on the gold stock—the United States was, of course, no longer on a gold exchange standard—there sure was on the dollar.

Just two days earlier, Russia had made a sudden and shocking policy announcement that it was introducing a new global currency, the dolar, which would be fully convertible into gold at a fixed rate of 1 dolar per kilogram. Russia had been accumulating gold reserves for some time, although precisely how much was a closely guarded state secret. Clearly, they now believed they had accumulated a sufficiently large gold reserve to credibly back this new currency at a level close to the prevailing market rate.

To bolster the attractiveness of this new currency, Russia took the additional step of easing dolar-gold convertibility by allowing it to take place in the neutral locations of Zurich and Singapore. Moreover, the currency was to be administered by a bank in London, and financial markets would not need to work through the Russian banking system. Finally, English law was to prevail in any dispute over dolar contracts. Overnight, Russia thus presented the world with a liquid, convertible, gold-backed alternative to the unbacked fiat dollar reserve currency from which the world had been struggling to wean itself.[60]

---

60 Jim Rickards posited this scenario back in 2009 at the Johns Hopkins Advanced Physics Laboratory Unrestricted Warfare Symposium, as documented in the published proceedings, which includes the mock Russian press release reprinted with permission here. I thank him for permission to use this scenario, which he also includes in his new book, *Currency Wars* (New York: Penguin Group, 2010).

The Central Bank of the Russian Federation (Bank of Russia)

Press release, Moscow, August 15, 2020

The Central Bank of the Russian Federation (CBR) hereby announces the following facilities and processes, which are in place and available for counterparty inquiry immediately:

Point 1. CBR has arranged long-term use of vaults in Zurich and Singapore capable of holding up to 10,000 metric tonnes of gold. Security is provided by G4S and is state-of-the-art, including multiple security perimeters, biometric scanning, advanced encryption standard 264-bit encryption of communications channels, blast-proof construction, and redundant power supplies. CBR has moved the gold component of the Russian Federation international reserves to these vaults amounting to approximately 500 metric tonnes.

Point 2. CBR announces the issuance of the Gold Reserve Dolar (GRD) to be issued in book-entry form by the Global Dolar Bank plc in London (SWIFT: GDBAGB) acting as fiscal agent of CBR. One GRD is equal to one kilogram of pure gold (the Fixed Conversion Rate, or FC Rate). The GRD is freely convertible into gold at the FC Rate and is freely transferable to any designated party on the books of the Global Dolar Bank or any other approved bank maintaining GRD accounts. CBR invites creditworthy and prudently regulated banks worldwide to open GRD accounts and facilities on their books that can be cleared on a real-time gross settlements basis via Global Dolar Bank. The Global Dolar Bank clearance, settlement, and accounts systems are operated on IBM Blade Servers using Logica CAS++ payments solution software.

Point 3. The Gold Reserve Dolar may be acquired in any quantity by delivery of the appropriate amount of gold at the FC Rate to any one of the vaults noted in Point 1. Upon receipt of good delivery, the pertinent number of GRDs will be credited to the delivering party's account at Global Dolar Bank. Gold Reserve Dolars are freely redeemable into gold in any quantity by instruction to Global Dolar Bank and by providing delivery instructions to one of the vaults.

Point 4. All matters pertaining to title, transfer and operation of GRDs and Global Dolar Bank plc are determined solely under English law and heard exclusively in English courts. All matters pertaining to physical possession, delivery and receipt of gold in the vaults will also be determined solely under English law and may be heard either in English courts or courts located in Switzerland and Singapore respectively. Opinions of law from Queen's Counsel and leading counsel in Switzerland and Singapore respectively are available for inspection.

Point 5. Effective immediately, all sales of Russian exports may be negotiated, denominated and paid for in GRDs only. The existing Russian Ruble will continue to be legal tender for domestic

TRANSACTIONS CONDUCTED SOLELY BY PARTIES WITHIN THE RUSSIAN FEDERATION.

POINT 6. EFFECTIVE IMMEDIATELY CBR ANNOUNCES A TENDER FOR UNLIMITED QUANTITIES OF GOLD. ANY GOLD TENDERED UNDER THIS FACILITY WILL BE PAID FOR BY DELIVERY TO THE SELLER OF US TREASURY BILLS, NOTES OR BONDS AT AN EXCHANGE VALUE CALCULATED BY REFERENCE TO THE MARKET VALUE OF SECURITIES DETERMINED IN USD CLOSING PRICES ON BLOOMBERG AND THE MARKET VALUE OF GOLD DETERMINED IN USD BY THE LONDON FIXING, BOTH FOR THE AVERAGE OF THE THREE BUSINESS DAYS IMMEDIATELY PRECEDING THE SETTLEMENT DATE OF THE EXCHANGE.

POINT 7. CBR WILL PROVIDE GRD LENDING FACILITIES AND GRD SWAP LINES VIA GLOBAL DOLAR BANK PLC FOR APPROVED COUNTERPARTIES WITH ELIGIBLE COLLATERAL AS DETERMINED IN THE SOLE DISCRETION OF CBR.

END OF PRESS RELEASE.

While it was impossible to know exactly how this decision had come about—not one of the various US intelligence agencies had warned the president or relevant members of Congress of the possibility—it was understandable, given the context, that Russia was willing to confront the United States. Recently, in response to Iran successfully testing a ballistic missile, the United States had threatened to impose strict new sanctions on Iran and enforce them by a blockade if necessary. This could conceivably provoke a military confrontation that could draw in regional nuclear powers, such as Israel, Pakistan and India. Iran was also an important trading partner for Russia. The perceived dangers to Russia, economic and military, were close to home.

And so it was, amid the growing threat of another, possibly now nuclear Mideast war, rising oil prices, and a chronically weak, stagflationary US economy, that by making the ruble convertible into gold, Russia sparked a global run out of the US dollar and, by extension, US financial markets and banking systems.

The New York Fed was in the front line. As central banks around the world began to sell a portion of their holdings of US Treasury bonds in exchange for the preferred new alternative of gold-backed, ruble-denominated securities, interest rates rose sharply. Naturally, the Fed responded to this unwelcome development by creating more reserves, but, while this did maintain a degree of liquidity in the banking system, it had a devastating effect on the dollar. Now that there was a credible, gold-backed alternative to the dollar, the injection of fresh reserves had a direct, immediate impact on the dollar's value in the foreign exchange markets. Banks were taking their fresh dollar reserves and exchanging them for rubles, euros, yen, and Swiss francs; the point was to try and minimize their exposure to the recently deposed fiat dollar reserve currency.

Within twenty-four hours, the dollar lost some 20 percent of its value in broad, trade-weighted terms. Oil, gold, and other commodity prices soared by even more as global investors fled into liquid real assets, anticipating shockwaves throughout the global financial system.

The president's advisers made it clear that he needed to take immediate, probably rather bold action, if a full-scale US financial market meltdown was to be averted. The dollar might have just lost its preeminent global reserve status, to be sure, something that could not be restored by executive order or legislative action. But there were still things that would need to be done to stabilize things on the home front and avoid a level of domestic economic chaos that, if not managed effectively, might morph into political chaos before long.

Dollar déjà vu: crisis meeting at Camp David, 49 years later…

Having reached a quorum by just after 6:00 p.m., the president entered the lounge, welcomed the attendees, and briefly explained his appreciation for the gravity of the situation. He then handed the floor over to the Treasury secretary, who was tasked, much as his predecessor John Connally had been nearly fifty years earlier, with crafting some plan whereby confidence in the US dollar, financial markets, and banking system could be quickly restored.

"Thank you, Mr. President," the secretary began. "We appreciate that this is the greatest crisis of your presidency and probably the greatest economic policy challenge faced by any administration since at least President Nixon and possibly even FDR.

"Before we begin our discussion, I have asked the undersecretary for Monetary Affairs to provide some background on recent events."

"Thank you, Mr. Secretary," he began. "Global financial markets have been jittery for weeks due to growing concerns of a US–Russian showdown over Iran, which had recently formally announced that it had acquired an intermediate-range ballistic missile capability to augment its recently successful bomb-testing program with a proven delivery mechanism. As you all know, we took the decision to push for the UN to apply immediate sanctions on Iran via the UN Security Council, prohibiting any and all trade with Iran. However, we were met with stiff, immediate, coordinated resistance by Russia, China, the other BRICS, and even France and Germany, who expressed their joint preference to negotiate a treaty with Iran that would limit the size and scope of Iran's future nuclear ambitions to primarily defensive purposes. Among other reasons given, they mentioned that Pakistan and Israel, both nuclear powers, were in the front line vis-à-vis Iran and easily within range of its new missiles. Russia and China believe strongly that this, combined with their own, massive retaliatory capabilities and modest IRBM interception capabilities, will deter Iran from ever using nuclear weapons for offensive purposes. Thus, they believe that such a treaty would be effective and thereby would obviate the need for sanctions.

"While we are accustomed to sanctions on Iran, which have been in place in some form since 1979, this cannot be said of either Russia or China. They have only ever supported sanctions on Iran when the United States declared it was of a critical national interest, most recently to prevent Iran acquiring a nuclear capability. Now that Iran has presented the international community with a fait accompli, neither Russia nor China sees any logic in continuing to impose sanctions, much less expand them. Indeed, China and Iran are in negotiations at this very moment regarding the upgrading of an Indian Ocean container port facility and associated rail and transport links in southeastern Iran.

"Turning now to the economy, the tensions associated with the arrival of the 'Persian Bomb' have sent oil prices sharply higher, to the detriment of financial market sentiment. It doesn't help matters that the global economy has still failed to recover properly from the prolonged slump that began in 2008, notwithstanding historically unprecedented amounts of fiscal and monetary stimulus by the US and most other developed economies.

"Abroad, currency volatility and economically destabilizing rates of inflation have been afflicting many countries, including all five of the BRICS. They argue that this is the inevitable consequence of US Federal Reserve policy. As you well know, we disagree. With this action by Russia, however, which implies a stronger ruble, we are also already seeing the other BRICS currencies appreciating."

At this point, the president interjected, "You mean that the dollar is depreciating, of course. And don't forget that it has been our policy since at least 2004 that China and certain other countries should allow their currencies to appreciate more substantially."

"Well, yes, there are two sides to any exchange rate. And yes, that has been our policy."

"Not entirely," continued the president. "What I mean is that the dollar is depreciating not only relative to other currencies but also in absolute, purchasing-power terms. Look at oil and gasoline. Look at wheat and corn. My God, look at cotton! Was this our policy too?"

The president glared over at his Treasury secretary, visibly annoyed with the undersecretary. "Yes, Mr. President," the undersecretary continued in a less certain voice, "the dollar is depreciating. Hence the upward pressure not only on commodity prices but also on interest rates, which threatens the solvency of our banking system, our ability to service our national debt, and the health of our economy in general."

"Quite. Now we have expressed for years our desire that the BRICS, in particular China, would allow their currencies to appreciate. Well, Goddammit, now they're doing it, and look at the result! How are we going to explain to the American public that a policy that we have been pushing for years is now threatening us with the second banking crisis in a decade!"

"Please, Mr. President," interrupted a defensive Treasury secretary. "We never pushed for Russia or any other country, for that matter, to suddenly make its currency convertible into gold."

Now the director of National Intelligence chimed in. "Mr. President, I can assure you that none of the US intelligence agencies anticipated this, nor could they have. There was no evidence of such planning received by the NSA or from anywhere else in the broad intelligence community."

"Excuse me," interrupted the president, "has it not occurred to you that although Russia may have chosen the precise timing of this action, there is clear and present evidence that the other BRICS were fully prepared for this? Haven't you noticed that their currencies have all risen by a comparable amount versus the dollar? This looks like a coordinated action!"

"We all know—indeed, we are among those who criticized them at the time—that the US intelligence community completely failed to anticipate the rapid implosion of the Soviet Union in the early 1990s. Well, at least that was a failure to anticipate developments in a single, albeit highly secretive country. Now, we have a failure to properly identify that any one of five countries, including two we have supposedly penetrated to the highest levels of government, have spent at least a number of months and more probably a number of years planning the greatest global economic policy coup in, well, in history! How am I supposed to explain that to the American people?"

The room fell silent. No one knew how to respond or had the courage to do so. The president was right. The United States had not only completely failed to anticipate a major Russian economic and monetary policy shift, clearly supported by the other BRICS and quite possibly Germany and France, but the United States was, suddenly and glaringly obviously, economically and politically isolated. Russia might be in the lead at this particular moment, but the bulk of US major trading partners were clearly in the convoy.

The president continued, "Now, gentlemen. We need to restore confidence in our currency, in our financial markets, in our banking system, and in our economy. And we need to do so right now. Before Monday morning in Asia, when financial markets reopen, I am going to make the announcement that accomplishes these things. You lot are going to craft it. I want a draft on my desk by 6:00 a.m. tomorrow morning. Mr. Secretary, you are in charge. Good night."

The president departed the lounge. Everyone stood aghast. They had never seen the president so angry. But then the president had never faced a crisis of this magnitude. While there were certain parallels to August 1971 and 1933, there were also differences, the most important of which was that the government was far larger now, relative to the economy, and thus so was the associated tax and debt financing burden. The population was older with far more recipients of Social Security, Medicare, and other such programs introduced in prior decades amid less challenging demographics. Prolonged global military commitments, including the wars in Afghanistan, Libya, Somalia, Yemen, and Syria and major policing actions elsewhere were claiming by far the largest share of the federal budget since the Vietnam War. The trade balance was negative, not only because the United States imported much of its oil but also because most manufacturing now took place in more competitive economies abroad.

To make matters worse, with the economy still so weak—the work force had not grown at all since 2008—not only was defense a burden but jobless benefits, food stamps, and other such counter-cyclical financial assistance programs were also taking up a huge portion of the federal budget. Moreover, chaos in state and local government finances was resulting in a huge reduction of those services and a growing risk that, at some point, the federal government might need to step in and provide certain guarantees to restore some degree of stability in the market for state and municipal borrowing. While each of these factors alone posed a major economic challenge, taken together they implied that the United States was simply no longer in a dominant economic position able to dictate terms in international monetary matters.

No one really knew where to begin. But then the deputy director of the CIA spoke. "You may not believe this, but we sorta 'war-gamed' this scenario back in 2009. It didn't go anywhere, mind you. Not enough people took it as a serious threat. But we did war-game it, and I recall roughly how it was resolved."

"How?" asked an astonished Treasury secretary, who indicated that he was prepared to retake the floor.

"Well, in brief, we restored gold convertibility."

"You mean as under Bretton Woods?"

"More or less. But mind you that we did so at a far higher gold price. This unilateral devaluation of the dollar implied a large reduction in the real debt burden and an improvement in the terms of trade with other countries. This helped to stabilize the financial system and ended the run on the currency."

"We can't recommend such a course of action to the president."

"And why not?"

"It would be too sudden. Too disruptive. It would lead to a burst of inflation. It would require an immediate rationalization of government finances. It would be akin to reaching the debt ceiling. We all know how that almost sparked a dollar crisis back in 2011."

"Excuse me, but the crisis has already been sparked. This discussion is about how we respond. You heard the president. As far as he knows, we never war-gamed this scenario. But we did. And we resolved it. No one took it seriously then, but it has happened now. And so we have a potential road map. I strongly recommend that all of us familiarize ourselves with it. Mr. Secretary, with your permission, I will have all the relevant documents sent to all present for their staffs' immediate consideration, subject to security clearances."

"Fine. Now we are going to need to present the president with at least two and preferably three proposals in total. It appears we may have one, however unpalatable. I want two more."

The room fell silent again.

"Mr. Secretary," the secretary of defense said quietly, "the Department of Defense has also war-gamed something along these lines."

"Really? I can't believe I'm hearing now that multiple agencies of the federal government that has just been blindsided had in fact previously imagined and war-gamed just such a scenario. Whatever, it is too late to worry about that now. Well, then, how does your scenario play out?"

"Well, it doesn't result in a return to the gold standard. But I'm afraid it does lead to a war with Iran, Russia, and China, with a high risk of going nuclear and, at a minimum, resulting in the loss of three carrier groups and several key military bases in the Pacific and Indian Oceans."

"I see. Would anyone else like to make a proposal?"

Chapter 13:
Golden Preparations

> "Money—capital—has a life of its own. It's a force of nature, like gravity. Like the oceans, it flows where it wants to flow. This whole thing with gold is inevitable, we're just going with the tide. The only question is whether you want to let it go like an unguided missile and raise hell, or whether you want to keep it in the hands of responsible people."
>
> — Maxwell Emery, fictional financier, *Rollover,* 1981

Jim Rickards is not the first person to envision the general scenario described in the previous chapter, in which some country, or group of countries, decides to divest its dollar reserves in favor of gold or a gold-backed alternative. Indeed, something right along these lines was turned into a screenplay and major Hollywood motion picture back in 1981, a time when confidence in the dollar had been badly shaken by a prolonged period of US economic underperformance and monetary policy misdeeds in the aftermath of the Bretton Woods breakdown. As we observed in Section II, these culminated in the brief, parabolic rise in the gold price to $850 and a rise in US Treasury yields to the unheard of level of over 15 percent amidst the deepest recession since WWII.

Rollover starred Kris Kristofferson as Hubbell Smith, a young, gifted financier and protégé to an elder financial statesman, Maxwell Emery, played by the late Hume Cronyn. Jane Fonda also starred, as Lee Winters, an ambitious young businesswoman and Hubbell's eventual love interest. Here is the plot summary, courtesy of the Internet Movie Database (IMDb):

> While working on an important international financing deal with Winters, Smith discovers Emery is moving money belonging to the Arabs into gold as a safe haven against potential losses if the dollar collapses. The Arabs are extremely worried that if anyone finds out their assets will vanish in a public panic as American currency becomes worthless.
>
> Winters also discovers the plot, and wants to change the terms of the financing deal in exchange for her silence; she has overheard part of Smith's conversation with Emery and mistakenly believes he was double-crossing her. A fake limo driver who is actually working for the Arab investors tries to kidnap her with the intent of killing her—as it turns out they did to her husband—to prevent her from disclosing what she knows, and when the attempt on her life fails, the Arabs panic and pull all of their money out of every bank in America, and possibly the entire world.
>
> The globe is gripped by panic and rioting occurs as people discover all of their money is now worthless. Emery is shown in his office—dead, an apparent suicide. The economic crisis paralyzes the world, but by spilling over boundaries between east and west blocs, and between developing and industrialized nations, it also unites the world in common cause. In the penultimate scene, workers at Borough National stand idle while listening to a report of the growing economic crisis. As the camera pans across the trading floor of the bank, the viewer sees that it's now empty of workers, the lights off, the

> desks and machines covered—completely inactive. Only Smith remains.

While in *Rollover* the instigators of a run on the dollar are the Arab oil-producing countries, rather than Russia, and their intention is not to crash the US financial system, they nevertheless accidentally bring this about in their attempt to surreptitiously divest their dollar reserves and accumulate gold instead. As such, we have a scenario that, while perhaps best suited to Hollywood, is nevertheless worth contemplating. As Rickards puts it:

> Notwithstanding an earlier period of globalization during 1880–1914, there can be little doubt that the current period of globalization from 1989–2009, beginning with the fall of the Soviet Union and the end of the Cold War, represents the highest degree of interconnectedness of the global system of finance, capital, and banking the world has ever seen. Despite obvious advantages in terms of global capital mobility facilitating productivity and the utilization of labor on an unprecedented scale, there are hidden dangers and second-order costs embedded in the sheer scale and complexity of the system. These costs have begun to be realized in the financial crisis that began in late 2007 and have continued until this writing and will continue beyond.
>
> Among the emergent properties of this complexity are exponentially greater risks of catastrophic collapse leading to the complete insolvency of the global financial system. This dynamic has already begun to play out and will continue without the implementation of appropriate public policies, which, so far, are not in evidence.[61]

61 From the Unconstrained Warfare Symposium Proceedings, edited by Robert

The point is that the existing, fiat dollar-based global monetary system is both highly complex and inherently unstable. It could be undermined, deliberately or not, in any number of ways. We have already explored two hypothetical examples. There are more, including some that are perhaps more plausible. In this chapter, we explore how the United States, wary of losing the initiative to Russia, to other oil-producing nations, to China or to anyone else for that matter, might instead choose to prevent a disorderly return to some form of gold standard by moving first, on its own initiative and terms. Indeed, this is precisely what Rickards proposes.

> The US could prevent this by preempting it—just by issuing a gold-backed dollar itself using the 4,600 metric tons available in Fort Knox (over nine times the Russian gold supply). Another approach is to convene a Bretton Woods II Conference, likely a G-20 meeting in today's world, and implement this on a global basis.[62]

As with many informed observers, Rickards understands that the fiat dollar cannot long remain the dominant global reserve currency due to the deteriorating US fiscal and trade position and its economic underperformance relative to the rest of the world. It is, therefore, in its best interest to be the first mover and to minimize the associated disruption to the domestic and global economy.

Interestingly, back in the late 1980s, when the former Soviet Union was falling apart and the threat of an imminent hyperinflation and economic collapse loomed, two prominent US economists, former Fed Governor Wayne Angell and Jude Wanniski, traveled to Leningrad (now renamed St. Petersburg) and Moscow and met with several Soviet economic and finance officials. They urged, among other measures, that

Lumin, Applied Physics Laboratory, Johns Hopkins University, 2009.

62 IBID.

the Soviets immediately move to shore up the rapidly devaluing ruble by backing it with their gold reserves. They also published this view in the US financial press.[63] Back then, as now, the way to restore monetary stability is to restore credibility. What is good for the goose is, of course, good for the gander. While the US economy of today is not falling apart, nor has hyperinflation set in, its financial system is quite clearly dysfunctional, a problem with acute relevance for the entire world. Moving preemptively to restore credibility and, therefore, stability in global monetary affairs makes increasingly evident good sense.

Should the United States seek to take the initiative in restoring global monetary stability and eliminate the risk that the fiat dollar will be deposed in a disorderly fashion, there is a series of concrete steps that could be taken.

Most important is the acceptance of the fact that, at the current official accounting price of $42.50, a return to gold convertibility would be hugely deflationary and most probably destroy the United States and global financial system in short order. Fortunately, history offers up a useful lesson for how *not* to restore gold convertibility, namely, the ultimately unsuccessful attempt by Great Britain to do so in 1925.

"The Economic Consequences of Mr. Churchill"

Winston Churchill was nothing if not resolute in his war and defense policies and politics, such as his program of naval modernization while first lord of the Admiralty, the disastrous Gallipoli campaign, the Blitz and Battle of Britain, the Harris bombing program of German cities, or his perennial unwillingness to contemplate the loss of the empire built with the blood, sweat, toil, and tears of the previous generations. But what was true of Churchill's policies in war was equally true in peace.

63 J. Wanniski, "Gold-Based Ruble? Two U.S. Economists Urge Hard Money on the Soviet Union," *Barron's*, September 25, 1989, 9; W. Angell (interview), "Put the Soviet Economy on Golden Rails," *Wall Street Journal*, October 5, 1989, A28.

In 1925, convinced that there was no other appropriate policy choice, Churchill, while serving as chancellor of the Exchequer, placed the United Kingdom back onto the gold standard. Britain had suspended gold convertibility shortly after the outbreak of war in 1914 to facilitate war financing through inflation. But rather than consider the economic and monetary developments, including the inflation, that had taken place in the interim, he chose to restore gold convertibility at the pre–World War I parity. Never mind that World War I had been hugely expensive, that it had destroyed a good portion not just of the British but of the Continental European economy, that Germany and the other defeated powers had all recently experienced hyperinflationary currency crises, and, most important, that Britain itself had expanded the sterling monetary base dramatically in the years 1914 to 1925 such that, in restoring convertibility at the previous parity rate, a severe deflation was assured.

Now, it could be that Churchill and his advisers were unaware of the dangers of a severe deflation. After all, deflation in prices was the norm, rather than the exception, for much of the century leading up to World War I. Sterling had been fixed to gold, yet industrial productivity rose dramatically. With sterling stable but output rising, prices necessarily fell. This sort of deflation was not damaging; rather, it was entirely healthy. It also implied a gradual rise in living standards, as wages tended to remain more or less stable but, for any given wage, purchasing power steadily increased.

John Maynard Keynes was among those who warned of the deflationary dangers of restoring sterling to the pre–World War I convertibility rate. In his famous treatise, "The Economic Consequences of Mr. Churchill," he writes satirically, as if he were advising the chancellor:

> If… you fix the exchange at this gold parity, you must either gamble on a rise in gold prices abroad, which will induce foreigners to pay a higher gold price for our exports, or you are committing yourself to a policy of

> forcing down money wages and the cost of living to the necessary extent.
>
> We must warn you that this latter policy is not easy. It is certain to involve unemployment and industrial disputes. If, as some people think, real wages were already too high a year ago, that is all the worse, because the amount of the necessary wage reductions in terms of money will be all the greater...
>
> To begin with, there will be great depression in the export industries...
>
> Nevertheless, the cost of living will not fall sufficiently and, consequently, the export industries will not be able to reduce their prices sufficiently, until wages have fallen in the sheltered industries... When the process is complete the cost of living will have fallen too; and we shall then be, with luck, just where we were before we started.[64]

Notwithstanding the objections of probably the single most influential UK economist of the day, Churchill carried through his plans. Convertibility at the pre–World War I parity was restored. The result was an immediate and severe recession, soaring unemployment, wage deflation, and widespread industrial action and social unrest.

Finally, in 1931 the United Kingdom capitulated to the deflationary pressure of its decision to restore the pre-1914 sterling parity and went off the gold standard, never to properly return. As sterling devalued versus the dollar by 25 percent, the deflationary pressure was transmitted across the Atlantic to the United States, where it exacerbated the stress

64 John M. Keynes, "The Economic Consequences of Mr. Churchill" (1925), 10–13, www.gold.org/government_affairs/gold_as_a_monetary_asset/historical_records_back_to_the_17th_century/the_heyday_of_the_gold_standard/.

on the domestic banking system. In 1932, hundreds of US banks failed. In 1933, the number of failures was even greater.

President Franklin Delano Roosevelt was convinced that something had to be done. It was unfair, of course, for the United Kingdom to try to pass on the deflationary consequences of its disastrous, botched return to sterling-gold convertibility to the United States. In 1934, he devalued the dollar by some 40 percent, although the United States remained on the gold standard. This was sufficient, however, to end the monetary and associated price deflation that had set in, beginning in 1929, and became particularly acute by 1932.

How to avoid a repeat of Churchill's error and risk another Great Depression

If the United States took the initiative and preemptively restored dollar convertibility, placing itself and, by implication, much of the world back on a gold standard, this would be far less disruptive to the current global financial system and the US economy specifically than it would be if the United States was in some way surprised and overtaken by the actions of others. That said, no economic policy change of that magnitude can go entirely smoothly, and, as with any major policy initiative, there would be winners and losers, notwithstanding that it best serves the national interest.

While it would certainly take an unusual degree of unity, vision, and leadership for a sitting US president and Congress to take a step back from the incessant crisis fighting required by the faltering fiat dollar reserve standard and to consider rationally that it is in the best interest of the United States to be the first to move back to gold, we should hardly rule out that possibility. There are some in Congress and government generally who are supportive, and it does seem that their voices are being more widely heard at present than at any time since the Reagan Gold Commission studied the issue at length in the early 1980s. Moreover, multiple Republican candidates for president in recent years have expressed support for exploring the idea of repegging the dollar to gold.

As difficult a decision as it would be, were the United States indeed to restore convertibility, how might it go about it? We have already pointed out what *not* to do, that is, try to restore convertibility at a previous, pre-devaluation rate, which in the case of the United States today would be $42.50, the rate prevailing in 1973 when the United States formally adopted a policy of allowing the dollar to float independent of the price of gold.[65] That would be so massively deflationary that it would almost certainly destroy the existing financial system, much to the detriment of the economy generally. More sensibly, the United States would restore convertibility at a rate that increased, rather than reduced, global confidence in the US financial system and economy generally. This would imply a conversion rate that substantially reduces the US real debt burden, public and private, to one that would be widely regarded as serviceable and thus sustainable by holders of dollars and dollar-denominated assets.

This goal would have to be balanced, however, against the rather obvious implied loss of purchasing power (price inflation) that would occur due to a large devaluation. Beyond a certain point, the devaluation would be so large that, while it would be economically sustainable in principle, it would be politically unpalatable in practice, as it would result in such a large surge in consumer price inflation that a substantial portion of the middle class would see their savings wiped out. This could well lead to social unrest, which could damage rather than restore credibility in the ability of the United States to service its accumulated debts. (There might be other ways to assuage the potential social unrest, such as providing each citizen with a modest amount of gold, allowing each to participate favorably in a revaluation of gold, rather than merely suffer from a devaluation of the dollar. Intriguingly, the Chinese and

65 While the gold window may have been closed by executive order by president Nixon in 1971, it was not until 1973 that there was accepted formal international recognition that the Bretton Woods arrangement had ended and that the international monetary system would henceforth be one of floating fiat exchange rates.

several other governments encourage their citizens to accumulate gold and as savings. The US government should take note.)

What rate might best balance these two important concerns? There are several approaches to determining the ideal conversion rate. We have already pointed out the danger of repegging to the pre-devaluation rate of $42.50. What about the current market price? In my opinion, this would also imply a substantial deflation, as by repegging to gold the Federal Reserve would no longer be able to maintain an artificially low or zero rate on dollar deposits. Sharply higher interest rates would be highly deflationary. A better approach would be for the United States to choose a conversion rate that adjusted for the interim growth in the money supply since the gold window was closed. For example, the United States could return to a 40 percent money supply M0 coverage ratio, as per the Federal Reserve Act of 1913. Alternatively, the United States could use a coverage ratio related to a broader monetary aggregate. Finally, and not mutually exclusive to the above, the United States could choose a level high enough to imply a dramatic reduction of the current debt burden. While these latter proposals would result in a sudden burst of inflation, they all nevertheless have the important benefit of containing future inflation expectations and thereby stabilizing the dollar's future value, as they would be regarded as more sustainable and, hence, credible. And credibility is really the key to any successful attempt at monetary reform.

Historical Examples of Restoring Currency Credibility

Once lost, trust is difficult to regain. What is true at the personal level is also true at the social, national, and international levels. Yet as the size of the system grows, so does the difficulty. Indeed, it is precisely the relative lack of trust pervading the international system that makes it essential to have objective points of reference to maintain any degree of equilibrium, be it a recognized border between states or, when it comes to monetary affairs, an objective convention such as a credible gold standard.

While it is beyond the scope of this book to discuss it in any detail, there is always the chance that, whatever the transition to gold looks like, it becomes so disorderly that there is a wholesale run on the dollar and quite possibly also other fiat currencies, in favor of gold. If not addressed quickly with credible policies, a general run on fiat currencies could lead to a general global hyperinflation, which would be enormously destructive not only to the global economy but also to the very fabric of global society. If history is any guide, it is difficult to imagine that a general global hyperinflation would not result in at least one revolution and at least one war. More probably, it would result in several.

Should this occur, restoring currency credibility would be extraordinarily difficult. While in principle, restoring a monetary role for gold would be part of any viable solution, a broader range of policy actions would no doubt be required to make a gold standard credible. In this regard, it is instructive to look at past hyperinflations and how they were successfully brought under control.

A recent winner of the Nobel Memorial Prize in Economics, Thomas Sargent, did just this in a study some years ago. He looked at some of the twentieth century's most severe hyperinflations and examined the full range of policies that were implemented to try to restore currency stability. What he found, interestingly, was that quantitative factors, such as growth in the money supply, for example, were relatively less important than qualitative actions that demonstrated a clear commitment, on the part of policy makers, to restoring stable money.

Of particular importance was action on the fiscal side, due most probably to the fact that central banks, even those ostensibly highly independent, have historically come under enormous pressure to accommodate large government deficits with future, if not present, monetary expansion. As such, running a tight monetary policy alongside a highly expansionary fiscal policy is not considered a sustainable, credible situation. Action on the monetary front alone thus cannot end hyperinflation once it is under way. However, after there has been a clear, well-communicated swing back toward fiscal prudence, then monetary policy need not be highly restrictive, although it can help at the margin. As these changes in fiscal policy are necessarily large, they normally occur only after a change in government. At a minimum, there needs to be a change of leader and party. In more extreme cases, a revolution is necessary.

Hyperinflation, while naturally associated with high rates of money supply growth, is thus understood by Sargent to be more a fiscal than a monetary phenomenon, in terms of both how it begins and how it ends. I leave it to the reader to ponder what changes of government the admittedly remote risk of hyperinflation would imply for various countries today.[66]

How best to determine a credible and sustainable price for re-pegging the dollar to gold?

The price of gold has generally trended higher ever since the dollar left gold in 1971 and stands near $1,200 per troy ounce today. But let's place this price in its proper economic context. Deflated by the US Consumer Price Index, the price of gold is currently only about $600 per ounce, well below the $850 peak reached briefly in 1980, a time when the US money supply and debt burden were far, far smaller than they are today. Looked at in a few other metrics, gold currently buys about as much crude oil as it did in 1971 and about as much wheat and about as much cotton. That is, the purchasing power of gold hasn't changed materially since 1971. What has changed, of course, is the purchasing power of the dollar, which has plummeted dramatically.

It may be difficult for readers to think this way, but consider: When you watch those classic TV shows about the United States in the nineteenth or early twentieth centuries, such as *Little House on the Prairie* or *The Waltons,* for example, most basic household goods were

66 Thomas J. Sargent, "The Ends of Four Big Inflations," in Robert Hall, ed., *Inflation, Causes and Effects* (Chicago: University of Chicago Press, 1982).

still priced in pennies rather than dollars. But does that really mean that things were less expensive back then? That somehow the standard of living was higher? Of course not. Real wages were far lower. People had to work longer to purchase a comparable basket of consumer goods. The standard of living was far lower than we enjoy today, notwithstanding the rather poor performance of the US economy in recent years. Once again, what has changed is the purchasing power of the dollar, which is so much lower today than it was back then that it almost seems like a currency from another world.

By contrast, gold may seem a barbarous relic to some, but in my opinion, there is nothing barbarous about something that has more or less retained its purchasing power over the same time frame. Indeed, for those willing to look at the longer history of gold through the centuries, what becomes clear is that gold has done remarkably well at holding on to its purchasing power. War, famine, and revolution on the one hand or peace, prosperity, and stability on the other, gold has been the preserver of purchasing power par excellence.[67]

Now, some might argue that as gold is a zero-yield asset (slightly negative, in fact, considering storage costs), an investor would have forgone the interest available on dollars over this long time period. This is true. Dollars placed in the bank would have earned some interest. But of course, during the Great Depression, many banks failed, wiping out dollar depositors in the process. And ever since the Bretton Woods arrangements in 1944, the after-tax rate of interest on dollar deposits and T-bills has been insufficient to compensate the holders of dollars for the exponential loss of purchasing power they have suffered. During the 1970s, US dollar real rates of interest were generally negative. The same has been the case since 2008. As such, cash is, in effect, a

67 The classic study on gold's remarkable ability to maintain its purchasing power over long periods of time, even those characterized by a broad variety of economic and political conditions, is *The Golden Constant* by Roy W. Jastram. Jill Leyland completed a revised edition of this 1970's study in 2007 for the World Gold Council.

negative-yield asset. And inflation is thus a *de facto* "regressive tax" falling disproportionately on the poor, who tend to hold proportionately more of what savings they have as cash balances, rather than portfolios of stocks, real estate, and other investments, the nominal value of which tends to rise as a result of monetary inflation.

There have been times, to be sure, when dollar interest rates were attractive, such as the early 1980s, for example. Indeed, high-dollar interest rates were precisely what ended the gold mania of the late 1970s. With the United States and parts of the global banking system poorly capitalized or possibly even insolvent, however, and central banks implementing all manner of unconventional, inflationary policies to try to prop them up, it might be a long time, if ever, before dollar interest rates again provide investors with a positive real rate of return.

When taking all factors into account, the current spot price of gold is simply much too low to provide a sufficient degree of credibility for a restoration of convertibility. It would imply substantial deflationary pressure, an outflow of gold, and threaten the solvency of the banking system with sharply higher interest rates. A somewhat higher price, one that accounts for the interim growth of the money supply, would be far more credible.

Adjusting for Growth in the Narrow Money Supply

Although the US money supply has grown dramatically during the four decades of the fiat dollar, much of this growth has occurred since 2008, when the Fed created a huge quantity of dollar reserves to help liquefy the US and global financial system and prevent a systemic meltdown. It has not subsequently drained these reserves and, given that much of the US financial system is essentially insolvent, it is highly unlikely to ever do so. Therefore, when considering what gold price would be appropriate for a return to conversion today, we need to consider what price would be implied, were the US narrow money supply to be 100 percent backed by gold. Taking the current narrow money supply, defined as bank reserves plus cash in circulation, of about $3.5 trillion, and dividing this by the official US gold reserve of some 8,133 metric tons, yields a current, 100 percent–backed US dollar gold price of about $13,600 per troy ounce.

Figure 13.1: Imputed dollar gold prices for various measures of the US money supply, 100 percent backed

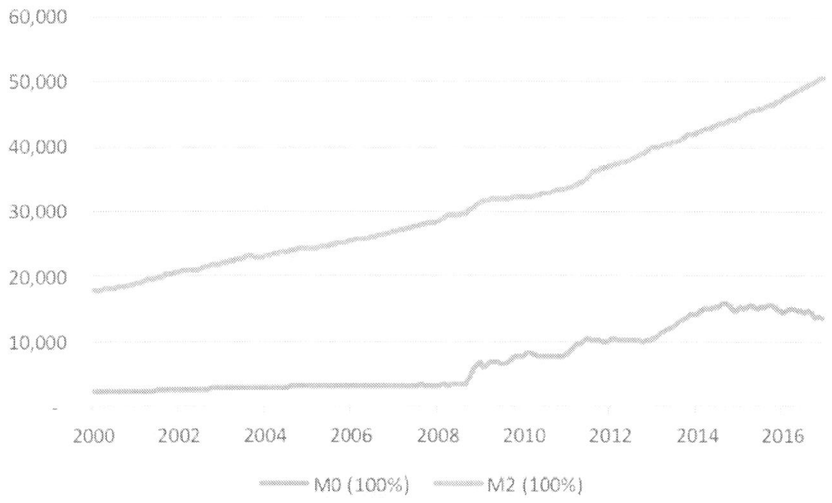

Source: Federal Reserve, US Treasury.

As can also be seen in the chart above, the implied gold price required to back fully 100 percent of the broad money supply M2 with gold is a whopping $50,000 a further order of magnitude higher. However, as M2 is in effect a combined measure of narrow money plus interbank credit, 100 percent backing is probably excessive. However, it does help to establish what might be considered a reasonable "ceiling" on the rise in the gold price that would be required, holding other factors equal, to provide sufficient gold backing for the dollar on the return to a gold convertibility.

Adjusting for Growth in the Broad Money Supply

Today's market gold price is thus at an unreasonably low level to start when considering at what rate the United States would fix dollar convertibility, were it to move back to a gold standard, because it would probably be highly deflationary and risk a general economic and financial collapse. But even the 100 percent–backed dollar price of $13,600 per troy ounce might not be high enough because even this price does not adjust properly for the dramatic potential future decline in the dollar's purchasing power implied by the surge in the broad dollar money supply in recent years.

No one can know exactly under what conditions banks might start lending money again, and the huge increase in narrow money created by the Fed in recent years would enter general economic circulation, but if it does, there will be a surge in inflation and, naturally, in the price of gold as well. But if the dollar is fixed versus gold, then to the extent that these dollars begin to circulate, this will reduce the implied gold coverage ratio for the broad money supply. And if that ratio should fall sufficiently, it will place upward pressure on interest rates. That will choke off economic growth and place deflationary pressure on the economy.

While this process of credit constraint is what a gold standard is all about, we must consider whether a general price deflation is what US policy makers would want to achieve by a return to a gold standard. Indeed, this is the mistake that Churchill made when he placed Great Britain back on the gold standard in 1925 at the pre- rather than post-war parity, causing an immediate and severe recession. If the goal, however, is to stabilize the US economy and financial system and maintain the US dollar's acceptance as an international reserve currency, the convertibility rate is going to have to be credible. Any rate that threatens the solvency of the US financial system will simply not be regarded as credible and thus will fail to restore lasting confidence in the dollar. By implication, it is important to consider what gold price would allow for a substantial portion of the broad money supply to also be backed by gold and to consider what coverage ratios have historically provided general economic and monetary stability.

To allow for previous Fed narrow monetary expansions to actually flow through the economy—that is, through the growth of broad money, thereby facilitating the service of already incurred debt—the gold price would need to be fixed at a price somewhat higher than the $13,600 that backs only the narrow money supply. Perhaps much higher. Indeed, the price that might best suit policy makers would be that which implies that the real total economy debt burden declines to a level that can be adequately serviced by the current level of national income or, from the perspective of the government specifically, that level of tax revenue that is available to service the accumulated Treasury debt.

If the debt burden is seen as too large to be sustainably serviced through current tax revenue, then either the government will have to raise taxes, reducing growth, hurting competitiveness, and potentially leading to an outflow of gold, or alternatively, the government will begin to accumulate additional debt straightaway, leading to a loss of confidence in the ability of the United States to maintain a stable gold exchange rate for the dollar, which would also lead to an outflow of gold. There is no point fixing to gold at all if the rate does not stabilize the US debt level and prevent the implied outflow of gold. A sufficiently high gold coverage ratio is thus essential if economic stability is to be achieved. As it stands today, the continuing rise in the money supply in recent years, combined with a generally sideways move in the dollar gold price, has taken the dollar narrow money supply gold coverage ratio down to the historic lows that pertained at the beginning of the big bull market that began in the early 2000s. In the case of broad money, the coverage ratio stands roughly where it was prior to the 2008 financial crisis.

Figure 13.2: Implied gold coverage ratio of the US money supply, narrow and broad

Source: Federal Reserve, US Treasury.

Now it is difficult not to get overtly political when talking about marginal tax rates—one of the more popular political footballs to kick around—but there are some simple realities implied by a gold standard. Basically, once you are on it, if you are going to stay on it, you can't print more money than enabled by the real, sustainable growth of your economy. Print too much, and financial markets drain your gold; print too little, and gold reserves swell but at the expense of growth and tax revenues. Given that the US economy is so weak and has been for so long, significantly higher taxes from this point forward are likely to be politically unpopular and, I would argue, damaging for US economic competitiveness. But then higher tax rates are also entirely unnecessary if the dollar convertibility rate is set at a level that makes future debt service manageable at the current level of taxation.

There is good reason, therefore, why politicians might prefer to fix not at today's market price but at a price somewhat higher and, in particular, one derived from a broad rather than narrow measure of the money supply. For example, let's target a 40 percent coverage ratio for M2. I suggest 40 percent because this was the original stipulated limit coverage ratio for Federal Reserve notes prior to the Banking Act of 1935. With M2 now exceeding $13 trillion, a 40 percent coverage ratio implies a $20,000 per troy ounce target price for gold.

Figure 13.3: Imputed dollar gold prices for various measures of the US money supply, 40 percent backed

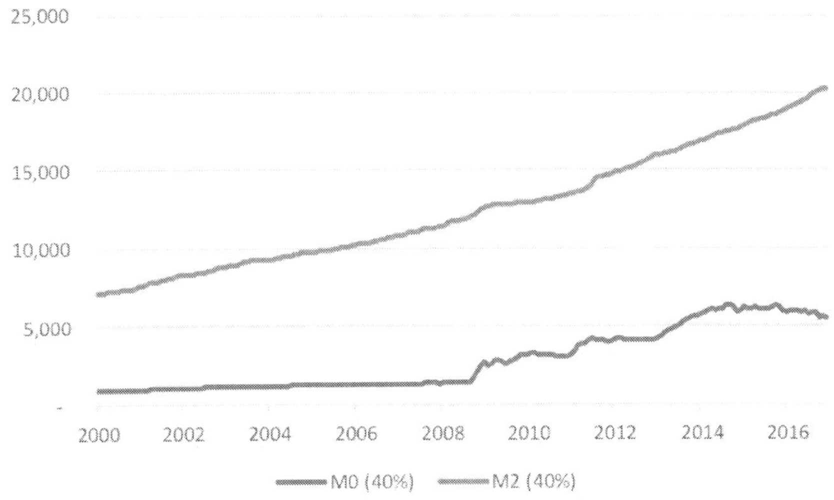

Source: Federal Reserve, US Treasury.

Some readers might express disbelief at the prospect of a gold price of $20,000 on any relevant time frame. I would advise these readers rather to express their disbelief at how the Federal Reserve has grown the money supply by such a colossal amount since President Nixon closed the gold window in 1971. All that we have done here is to run the numbers as they are. The alternative to revaluing gold to the levels discussed here is to force an outright contraction of the United States' broad or possibly even narrow money supply, which would wreak havoc with the banking system and economy, exactly the opposite of what is needed to restore a degree of monetary stability not only to the United States but also to the global economy.

Having thus explored various ways in which to estimate what gold price would be appropriate for a future, sustainable restoration of dollar-gold convertibility, we can consider more specifically the actions that would be required to implement this historic and salutary regime change in US monetary policy and international monetary relations.

Chapter 14: Long-Forgotten Suggestions for How the United States Could Return to Gold

> "The major roadblock to restoring the gold standard is the problem of reentry. With the vast quantity of dollars worldwide laying claims to the US Treasury's 264 million ounces of gold, an overnight transition to gold convertibility would create a major discontinuity for the US financial system. But there is no need for the whole block of current dollar obligations to become an immediate claim."
>
> —Alan Greenspan,
> writing in the *Wall Street Journal*, September 1981

THE FIAT DOLLAR IS FORTY-FIVE years old. Those in favor of a return to a gold standard have never ceased arguing their case. A number of these gold standard advocates have also provided specific recommendations for how to get the United States back onto a gold standard, with minimal disruption to the economy and financial system. Some of these advocates happen to have ties to individuals in President Trump's inner circle of economic advisors. It is conceivable that one or more of them have already had the opportunity to make their case for gold and, quite possibly, President Trump is favorably inclined to at least seriously explore the possibility of rescinding President Nixon's "temporary, emergency" executive order from August 1971 suspending dollar-gold convertibility.

However, the history of the return-to-gold advocates goes back somewhat further. This is because, for some, the Bretton Woods arrangements themselves were flawed. Consider that, under Bretton Woods, the dollar was fixed to gold at $35 per ounce. But actual convertibility was provided only to foreign governments in official transactions with their central banks. Indeed, from 1933, US residents had been forbidden from owning monetary gold by executive order. Although President Franklin D. Roosevelt claimed that this was an emergency measure to help stabilize the failing US banking system in the depths of the Great Depression, the order had never been rescinded. It was only natural that some commentators would wonder why US residents were still forbidden to own gold decades later, when the US economy and financial system were clearly much more robust.

One prominent economic commentator of the 1950s and 1960s who argued for a restoration of gold convertibility for US residents was Henry Hazlitt, a columnist for both *Newsweek* and the *New York Times*. In his 1960 book, *What You Should Know about Inflation,* he made the case, now associated primarily with Milton Friedman and the Chicago School, that "inflation is, always and everywhere, a monetary phenomenon." The first chapter of the book, "What Inflation Is," contains the following:

> Inflation, always and everywhere, is primarily caused by an increase in the supply of money and credit. In fact, inflation *is* the supply of money and credit. . . .
>
> In recent years, however, the term has come to be used in a radically different sense. This is recognized in the second definition given by the American College Dictionary: "A substantial *rise in prices* caused by an undue expansion in paper money or bank credit." Now obviously a rise of price *caused* by an expansion of the money supply is not the same thing as the expansion of the money supply itself. A cause or condition is clearly not identical with one of its

> consequences. The use of the word "inflation" with these two quite different meanings leads to endless confusion.[68]

Why do you think that Hazlitt went to the trouble in 1960 to write a book about what inflation is? Well, believe it or not, inflation was becoming an issue already in the late 1950s. Hazlitt and others were concerned that inflation, if unchecked, could lead to severe economic consequences. In his view, the most effective way to prevent inflation from becoming a serious problem in the future was to restore domestic gold convertibility. Whereas Bretton Woods allowed for international gold convertibility, US residents and businesses were not permitted to exchange their dollars for gold, at any price. Hazlitt believed a full repegging of the dollar to gold would be a strong check on the temptations of government to spend and borrow in amounts that are not compatible with stable money.

He was hardly alone in this. Nor was he the first to voice such concerns. In Chapter 9, "Gold Goes with Freedom," he quotes W. Randolph Burgess, former chairman of the executive committee of the National City Bank of New York (today known as Citibank), from a 1949 speech:

> Historically one of the best protections of the value of money against the inroads of political spending was the gold standard—the redemption of money in gold on demand. This put a check-rein on the politician. For inflationary spending led to the loss of gold either by exports or by withdrawals by individuals who distrusted government policies. This was a kind of automatic limit on credit expansion. . . .

---

68 Hazlitt, *What You Should Know about Inflation* (New York: D. Van Nostrand Company, 1960), Chapter 1.

> There is a group of people today asking for the restoration of the full gold standard immediately in the United States. Today we have a dollar that is convertible into gold for foreign governments and central banks; these people are asking for the same rights to hold gold for our own citizens.[69]

We can see, therefore, that already in the immediate post–World War II period, there were prominent people supporting a restoration of full gold convertibility, primarily because they did not necessarily trust government or central bank economic and monetary policies.

Yet even back then, these people also understood that restoring convertibility could be disruptive and should be done with care so as not to discredit the very concept of a full gold standard. Hazlitt quotes further from the Burgess speech thus:

> If you try to force the pace by resuming gold payments before the foundations are laid through government policies on the budget, on credit, and on prices, the gold released may simply move out into hoards and become the tool of the speculator.
>
> Gold payments are only part of the building of sound money, and they are in a sense the capstone of the arch. . . .[70]

Hazlitt understood well the nexus where government policies on the economy, generally, and on the gold standard, specifically, meet. As such, while he believed strongly that a return to a full gold standard was highly desirable to check the implementation of unsustainable and economically destructive government policies, it was important to recognize that it is

69 Hazlitt, *What You Should Know about Inflation* (New York: D. Van Nostrand Company, 1960), Chapter 9.

70 IBID.

the policies that can be destructive, and thus the policies themselves need to be sorted out. Hazlitt therefore advocated gold convertibility as an important means to an end rather than an end in itself:

> The gold standard is not important as an isolated gadget but only as an integral part of a whole economic system. Just as "managed" paper money goes with a statist and collectivist philosophy, with government "planning," with a coercive economy in which the citizen is always at the mercy of bureaucratic caprice, so the gold standard is an integral part of a free-enterprise economy under which governments respect private property, economize in spending, balance their budgets, keep their promises, and refuse to connive in overexpansion of money or credit. Until our government is prepared to return to this system in its entirety and has given evidence of this intention by its deeds, it is pointless to try to force it to go on a real gold basis. For it would only be off again in a few months. And, as in the past, the gold standard itself, rather than the abuses that destroyed it, would get the popular blame.[71]

Did Alan Greenspan Read Hazlitt?

Alan Greenspan wrote and spoke on economic matters long before he became world famous as chairman of the US Federal Reserve. Indeed, in 1966, he wrote a provocative essay, "Gold and Economic Freedom," in which he echoes rather clearly several of the key arguments put forward by Hazlitt in his various prominent columns and books in the early 1960s. Readers might wish to compare the following quote from Greenspan's essay with the prior quote by Hazlitt:

71 Hazlitt, *What You Should Know about Inflation* (New York: D. Van Nostrand Company, 1960), Chapter 14.

Under a gold standard, the amount of credit that an economy can support is determined by the economy's tangible assets, since every credit instrument is ultimately a claim on some tangible asset. But government bonds are not backed by tangible wealth, only by the government's promise to pay out of future tax revenues, and cannot easily be absorbed by the financial markets. A large volume of new government bonds can be sold to the public only at progressively higher interest rates. Thus, government deficit spending under a gold standard is severely limited. The abandonment of the gold standard made it possible for the welfare statists to use the banking system as a means to an unlimited expansion of credit. They have created paper reserves in the form of government bonds which—through a complex series of steps—the banks accept in place of tangible assets and treat as if they were an actual deposit, i.e., as the equivalent of what was formerly a deposit of gold. The holder of a government bond or of a bank deposit created by paper reserves believes that he has a valid claim on a real asset. But the fact is that there are now more claims outstanding than real assets. The law of supply and demand is not to be conned. As the supply of money (of claims) increases relative to the supply of tangible assets in the economy, prices must eventually rise. Thus the earnings saved by the productive members of the society lose value in terms of goods. When the economy's books are finally balanced, one finds that this loss in value represents the goods purchased by the government for welfare or other purposes with the money proceeds of the government bonds financed by bank credit expansion.

> In the absence of the gold standard, there is no way to protect savings from confiscation through inflation. There is no safe store of value. If there were, the government would have to make its holding illegal, as was done in the case of gold. If everyone decided, for example, to convert all his bank deposits to silver or copper or any other good, and thereafter declined to accept checks as payment for goods, bank deposits would lose their purchasing power and government-created bank credit would be worthless as a claim on goods. The financial policy of the welfare state requires that there be no way for the owners of wealth to protect themselves.
>
> This is the shabby secret of the welfare statists' tirades against gold. Deficit spending is simply a scheme for the confiscation of wealth. Gold stands in the way of this insidious process. It stands as a protector of property rights. If one grasps this, one has no difficulty in understanding the statists' antagonism toward the gold standard.[72]

Even more curious than the possibility that the young Alan Greenspan borrowed heavily from Hazlitt in "Gold and Economic Freedom" is the conundrum of Greenspan's complete transformation from gold standard advocate to champion of the fiat dollar in his role as Federal Reserve Chairman. As late as 1981, he was still openly advocating the gold standard. For example, in a *Wall Street Journal* editorial from that year, he wrote about how the United States might go about getting back on gold in gradual fashion:

72 Alan Greenspan, "Gold and Economic Freedom," as featured in Ayn Rand, "Capitalism: The Unknown Ideal," (New York: Penguin Group, 1967).

> Convertibility can be instituted gradually by, in effect, creating a dual currency with a limited issue of dollars convertible into gold.[73]

It is worth noting that one of Greenspan's early mentors was none other than Ayn Rand, who once quipped that he was "a social climber." He did, indeed, manage to climb all the way to the top of the US Federal Reserve, arguably the most powerful economic policy post in the entire world. But one wonders, to what purpose? Did he ever use his enormous power or influence to try to move the United States back toward a gold standard? If not, why not? Did he simply decide at some point that he was wrong about gold and that the fiat dollar was superior? That unchecked government was better than checked? That welfare statism and associated inflationism was preferable to a free market, sound money economy? Or alternatively, was Greenspan severely disappointed that another one of his mentors, Arthur Burns, failed in his attempts to prevent President Nixon from closing the gold window and that he would continue to try, behind the scenes, to move the United States back toward gold?

In recent years, Greenspan has spoken on multiple occasions about the possibility of reinstating some form of gold standard and in his early 2017 interview with the World Gold Council, he comes close to recommending it.[74] This Dr. Jekyll–Mr. Hyde aspect of Greenspan's career has led some to speculate that, perhaps, while at the Fed, Greenspan deliberately and surreptitiously sowed the seeds of the financial crisis of 2008 with easy money and lax banking system regulation. In this way, single-handed and in secret, he undermined the welfare statists' fiat dollar, perhaps fatally, laying the groundwork for a future return to gold. If true, this would be a classic example of truth indeed being far, far stranger than fiction.

---

73 Alan Greenspan, "Can the U.S. Return to a Gold Standard?" *The Wall Street Journal*, September 1, 1981.

74 The World Gold Council, Gold Investor, February 2017.

Let the market decide

Hazlitt devotes much space in his book to describing how he believes the United States should go about restoring full gold convertibility. In Chapter 15 of *What You Should Know about Inflation,* "What Price for Gold?" he considers the obvious importance of restoring gold convertibility at a price that will lead to maximum economic and financial stability and, therefore, have the greatest chance of lasting success.

First, he points out how important it is to choose a price that does not lead to a deflationary run on gold that would potentially crash the economy, which, as we have seen, happened with Great Britain following Churchill's decision to restore the pre–World War I gold convertibility rate in 1925:

> In periods when public confidence exists in the determination of the monetary managers to maintain the gold standard, as well as in the prudence and wisdom of their policy, gold convertibility may be maintained with a surprisingly low reserve. But when confidence in the wisdom, prudence, and good faith of the monetary managers has been shaken, a gold reserve far above "normal" will be required to maintain convertibility. And today confidence in the wisdom, prudence, and good faith of the world's monetary managers has been all but destroyed.[75]

No doubt Hazlitt would not think particularly highly of the wisdom, prudence, and good faith of today's monetary managers. As such, he would almost certainly recommend erring on the side of restoring convertibility at a much higher gold price than that observed today. This is because, at the current price, the implied gold coverage ratio would

75 Hazlitt, *What You Should Know about Inflation* (New York: D. Van Nostrand Company, 1960), Chapter 15.

be less than 10 percent of money supply M2, far lower than what was generally observed back when the United States was officially on a gold standard, yet amid a far, far lower level of monetary credibility.

Given his faith in free markets, it should be no surprise that Hazlitt, while having some idea of what a sensible price for gold convertibility might have been when he wrote his book in 1960, thought that it would be preferable to use the free market to determine an ideal convertibility price before returning to a fully operational gold standard. His specific recommendation is presented in Chapter 19, "How to Return to Gold":

1. The Administration will immediately announce its intention to return to a full gold standard by a series of steps dated in advance. The Federal Reserve Banks and the Treasury will temporarily suspend all sales or purchases of gold, merely holding on to what they have. Simultaneously with this step, a free market in gold will be permitted.
2. After watching this market, and meanwhile preventing any further inflation [i.e., growth in the money supply], the government, within a period of not more than a year, will announce the dollar-gold ratio at which convertibility will take place.
3. On and after Convertibility Day, and for the following six months, any holder of dollars will be entitled to convert them into gold bars, but at a moderate discount on the paper dollars he turns in. To put the matter the other way, he would be asked to pay a premium on gold bars above the new valuation—equivalent, let us say, to ½ of 1 percent a month. The purpose of this would be to spread out the first demands for conversion and discourage excessive pressure on reserves at the beginning. . . .
4. Six months after Convertibility Day, the country will return to a full gold-bullion standard. Conversion of dollars into gold bars, or vice versa, will be open to all holders without such discounts or premiums and without discrimination.

5. One year later still, the country will return to a full gold-coin standard, by minting gold coins and permitting free conversion.[76]

There you have it. A detailed road map for how the US government, if it desired, could go about restoring a full gold standard in a way that would not cause undue deflationary pressure or threaten the financial system but would, in fact, ensure that, going forward, confidence in the US dollar and US economic policy generally was restored. While there would be nevertheless some economic disruption during the transition, including a wave of inflation as the dollar was devalued sharply versus gold, as discussed earlier, this would be far, far less disruptive than for the United States to wait to be overtaken by events elsewhere.

There is no reason why a future US president must face a sudden dollar crisis far greater than that faced by President Nixon in August 1971. With foresight, US policy makers can make a choice to unilaterally go about restoring gold convertibility. Yes, it will restrict their future freedom of action. But if the dollar suddenly loses reserve currency status, falls sharply in value, and forces up US interest rates, freedom of action will be restricted anyway. Yet in the latter case, this will take place at a time of one or more foreign governments' choosing. United States officials should ask themselves whether they really want to leave something potentially this disruptive and economically damaging up to foreign governments, some of whom might not be on friendly terms with the United States, or whether they would, in fact, retain greater freedom to act in the future, were they to set about restoring gold convertibility on their own terms sooner rather than later.

The American people also need to ask themselves this important question. In 2010, the deficit arrived on the stage as the crisis issue du jour, with the Republicans in Congress refusing to raise the federal debt ceiling. More recently, criticism of the Federal Reserve has grown,

76 Hazlitt, *What You Should Know about Inflation,* (New York: D. Van Nostrand Co., 1960), Chapter 19.

and in both major US political parties. In the UK, the government has criticized the Bank of England for implementing monetary policies that have exacerbated inequality, although the Bank disagrees.

William Jennings Bryan won the 1896 Democratic presidential nomination with his "Cross of Gold" speech about the dollar and monetary policy. It may be difficult to imagine a US presidential candidate today securing a party nomination or winning an election with a speech about the dollar and about whether the United States should restore the gold standard. But at some point, it is likely to happen. The issue will become so immediate, so unavoidable, that a US presidential candidate will be nominated and perhaps subsequently elected or reelected due primarily to whether the candidate supports or opposes a restoration of dollar-gold convertibility.

It is my hope that the voters choose wisely.

A Golden Windfall

One of the more obvious, practical investment implications of those who agree with the view that the nominal price of gold is going to rise dramatically as the world moves back to some form of gold standard is to acquire a position in gold in some investment form. There are investors, foreign and domestic, who already have had the foresight to invest in gold and other precious metals and dollar hedges and have prospered as the price of gold has risen. Naturally, these are likely to be relatively wealthy people, but there are many so-called gold bugs out there who are not particularly wealthy but, for whatever reason, have long regarded gold as a sensible asset to own to protect against what many have considered an unsustainable path of US finances. So there are no doubt a large number of individuals out there owning a few coins or who have purchased various gold-linked or gold-derivative investments, such as exchange-traded funds (ETFs) or gold mining shares, all of whom would all reap a windfall gain, at least in nominal terms, from a dollar devaluation.

Naturally, these gains would be taxable once cashed in, providing the government with a source of tax revenue over time. But the bulk of the gain would remain in the hands of private investors who took a sensible view of their government's limited options for dealing with the debt problem and were proven right by events. It is hard to argue why they should not be among the beneficiaries of a return to gold convertibility.

Chapter 15: The Golden BRICS

> "In the most profound financial change in recent Middle East history, Gulf Arabs are planning—along with China, Russia, Japan and France—to end dollar dealings for oil, moving instead to a basket of currencies including gold."
>
> —Robert Fisk, "The Demise of the Dollar," *The Independent*, October 6, 2009

IN PREVIOUS CHAPTERS, WE HAVE described the relative decline of the US economy since the end of World War II and, in particular, since the start of the twenty-first century. There are, however, two sides to relative shifts, and, in this chapter, we explore the possibility that the larger of the rising global economies, collectively known as the BRICS (Brazil, Russia, India, China, South Africa), will collectively take the initiative in moving the global economy back to a gold standard.

The relative growth of the BRICS in recent years has been dramatic. As a group, they are already larger than the US economy and, by extrapolating recent trends, will continue to outpace the US and other developed economies in the coming few years. Importantly, they also trade increasingly with each other, rather than bilaterally with the United States. Taken together, these trends imply a growing preference to use their own currencies in bilateral trade, rather than the dollar. But with no single BRICS economy in a position to dominate the others, it is far more logical for them to move toward the use of an objective reference currency that can be trusted and accepted by all. A gold-backed currency of some sort would be ideally suited for that.

As discussed in Section II, the dollar reserve standard is destabilizing the BRICS economies through monetary, asset, and consumer price inflation. It also threatens them with huge losses on their substantial accumulated dollar reserve assets at some future point in time. This helps to explain why the BRICS are already accumulating gold reserves, as well as other real assets such as natural resources. China has been particularly aggressive in this regard, buying up oil and mining companies, acquiring mineral rights, and building real economic infrastructure, such as ports and railways, that facilitates the transport, processing, and manufacture of basic materials into capital and consumer goods. Collectively, these efforts are sometimes referred to as the "New Silk Road" in which Russia is a strategic partner. Russia, too, has accumulated a large gold reserve. Both countries run large trade surpluses, resulting in the unwelcome, indirect importation of inflation from expansionary US monetary policies.

Figure 15.1: The Russian trade balance is chronically positive

Figure 15.2: Russian gold reserves are growing steadily

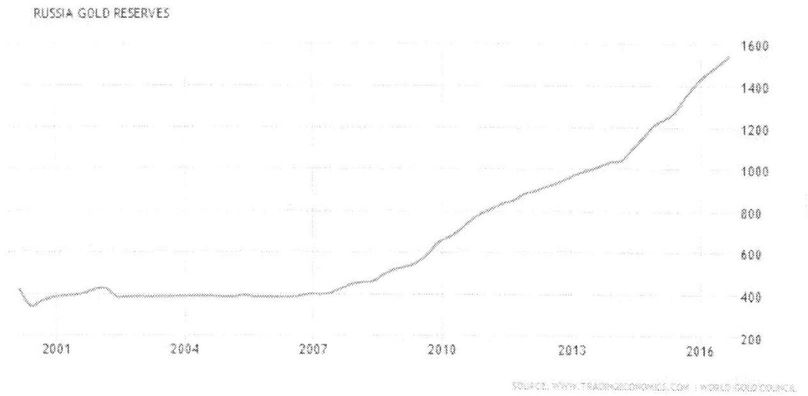

The BRICS have also been increasingly assertive in recent years with respect to global monetary arrangements. In the introduction to this section, we pointed out that in spring 2011 they issued a joint statement that they would prefer for their currencies to be used more widely in global commerce and to be held more widely as foreign exchange reserves.

Indications that the BRICS and other countries have long been dissatisfied with the fiat dollar reserve standard go back to the immediate aftermath of the 2008–2009 credit crisis, when several countries explicitly blamed US economic policy for the near-meltdown in the global financial system. In October 2009, veteran journalist Robert Fisk wrote a provocative article, "The Demise of the Dollar," in which he claimed there had been some high-level, behind-the-scenes discussions between the BRICS, oil producers, and a handful of other countries, regarding plans to move away from the dollar as the primary currency for the global oil trade.

If true, this would represent an even more significant shift in international monetary relations than when French President De Gaulle made his famous comments attacking the Bretton-Woods arrangements in 1965. Whereas De Gaulle's actions were essentially unilateral—it is unclear to this day to what extent other European countries supportive his efforts—what Fisk is describing is a truly international effort to move away from dependence on the fiat dollar and toward a basket of currencies, including gold.

Absent the Bretton Woods legacy, it would be entirely logical for global trade to be denominated in something other than dollars. Among other things, Fisk observes in his article that China imports 60 percent of its oil from the Middle East. Moreover, China's non-US exports now significantly exceed those to the United States. A similar situation exists with Brazil. That the fiat dollar should be the transactional currency for such commerce is explained only by historical convention, not contemporary economic logic.

Finally, Fisk also notes that these countries are well aware that, as a result of the fiat-dollar reserve standard, they suffer the consequences of US monetary policies that are increasingly not in their domestic interest:

> America's trading partners have been left to cope with the impact of Washington's control and...the hegemony of the dollar as the dominant global reserve currency.[77]

Of course most countries implement monetary policies that are not necessarily appropriate for others. But few currencies are widely held as reserves and none anywhere near the scale of the dollar. In any case, it would be a nonsolution to the BRICS and others' problems to simply replace the fiat dollar with another fiat reserve currency.

Even a basket of currencies could be problematic, as all major economies are currently suffering various forms of economic and financial crises, which raise the temptation to inflate away their debts. The euro area, UK, and Japan all fall into this category. Hence, the explicit reference to gold in the article is of particular note. Gold is the only alternative to the dollar, which is not at risk of arbitrary and expedient devaluation. From the perspective of exporting countries, in particular the large oil exporters, with their vast accumulated wealth and

77 Robert Fisk, "The Demise of the Dollar," *The Independent,* October 6, 2009.

large export revenues, transacting in gold, or in an explicitly gold-backed currency, would be most desirable.

Regardless of whether the specifics of this article are true—no official sources have ever confirmed its claims—it is perfectly reasonable to assume that, at a minimum, some of the countries mentioned in the article have considered what to do if, for example, the US Fed continues to print money aggressively or if the United States deliberately chooses to weaken its currency as a matter of policy. By acting in concert, rather than individually, the BRICS and others could probably more effectively deal with the increasing global monetary disruption that such actions would cause. It is thus entirely plausible to assume that there have been some cross-border discussions on the possibility of coordinated action.

Indeed, there have been other, less provocative but nevertheless pertinent reports in the press during the past year or two regarding cross-border arrangements to reduce dependence on the dollar. A few years back China and Japan announced that they would begin to rely more on yuan and yen in bilateral trade and less on the dollar.[78] China has also been negotiating with Thailand regarding increasing bilateral trade in their domestic currencies.[79]

In the immediate wake of the 2008–2009 global credit crisis, there were also a handful of such reports. In March 2009, China and Argentina announced a currency swap arrangement.[80] Prior to the Fisk article above, in July 2009, Reuters reported that Russia, China, and Brazil had prepared to push the idea of a new global currency at the upcoming G8 Summit.[81]

There have also been reports of increased official gold purchases in recent years, an implicit indication that a growing number of countries

78 "China, Japan to back direct trade of currencies," *Bloomberg*, December 26 2011.

79 "China, government sign currency swap deal," *Bangkok Post*, December 23, 2011.

80 "China, Argentina reach agreement on currency swap," *Bloomberg*, March 30, 2009.

81 "Russia, China to push global currency at G8 summit," *Reuters*, July 7 2009.

are seeking to reduce their dependence on dollar reserves. Unlike currency swap and bilateral trade arrangements, the accumulation of gold reserves need not be coordinated. Indeed, a growing preference for gold reserve accumulation could be an indication of a relative lack of global cooperation in monetary affairs. Notwithstanding the various bilateral agreements cited above, these are hardly sufficient to restore the degree of confidence and credibility in global monetary arrangements, which prevailed prior to the undermining of the US economy and financing system from 2008, and to which this book argues there is no return absent gold.

Let's return briefly to the provocative scenario posed at the start of this section, in which Russia unilaterally established a new, credible, gold-backed currency. Having been presented with a viable, liquid, gold-backed alternative to the increasingly undesirable US dollar, we assumed that other countries would be quick to adopt the new currency for use in international transactions and as reserves, the most obvious advantage being that this would prevent their economies from being further destabilized by inflationary US monetary policies.

But if the evidence indicates that many countries share a common goal of moving away from the fiat dollar toward something more credible, stable, and reliable, why does one of them need to be a first mover? Indeed, as bilateral commercial ties between several countries are now greater than those they have with the United States specifically, were a group of countries to move away from the dollar in concert, it would be much less disruptive for any single one of them. Consider also the danger that if a single country moves first and establishes a gold-backed currency it might suddenly face huge pressure to revalue as other countries seek to swap a portion of their dollar reserves for the new, gold-backed alternative. That would, of course, hurt relative economic competitiveness.

Recall our previous discussion of the Nash equilibrium: it represents the most desirable collective outcome when each player takes full account of the other players' strategies. As the interests of a single player shift, so must others react, and the equilibrium shifts accordingly. Such is the case in our Russia as first-mover example. But what if Russia is in good company and the BRICS' interests are all shifting in similar fashion? Perhaps export-led economies such as Germany, South Korea and Taiwan are also tiring of accumulating dollar reserves in exchange for exports. Only the interests of one major player, the United States, remain essentially unchanged—to inflate the dollar money supply as required to ease the burden of financing its large trade and budget deficits and, if necessary, to re-liquefy it's financial system in the event of another crisis.

Therefore, it is entirely reasonable to assume that, at some point in the future, the BRICS and possibly a larger collection of countries finds a way to move away from the fiat dollar in concert. It would be less disruptive for each to do so in such fashion. The relative impact on each participant's economic competitiveness would be substantially less and the losses on the accumulated dollar reserve holdings would be more proportional, rather than any one country being stuck holding the "Old Maid" fiat dollar reserve pile, as it were.

In practice, this could be done by following a variation on the hypothetical, unilateral Russian example posed by Rickards. All four BRICS, joined perhaps by Germany and France and some oil-producing countries, could agree to the simultaneous implementation of gold convertibility for their currencies, at a conversion price that would be credible and, hence, sustainable. As is the case in our discussion regarding the United States, the key would be to make certain that, whatever price is chosen, that it does not require a deflationary adjustment that would threaten their respective financial systems.

Probably the best way to proceed would be to follow Henry Hazlitt's advice on the matter: announce your intentions, let markets adjust the relevant exchange rates and their gold exchange ratios for a time, and then allow actual convertibility from that point forward. His five-point plan for the United States could be adopted by any number of countries, in concert or individually. The more that participated up front, the less overall disruption to global commerce, and the sooner the world, having placed gold back at the center of the global financial system, could return to the business of generating sustainable economic growth, rather than continuing to fight the endless series of financial fires associated with the unstable fiat dollar.

Were other countries to take the lead, the United States would quickly find it had no alternative but to go along with whatever gold-backed arrangements this group of countries decided to implement. Gold-backed currencies are simply more credible in a world where trust is lacking. Indeed, if the United States resisted a global move back to gold, it would no doubt find that it faced higher interest rates as a result. Who would prefer to buy unbacked US Treasuries when they could buy gold-backed German, Brazilian, or Chinese government bonds instead?

Sure, the Fed could continue to buy ever-increasing amounts of Treasuries to keep interest rates as low as desired, but then the dollar would not only lose reserve currency status entirely but become a chronically weak currency, leading to persistent high inflation above and beyond that which would occur were the United States simply to bite the bullet now and restore gold convertibility at a credible rate, as discussed earlier in this section.

As is well demonstrated by history and as discussed above, rationality does not always prevail in policymaking. There are times when not just one, but a number of countries persist for years in pursing suboptimal or even seriously damaging economic policies. But that which can't go on, won't, and beyond a certain point, financial markets themselves will force the issue and drag the world, kicking and screaming if necessary, back onto a gold standard. Indeed, in the background of contemporary global economic and financial market developments, there is some evidence that this process is already underway. In the following chapters, we examine how some relevant new monetary and financial technologies may play an important role in what is to come.

Chapter 16:
Bitcoin, the Monetary "Touchstone"

"We must remember that bitcoin is not the byproduct of a blockchain—the blockchain is the byproduct of bitcoin. Private, permissioned blockchains and distributed ledgers serve only to erect barriers and advance the interests of restrictive cartels whereas the public Bitcoin blockchain works to disrupt, not enable, financial incumbents."

—Jon Matonis,
founding director of the bitcoin foundation

Back in 2011, when I was preparing the manuscript for the original edition of *The Golden Revolution*, bitcoin was still relatively unknown, having not yet received any material attention from the mainstream financial or other media. However, that all changed and rather abruptly so in early 2014, when suddenly multiple mainstream publications, including the *New York Times* and *Newsweek*, ran feature articles on the world's first and, at the time, only major "blockchain"-based currency.

The *Newsweek* article not only reported on the concept of blockchain and on the history of bitcoin specifically but went to far as to claim to have outed "Satoshi Nakamoto," the hitherto anonymous author of the 2008 paper explaining the "proof-of-work" algorithm behind what shortly thereafter became bitcoin. (*Newsweek* subsequently backed off their claim and to this day the identity of "Satoshi Nakamoto" remains uncertain, although there have been multiple additional claims since.)

The debate continues to rage as to whether bitcoin or other blockchain-based digital currencies are or are not potentially viable forms of alternative money. In this chapter, I survey a handful of prominent, diverging views on bitcoin and then share some of my own thoughts. In brief, I believe that bitcoin's blockchain technology indeed enables a low-cost payments system capable of disintermediating the banking industry, but I do not believe bitcoin presents a viable, alternative store of value on par with gold. In any case, bitcoin serves as a monetary "touchstone" of sorts, distinguishing those who lean toward monetary central planning from those who favor market-based economic organization instead.

In order to evaluate bitcoin's monetary properties and to compare it to either the dollar or gold, we need first consider why an alternative money would ever be necessary in the first place. Well, repeatedly throughout history, due to financial pressures, governments have chosen to debase their coins or inflate their paper currencies to service or settle their debts, by implication appropriating the wealth of prudent savers in the process. Wars for example can be expensive and most large debasements in history have occurred either during or following major wars, in particular in those countries on the losing side of the conflict. But even the winners can succumb, as Rome demonstrated in the third century or as the victorious WWI powers did in the 1920s and 1930s. [82]

Savers fearful of potential future currency debasement or inflation, therefore, naturally seek alternatives for protection. Gold and silver have

82 There are those who fail to draw the connection between WWI and the currency debasements that followed. While it is easy to understand why the defeated powers ended up hyperinflating in the period 1919–1924—they were broke and had reparations payments to make—it is harder to see how WWI contributed to the devaluations of sterling and the dollar in the 1930s. However, a close look at the 1920s reveals that inflationary policies, including the fractionally reserved "gold exchange standard" were implemented to soften the economic blow of the immediate post-war period. However, these led to asset bubbles, in particular in the United States, which burst in the early 1930s, inaugurating the Great Depression. FDR finally succumbed to the urge to debase the dollar in 1934.

historically been the most obvious choices. When governments sought to debase coins passing through the Treasury by clipping or by minting new coins with less gold or silver content, the higher quality coins would be hoarded out of existence by savers as per Gresham's Law. Individuals would subsequently transact using the inferior coins instead, which in time would fully replace the sounder coinage in commerce. In time, this would push up prices, as more and more economic agents became aware that the quality of the coinage had declined.

Another option for savers was to hoard foreign coins, for example, that were not being debased. This could restrict the amount of circulating medium in foreign countries, however, with deflationary effects on prices and possibly on output, something that the foreign governments might then seek to offset with debasement of their own. This could also lead to an aggressive "race to debase," or "currency war," which occurred in the 1930s, for example, and which is also arguably occurring again today, as James Rickards and others have argued.

Gold and silver hoarding is hardly the only way in which savers can go about trying to store wealth during periods of debasement and inflation. In theory, any goods of value can be hoarded. Wealthy individuals tend to hoard fine art and wine, or prestigious property. Middle-class individuals can purchase a modest home, or perhaps even a second home. Farmers can hoard their harvests for a time rather than release them directly into the marketplace. Producers of energy can do the same with oil and gas. Indeed, practically any business that holds inventory of any kind has the option to hoard some portion of that inventory, not in anticipation of increased real final demand, but merely as a hedge against debasement and inflation. Withholding goods from the marketplace in anticipation of higher prices in future rapidly becomes a self-fulfilling prophecy, however, as it constitutes a negative supply-shock, contributing to "stagflation," such as that of the 1970s in the United States, Britain, and a handful of other economies.

The problems and costs associated with hoarding real-goods inventory, however, are numerous, and it is far better if confidence in the official money declines for savers to have the option of just switching to an alternative. International businesses have some flexibility in this regard, switching their trading and invoicing between dollars, euros, yen or, increasingly, the yuan.

Unlike physical inventory, major currencies are fungible. Indeed, this is one of the definitions of money, that it is a convenient, efficient medium of exchange. Historically this has most frequently been metallic coinage. Why metallic coinage? Because metals were the most marketable commodities, accepted by everyone, everywhere, subject to a quick check of weight and authenticity in the event they were of dubious provenance.

The desire for an alternative money, therefore, is entirely natural when economic agents become uncertain as to the future purchasing power of any legally mandated tender. In this regard, we should not be so surprised why bitcoin has skyrocketed from obscurity to prominence in such a short period, notwithstanding its tiny market share as a globally available alternative medium of exchange. The context is key, and the current context of zero or negative interest rates and unusually high global uncertainly as to the future purchasing power of dollars or other fiat currencies is the ideal environment in which an upstart alternative can have a disproportionate impact. When combined with the perennial technological innovations of modern times, resulting in all but the oldest individuals now being comfortable with digital commerce for all manner of goods and services, why not a truly digital currency, created by computational power itself, to serve as the twenty-first century alternative medium of exchange?

The "Monetary Touchstone"

How one feels about bitcoin tells us much, however, about how one feels about money itself, making bitcoin a monetary touchstone. Those who embrace it likely do so out of some combination of uncertainty around existing legal tender and embrace of technological solutions to problems. Those who disparage bitcoin, by contrast, most probably do so either because they trust the legal tender, obviating any perceived need for an alternative currency, and/or because they are distrustful of technology as a solution. This could be due to a general distrust of technology, say in the case of Luddites who would prefer a simpler world absent of much if not all modern technology, or perhaps a distrust of market-based solutions, technological or otherwise.

For example, there are some who oppose the US Federal Reserve on the (entirely justifiable) grounds that its actions appear to favor large financial institutions over other economic actors, including most households; yet rather than replace the Fed with a market-based solution to money creation and interest rate determination, they think that the Fed, a federal agency, should be replaced by another agency instead, say the US Treasury.

Several prominent commentators have weighed in on this bitcoin debate, spanning the entire range of approval to disapproval. Before we review a broad, representative set of examples, let's start with the mysterious "Satoshi Nakamoto," whoever he or she or they might be.

Satoshi Nakamoto was not the first to propose a purely digital currency, an idea that has been occasionally discussed in tech forums for years. However, s/he was the first to publish a practical solution to a major problem: that of establishing proof of ownership without any third-party verification. The bitcoin algorithm includes a blockchain, linking bitcoins back to their origin, so that as the limited and known supply of bitcoins pass from person to person, their ownership remains certain and prevents the possibility of what could be termed "crypto-counterfeiting" in which an individual would fraudulently exchange the same bitcoin with two or more other individuals simultaneously.

The blockchain is thus an objective way to verify ownership comparable in principle to when a physical coin passes from one person's hand to another in exchange settlement. However, there is an important and controversial difference: When a coin passes between individuals, they can easily identify one another. When bitcoins pass between individuals, they need never know one another. Indeed, some argue that with a sufficient degree of encryption, bitcoin commerce can be 100 percent anonymous.

This potential for anonymity became a hot topic of debate around the controversial website Silk Road, an online marketplace for controlled substances, including various drugs, that transacted in bitcoins. For supporters of anonymity, it was disturbing to learn of the website's demise when its alleged founder was arrested on various criminal charges. If bitcoin guarantees anonymity, how did the authorities find the perpetrator? In another case, a prominent bitcoin advocate known in the community as "Bitcoin Jesus" went into hiding, claiming to be on the run from the US government for some unspecified, presumably bitcoin-enabled crime.

On the other hand, for those non-Libertarians embracing activist government regulation as an essential form of social protection, the 2014 demise of prominent bitcoin exchange Mt. Gox has led to the opposite concern, that bitcoin's anonymous nature enables wholesale fraud without possibility of compensation for victims. It is in this social aspect of the bitcoin debate that it becomes more than just a monetary touchstone; it becomes a social touchstone for how you feel about societal organization itself, not just the role of money within it. Thus, it should be no surprise that Libertarian and non-Libertarian types tend to have quite different views on bitcoin.

With that background, let's now begin exploring the views of a broad, representative handful of prominent bitcoin commentators.

Jon Matonis

(www.themonetaryfuture.blogspot.co.uk)

Currently serving as the executive director of the Bitcoin Foundation, and having worked for years in e-money payments, Jon Matonis was one of if not the earliest (non-pseudonymous) prominent champions of bitcoin. Indeed, he was active in the cryptocurrency debate long before bitcoin arrived on the scene and is thus on the record having anticipated the modern blockchain phenomenon.

Given this background, it should be no surprise that Matonis is a huge fan of bitcoin and sees enormous future potential for a complete transformation of our monetary and financial system. He has a vision of a future in which spontaneous market competition creates competing blockchain currencies and that perhaps, eventually, only a handful survive and become the dominant global media of exchange, entirely displacing today's national fiat currencies. For all intents and purposes, banks as we know them today will disappear, including central banks. The creation of money and the determination of interest rates would be largely unregulated, international and depoliticized. The bitcoin phenomenon is thus comparable or perhaps of even greater historical significance than the original, Lydian invention of coinage; the subsequent invention of deposit banking; and the more recent introduction of the modern, electronic money we all use today in some form: the credit (or debit) card.

Matonis goes even farther, however, envisioning what some detractors might disparagingly call a utopian "monetary nirvana" in which bitcoin enables a comprehensive economic and social evolution to a new stage in civilization, to the great benefit of humanity generally.

Regardless of whether you share Matonis' bitcoin enthusiasm and optimism, his website is a treasure trove of information and divergent opinions about bitcoin, not merely his own. As a first step for those genuinely interested in not only a thorough introduction but essentially comprehensive exposure to all things bitcoin, I strongly recommend you visit his website.

Marc Andreessen

As one of the most prominent innovators in the early Internet age, Marc Andressen's view of bitcoin, when published back in 2014 in the *New York Times*, drew much attention from the wider tech community.

As an inventor of a famous disruptive technology in his own right—the Netscape browser—Andreessen perceives a similar potential in bitcoin as an ideal Internet-based payments system:

> Bitcoin is the first Internetwide payment system where transactions either happen with no fees or very low fees (down to fractions of pennies). Existing payment systems charge fees of about 2 to 3 percent—and that's in the developed world. In lots of other places, there either are no modern payment systems or the rates are significantly higher. [83]

Even bitcoin's detractors normally acknowledge as much, as bitcoin does appear to have some promise as a low-cost payments system. We all know how broadband technology sank telecommunications costs to essentially nothing. Why shouldn't Internet payments also cost essentially zero?

Andreessen sees much potential for bitcoin and thinks it may catalyze a general transition from e-commerce based in dollars (or other national currencies) to e-commerce based in bitcoin. He is far from as sweeping in his perspective as Matonis, but this could be down to a relative unfamiliarity with the broader social concepts of money. That said, he does share a monetary insight that echoes that of founding Austrian School economist Carl Menger from the late 1800s:

> It is perhaps true right at this moment that the value of bitcoin currency is based more on speculation than actual payment volume, but it is equally true that that speculation is establishing a sufficiently high price for the currency that payments have become practically possible. The Bitcoin currency had to be worth something before it could bear any amount of real-world payment volume.

83 Marc Andreessen, Why Bitcoin Matters, *New York Times*, 21 January 2014.

> This is the classic "chicken and egg" problem with new technology: new technology is not worth much until it's worth a lot. And so the fact that Bitcoin has risen in value in part because of speculation is making the reality of its usefulness arrive much faster than it would have otherwise.

Those familiar with the Austrian School will notice immediately in this quote that Andreessen has apparently stumbled upon one aspect of the monetary "regression-theorem" concept formalized by Ludwig von Mises in the early twentieth century but originally postulated by Menger decades earlier.

Andreessen lists several other reasons to be bullish on bitcoin's future, and his explicit endorsement has almost certainly influenced a sizeable portion of the tech community, long-since acclimated to the concept of disruptive technologies. As Andressen himself acknowledges, however, his views are less likely to have much influence if any on the mainstream economics community. And so it is to that we now turn.

Robert Shiller

As one of the best-known mainstream economists of his generation and a Nobel laureate to boot, Robert Shiller's take on bitcoin has naturally been the subject of much consideration within the academic and financial market community. He also recently published his views in the *New York Times*. His perspective is that of a mainstream Neo-Keynesian economist, albeit one who has spent as much or more time studying financial markets specifically rather than the economy generally. (As an aside, isn't it curious that the *New York Times*, hardly an innovative, cutting-edge tech source, seems to have gone on a bitcoin binge early 2014. One wonders why.)

Shiller is not at all optimistic about bitcoin and in fact thinks that the level of hype is grossly misguided. The ultimate reason for this view he explains in his article thus:

> The central problem with Bitcoin in its present form... is that it doesn't really solve any sensible economic problem. Nor should it substitute for banks and the governmental institutions that regulate them. They are reasonably effective institutions, despite their flaws, and should not just be scrapped and replaced by a novel electronic system.[84]

He then goes on to specify that existing currencies work well as both media of exchange and stores of value. Well, if one doesn't see a problem with state-mandated legal tender in the first place, then naturally one sees little if any value in an alternative, in particular one that has invited a huge degree of pure speculation relative to any current practical use.

Somewhat curiously, perhaps, despite these sentiments, Shiller does see value in the broader debate around bitcoin. He draws particular attention to the concept of money as a unit of account and believes that there is substantial future promise for synthetic units that can serve valuable social functions. As an example, he cites Chile's inflation-indexed unitado de fundato (UF) or unit of development. This national reference point permits coordinated indexing to domestic price inflation, simplifying certain forms of economic calculation in which price inflation is a material risk factor.

Shiller then suggests that price baskets in general could be used as units of account. Thus, he appears to be drawing from Keynes, who advocated a commodity basket currency he termed a "bancor" and from Prof Jeffrey Frankel, who has done much theoretical work in the commodity-basket-currency area. He then goes one step further, suggesting that a useful electronic unit of account could also reference national account statistics, such as GDP or GNP, which rank among the most complicated economic statistics of all, subject to a large amount of estimation error and other possible flaws.

84 Robert Shiller, In Search of a Stable Electronic Currency, *New York Times*, 1 March 2014.

All of Shiller's proposed electronic units of account are, therefore, artificial constructs that would need to be specified and subsequently updated by some person or group of persons relying on an agreed statistical method and sample of certain identified and estimated variables. He indicates no role whatsoever for a natural, market-based process to determine the specifications most desired. As such, he is coming from a most different perspective than Andreessen or Matonis, one that requires a thick layer of bureaucratic intermediation, presumably from people with PhD's like himself.

Those distrustful of bureaucrats—always subject to some degree of political influence—to determine monetary convention and set interest rates are likely to reject Shiller's view from the outset. However, the current academic and policy mainstream, focused as it is on the core Keynesian precept of the necessity of a bureaucratic- rather than market-based money and monetary policy, is likely to consider Shiller's observations as a potentially useful way to incorporate bitcoin's technological innovation into their existing if deeply flawed economic paradigm.

Hugo Salinas-Price

(www.plata.com.mx)

A highly successful Mexican businessman, Hugo Salinas-Price has been active for decades in the cause of promoting sound money for Mexico. In more recent years, he has broadened his activities to promote sound money around the world, drawing up plans for how governments could remonetize gold or, as he specifically recommends for Mexico, silver.

Back in early 2012, while on business in Mexico, I conducted an interview with Mr. Salinas-Price. He explains his silver plan thus:

> My focus is on silver, because silver was formerly always the money of the great majority of the population in every country of the world. It has been and can again be money for everyday use and which can be saved by almost everyone. Silver is the ideal medium for "micro-

> savings," for millions upon millions of savers who can put away small amounts, day by day, and build up a personal or family capital, which can be passed on to the next generation.
>
> We have a tragic impoverishment of enormous numbers of humanity whose attempt at savings is continually undermined by the devaluation of paper money—its loss of purchasing power. We have to put a stop to this, out of justice and self-interest too: the wider the breach between rich and poor, the more dangerous life becomes for all. (Ed. note: Eminent historians Will and Ariel Durant observed that nearly all revolutions have occurred alongside extreme disparities in wealth.)

The above quote should make clear why, in principle, Mr. Salinas-Price is a strong advocate of a monetary alternative to the national fiat currencies of today. QE and related stimulus policies have coincided with a tremendous surge in wealth disparity across most of the developed world, as money has flowed primarily toward those who already held substantial assets when the global financial crisis arrived in 2008.

However, as he has made clear in his comment on the topic, he does not regard bitcoin satisfactory monetary alternative. Indeed, he argues that bitcoin is not really money at all, nor is there any realistic chance of it becoming so:

> An interesting point about the Bitcoin is that it is so important for it to have a price in dollars; it has had various prices, all totally speculative.
>
> I should like to point out that when real money—gold—was in use in the world, it had no price. All national currencies were only certain various amounts of gold, with various national names.

> The Bitcoin as a "digital currency" is an example of the enormous confusion which reigns in the world, regarding what money is and must be. Money—authentic money—must be the most marketable of all commodities. This is why gold is money! Silver follows in second place. The Bitcoin cannot be money because it is digital. Since it is merely a digit, which is as close to nothing as one can get, it cannot settle any debt. [85]

That is a rather categorical critique of bitcoin, and I think it would be difficult to convince Hugo Salinas-Price or anyone dismissing the entire concept of intangible money that bitcoin has any future as a monetary alternative. As it happens, there are many prominent economists of the Austrian School who completely agree and insist that, were money determination left to the marketplace, rather than imposed by governments from above, gold and silver would invariably be chosen as money, as indeed they have been since the dawn of recorded history. [86] Bitcoin, they claim, wouldn't stand a chance.

Detlev Schlichter

There are prominent Austrian School economists, however, who do not dismiss bitcoin out of hand but rather see it as something that, in key respects, satisfies the core Austrian School requirements for sound money.

In a 2014 article, "Bitcoin Has History and Theory on its Side," Detlev Schlichter lays out what I believe is the correct framework for

85 "Of Paper Money, Digital Money and Gold," by Hugo Salinas-Price, 7 March 2014.

86 It is true that there is much evidence of relatively primitive societies using local commodities as a form of money, in particular agricultural products such as carob, cocoa, or soybeans. Seashells have also served. However, it should be noted that in every single historical instance in which these societies came into commercial contact with other societies, they quickly adopted gold and silver as the preferred stores of value, even if they continued to employ the domestic commodity for day-to-day domestic trade.

considering the prospects for bitcoin and for blockchain money-technology generally:

> Any proper analysis has to distinguish clearly between the following layers of the Bitcoin phenomenon: 1) the concept itself, that is, the idea of a hard crypto-currency (digital currency) with no issuing authority behind it, 2) the core technology behind Bitcoin, in particular its specific algorithm and the "mining process"…
>
> Before we look at recent events and recent newspaper attacks on Bitcoin, we should be clear about a few things upfront: If 1) does not hold, that is, if the underlying theoretical concept of an inelastic, nation-less, apolitical, and international medium of exchange is baseless, or, as some propose, structurally inferior to established state-fiat money, then the whole thing has no future. It would then not matter how clever the algorithm is or how smart the use of cryptographic technology. If you do not believe in 1)—and evidently many economists don't (wrongly, in my view)—then you can forget about Bitcoin and ignore it.
>
> If 2) does not hold, that is, if there is a terminal flaw in the specific Bitcoin algorithm, this would not by itself repudiate 1). It is then to be expected that a superior crypto-currency will sooner or later take Bitcoin's place. That is all. The basic idea would survive.[87]

We can now use Schlichter's framework, (1) and (2), to summarize the previous bitcoin advocates and detractors:

87 This article can be found at www.detlevschlichter.com.

- Jon Matonis clearly sees the need for a monetary alternative and believes that both the concept of cryptocurrencies generally (1) and the specific properties of bitcoin are solid and have a bright future (2);
- Marc Andressen sees vast potential for bitcoin as a disruptive financial technology (2). He is agnostic, however, as to whether there is a need for an alternative money (1);
- Robert Shiller sees no need for an alternative money (1) but does see a role for widespread use of price and other index algorithms in facilitating the use of existing state-fiat media of exchange (2);
- Hugo Salinas-Price sees a vital need for an alternative to state-fiat but dismisses the entire idea of intangible money (1), thus the specific qualities of the bitcoin algorithm (2) are irrelevant to any monetary application.

Schlichter subsequently goes on to offer his own thoughts on bitcoin's potential. First, he observes that several recent attacks on the bitcoin concept are essentially baseless in that they assume that the existing monetary order is functioning well. This assertion is increasingly tenuous post-2008 even though the economic mainstream continues to defend it. Robert Shiller falls into this category, but he did leave open a door to algorithms augmenting the core of what he believes is a robust monetary system.

Second, as is the case with Salinas-Price, Schlichter points out that our current monetary system is quite young and that some historical perspective is in order. Unbacked state fiat money has existed for only about forty-five years, a mere bat of the historical eyelash. Indeed, the human eye has regarded gold (or silver) as money for 99 percent of history, and all previous experiments with unbacked fiat, without exception, have ended in failure and a subsequent de jure or de facto remonetization of gold and silver. Contemporary economists, including Shiller, who claim that state fiat is a robust system, have scant historical evidence at their disposal. Indeed, any objective look at the evidence strongly implies the opposite is true.

Third, and this is really the key point, Schlichter cogently argues that bitcoin far more closely resembles gold than state fiat money, subject as the latter is to state manipulation and control:

> Bitcoin—just like a proper gold standard—does not allow for discretionary manipulation of the monetary base. There was no "monetary policy" under a gold standard, and there is no "monetary policy" in the Bitcoin economy. That is precisely the strength of these concepts, and this is why they will ultimately succeed, and replace fiat money.[88]

It should be no surprise that Schlichter sees through all the rhetoric and hyperbole on all sides of the bitcoin debate. His first book, *Paper Money Collapse*, begins with the theoretical observation that what separates paper money from gold or silver is the elastic nature of its supply. This opens up paper money to political manipulation and, sadly, corruption. As mentioned above, the historical record on this is as clear as can be.

Regardless of how one feels about an intangible money, you can't deny that the bitcoin algorithm strictly determines its supply according to an inviolable and entirely transparent rule whereby new bitcoins are "mined" into existence. Applying Schlichter's approach, the entire bitcoin debate thus reduces quickly, to those like Shiller, who regard bureaucratic money as superior, even essential, and those like Matonis or Salinas-Price, who would prefer to do away with the monetary bureaucracy completely.

Schlichter does not go so far in his article as to advocate bitcoin specifically as a preferred monetary alternative (although over lunch back

88 Detlev Schlichter, "Bitcoin and Theory and History on its Side," www.detlevschlichter.com, February 2014.

in 2014 he did refer to bitcoin as "ingenious"). But is appears that he would in principle prefer a bitcoin-centric monetary system over that which we currently have.

By "in principle" I refer to another key point on which I completely agree: if you hold, as Schlichter and other economists of the Austrian School do, that the ideal money is that determined spontaneously by market-driven exchange processes, rather than by state edict, then it becomes not just presumptuous but even theoretically inconsistent to claim precisely what that money should be.

If the market chooses gold, fine. If both gold and silver, fine. If cocoa beans, peppercorns, or seashells, fine. And if bitcoin or another cryptocurrency, well that's fine too. If it so happens that a given money isn't performing adequately, well then the market will sort that out in short order, just as it does with uneconomic activities generally, rendering inefficient firms bankrupt, reordering the capital and labor stock, and moving on via creative destruction to more efficient production and innovation. Money is no exception to the fundamental laws of human action. As with all economic goods, it is best provided by the marketplace itself, not by a bureaucracy, government-run or otherwise.

Now, it's my turn

Having evaluated these various pro-, anti- and maybe-bitcoin arguments, it is now my turn to weigh in. Although I do agree with Schlichter that fiat money is flawed and that a non-manipulable, non-state money is highly desirable, I strongly believe that, when one goes one step farther and directly evaluates bitcoin and gold as potential monetary rivals, a free society, absent legal tender laws or other restrictions on money, would favor gold (or silver) over bitcoin and cryptocurrencies generally.

First, I think it is important to distinguish clearly between the medium-of-exchange and store-of-value roles of money. There can be no doubt that bitcoin is an innovative medium-of-exchange that, in principle, can bypass the existing payments system. In this sense, bitcoin is a disruptive technology that, if so allowed by regulators, could render a huge portion of existing transactional banking unprofitable, ranging from credit cards to bank transfers. Unless your bank charges you for making deposits and withdrawals, how could it make money from your future transactions if you first withdraw funds, purchase bitcoins, and transfer them instead? And if the counterparty, on receipt of the bitcoins, sells them and deposits the currency proceeds in the bank, then their bank can't earn any transactional fees either.

It is highly likely that some smart people working in strategic planning at banks are already aware of this danger. They are probably also aware that, if banks can't make money from processing transactions, they will have to make more money from idle deposits. But with interest rates on most types of accounts already near zero, how are banks going to do that, absent charging depositors to keep their money? And if banks start charging depositors, what are depositors going to do? Why, they will look for alternatives to traditional banking, such as using bitcoins or other blockchain currencies instead!

Do you see the vicious circle here? Absent regulatory action to impede or prohibit their use, or to somehow subsidize the banks, blockchain-based payments services are going to disintermediate the existing, bank-centric payments system. And it doesn't really matter which services gain market share. Indeed, the fact that bitcoin has invited as much competition as it has, as fast as it has, is strong evidence that those entrepreneurs familiar with the economics of disruptive technologies are now behaving like sharks (startups) that smell blood (profit).

For all their promise as highly efficient means of payment, however, I am unconvinced of blockchain currencies' collective role as a store of value. Indeed, it is precisely their suitability for use as an inexpensive, alternative payments system that, in my opinion, undermines their ability to provide a store of value.

Why should that be? Although bitcoin and other blockchain currencies are based on entirely transparent algorithms that strictly regulate their supply, there is nothing that regulates their replication. There might be only one blockchain for each currency, but there is no limit on the number of blockchains that can be created at will to satisfy growing demand. As one blockchain is preferred and gains market share, speculators may enter and drive the price higher. But beyond a certain point, around the speculative margins that exist in all markets, substitution effects will kick in and some will switch into a rival blockchain, programmed into existence at minimal cost, then another, then another…in a process that need never end.

This process, if market driven, can be entirely self-regulating, providing for an endlessly growing supply of nearly costless-to-create, competing media of exchange, based on replicate algorithms, each with its own blockchain. But do you now see the problem? A dynamic aggregate of replicate, competing blockchains would have a highly ELASTIC supply, not one strictly limited. In fact, the supply is theoretically infinite, more infinite than grains of sand, drops of water, molecules of oxygen or, indeed, any other substance on earth or, for those who think even more broadly, in the entire universe. The cyber "universe" is, by its very nature as a creation of the human mind rather than a naturally occurring substance, infinitely larger than the physical universe, vast as it is.

Gold or silver, by contrast, are strictly limited in supply, regardless of price, and cannot be replicated. Sure, they can be exchanged for one another and for other substances, such as copper or nickel, to use two real-world coinage examples. But regardless of which of these are used, note what they all have in common: they have a production cost. Indeed, they are expensive to locate, pull out of the ground, refine, and cast. Only when their market prices are sufficiently high does their production expand and, as supply rises to meet demand, their prices then stabilize. In other words, metallic monetary systems are also self-regulating, but in a context of real-world physical supply constraints and associated costs, rather than a cyber world of no theoretical supply constraints and the minimal costs associated with a few strokes on a keyboard and the imagination to conceive a new blockchain "brand." [89]

A second theoretical problem I have with cryptocurrencies as stores of value is that of physical security. I'm not talking here about the potential for fraud and abuse, which exists and will always exist where human exchanges take place. Rather, I'm talking about the ability of an authority of some sort, say one with the ability to operate entirely in secret, to trace blockchains as desired, from place to place, and to hack in to systems as required to effectively confiscate these in the event that the authority deems their use to be criminal or politically undesirable. While I don't in any way condone criminal behavior, I appreciate why criminals prefer physical over electronic cash, or physical gold or silver for that matter, as these exchanges are anonymous vis-à-vis third parties, even if not at all anonymous between the two parties involved in the transaction.

Some claim that encrypted bitcoin ensures complete anonymity vis-à-vis not only the parties to a transaction but also third parties. In my opinion, the opposite is true. The blockchain, if traced by sufficient computing power, provides a complete record of all transactions that can then be used or abused as desired by the authorities, who most probably could also covertly confiscate digital "coins" or somehow render them effectively unusable.

However, if the authorities want to confiscate your gold, for whatever reason, they are going to have to make a rather public matter out of it. If you keep some gold in a safe at home, they are going to have to break into your house. If you have it buried in your garden, they are going to have to trespass on your property in order to dig it up. Physical gold stored in a neutral jurisdiction, such as Singapore or Switzerland, will not be released to foreign authorities without extensive,

89 For those familiar with the concept of elasticity in economics, gold and silver supply are demonstrably highly price inelastic, whereas theoretical blockchain supply is highly price elastic. As stability of supply is an essential feature of sound money, this factor alone argues strongly in favor of precious metals generally vis-à-vis blockchain technology as an alternative store of value.

public evidence of criminal wrongdoing. And even then, it might only be released following public trials in public courts. In this sense, gold is a sort of monetary *habeus corpus*: there is no easy way for authorities to confiscate physical gold short of extensive, public legal action, including a presentation of the specific charges. Digital currencies, however, can be electronically (and secretly) "reassigned" if so desired.

Finally, I believe that there is a third important reason why gold and silver are likely to win out over bitcoin in the marketplace for money, namely culture and religion. Cultures don't change overnight; they evolve through the generations. The same could be said of major religions, each of which has a core canon of beliefs but one that, around the edges, can change over long spans of time. As Hugo Salinas-Price observes correctly, you don't just convince people overnight to use something new as money. Referring to Austrian School economist Ludwig von Mises, he writes that:

> [N]o fiat currency has ever been successfully introduced into circulation without a monetary value ultimately derived from when that currency was gold or silver money. Bitcoin does not fill the bill; it cannot circulate along with the established fiat currencies of the world because it has no history, no ancestry reaching back to its parent, gold or silver.[90]

The late Roy Jastram, who's magnum opus *The Golden Constant* is regarded as a modern classic amongst the gold investment community, opined that the reason why of all substances gold came to be money went beyond any purely rational explanation as to gold's unique physical properties.

I believe that Jastram was on to something. And I believe that Hugo Salinas-Price, Detlev Schlichter, and Austrian School economists

90 "Of Paper Money, Digital Money and Gold," by Hugo Salinas-Price, 7 March 2014.

generally are on to something too. That something is human nature. As Lord Acton observed, power tends to corrupt; absolute power corrupts absolutely. By corollary, monetary power tends to corrupt; absolute monetary power corrupts absolutely. So now I lay my monetary cards on the table. As I conclude Chapter 11, "No form of money can possibly replace that which transcends all government, all laws, and, indeed, all things created by man."

Conclusion: Towards A Digital-Golden Synthesis?

While I fully acknowledge blockchain's vast potential to power an alternative, non-bank payments system to disintermediate much of the increasingly archaic, dysfunctional, "too-big-to-fail" banking and payments system, I have also described several reasons why I do not believe that it will displace gold or precious metals generally as the preferred alternative stores of value, at least not on a relevant time horizon. This raises the question, therefore, of whether it might be possible to somehow combine the two in a way that instantaneously "sweeps" digital currency proceeds directly into allocated gold, at some market-determined exchange rate. That is, if you would like to transact in a digital currency but save in physical gold, is there a way in which to do so without using a fiat currency as an intermediate step?

While the technology to provide for some form of "gold-backed" bitcoin almost certainly already exists—or if it does not, a patent application is probably pending—the question is whether the legal-tender authorities would ever allow this. After all, payments systems compete with banks but don't compete with purely monetary power, at least not directly. Gold does. It will be interesting to see what happens when the first "digital-gold" service is launched, perhaps in a friendly monetary jurisdiction such as Singapore or Switzerland. If the local authorities allow it to go ahead, will residents of other countries adopt the service? If they do, will their domestic authorities try to prevent them in some way?

From the perspective of the state, the power to inflate is the power to tax. States do not take kindly to a reduction in their power to tax. Arguably, blockchain technology, if employed as state-mandated legal tender, would in fact increase the power of the state to tax, as taxes could be automatically withheld from the blockchain for each and every transaction according to some algorithm; or alternatively the blockchain authority could earn seignorage income as the supply grew.

Aspiring totalitarian regimes (and dystopian science fiction writers) take note. Use of physical cash or any unauthorized form of electronic exchange can simply be criminalized with severe penalties and replaced by "PatriotCoin." The PatriotCoin withholding algorithm can be modified so as to exempt favored individuals or qualifying transactions. State employees can share out any PatriotCoin mining seignorage income, as befits their privileged status. Children can be assigned personalized PatriotCoin serial numbers at birth and retain these until death, when they pass to their children...

Is this where the blockchain phenomenon is eventually going? In a totalitarian direction in which there is complete and total control of money, with inflation, taxation and wealth redistribution embedded in a government-imposed monetary algorithm? Who knows? As is the case with gold and silver on the one hand, and debasement and devaluation on the other, the war between economic liberty and authoritarianism never ends. And it certainly won't end with bitcoin and blockchain.

Chapter 17: The Promise of Digital Gold Ledger Technology and Real-Time Settlements

> "Gold has huge potential within the current global financial environment, whereby the presumed benefits of Bitcoin and other cryptocurrencies can be achieved without their drawbacks."
>
> —John Dwyer,
> 2016 Celent report on digital gold technology

One of the most common complaints leveled at those who would advocate a return to some form of gold-backed money is that gold is just too cumbersome for use in a modern economy. Moving it around from place to place is expensive and entails the risk of theft. Hence, paper banknotes, or electronic credit, debit or prepaid cards, or smartphone payment apps, are seen as superior.

This criticism is entirely specious, however, because if back on a gold standard, gold need only provide the monetary base. It does not need to provide the actual circulating medium. Indeed, a modern gold-backed monetary system could, in fact, function much as the fiat currency system does today. There is no difference in principle between various forms of electronic "payments protocols" overlaid on a fiat currency monetary base and those same forms overlaid on gold instead. What is entirely different, however, is the nature of the money itself: reserves created arbitrarily at will by a central bank on a computer or a highly stable supply of physical gold stored in a vault.

In the old days of banking, before electronic transaction processing or record-keeping came into being, paper ledgers were maintained in order to keep track of precisely how much money was moving where and who had what balance in their account, and the reserves in the vault the bank held against those balances. Today, of course, nearly all transactions processing and settlement and the record-keeping thereof is done electronically.

However, just because something is done electronically does not necessarily imply that it is done as efficiently as possible. Electronic systems can be cumbersome and based on technology that is now many decades old. Indeed, it is perhaps surprising to note that, even today, electronic securities trading settlements can take several days.

The so-called FinTech—financial technology—revolution is unfolding rapidly because there are so many modern functions of banking and the financial industry more generally that might be done more or less electronically but not using the latest, most efficient technologies. FinTech firms seek out inefficiencies wherever they can find them and then attempt to apply a superior technology that "disrupts" or perhaps outright "disintermediates" some aspect of banking or finance.

Foreign exchange offers a good example of this. There are now multiple nonbank foreign exchange providers that process a huge amount of cross-border payments. They have built market share by offering lower commissions than the banks, and this they can do because they operate fare more efficiently, with their better technology, lack of legacy issues, and more entrepreneurial mind-set.

Indeed, banks are now scrambling to keep up with what might be called the "payments revolution" in which not only foreign exchange transactions but payments services of all kinds are increasingly being done by nimble FinTech firms with better technology. In some cases, big banks are "onboarding" FinTech firms in order to acquire their technologies and apply them internally, thereby achieving greater efficiencies. But the larger of the FinTech payments firms enjoy their highly profitable independence and prefer continuing to compete with the banks, most of which do not have particularly innovative or entrepreneurial cultures. Indeed, in many cases quite the opposite is true, with banks spending more time seeking regulatory protections against these upstarts rather than working to improve the efficiencies of their services.

So far, however, the banks are not having much luck in stifling the growing competition. Regulators have little sympathy left for an industry that has been so riddled with claims of fraud in recent years and which naturally is still associated with the crisis of 2008 and legacy issues thereof. Banks have few friends, and those they do have tend to be paid lobbyists or politicians to whom they donate large sums of money. A brief look at the amount that US banks (and their employees) have contributed, in various ways, to the 2016 US federal election candidates is instructive in this regard. The numbers are in the many millions and the financial industry generally is by far the largest net contributor to US federal election candidates, including presidential.[91]

However, perhaps much as in the way that Amazon gradually took market share away from traditional retailers, notwithstanding regulatory pushback at times, FinTech is making much progress. Uber and AirBnB also offer examples of hugely successful tech companies disrupting industries notwithstanding major legal and regulatory hurdles. It would be naïve to think that, in time, those FinTech firms that truly have superior technologies will fail to grab market share and eventually become major, established players in the financial industry.

One example of a financial technology with many potential applications is Digital Ledger Technology (DLT). DLT relies on sophisticated algorithms to perform what can be quite complex tasks and in some cases perform multiple tasks simultaneously, in parallel. When it comes to payments, settlements, account maintenance, and record-keeping, DLT holds much promise indeed, as it can do all of the

91 Nonprofit political research group OpenSecrets maintains a database of contributions by industry and firm. Their website is www.opensecrets.org

above and is essentially infinitely scalable. In principle, if the necessary algorithms were developed, even the world's largest banks could migrate their internal systems entirely over to DLT and realize huge efficiencies. Yes, that is easier said than done, but that is due in large part to the legacy issues of relatively antiquated systems that are simply difficult to consolidate and to migrate. Starting afresh, as a FinTech firm can do, legacy issues are nonexistent. Relatively smaller banks would find such migrations easier, something that might help to explain why some small, upstart banks are successfully taking market share already as they simply have better, new-generation internal systems.

DLT could even provide for a next-generation interbank payments and settlements system at the national or even international level. SWIFT, based in Belgium, is the current global interbank settlements system. There is no reason why SWIFT could not at some point in future migrate to DLT. Alternatively, there is no reason why a more efficient competitor to SWIFT could not seek to take market share by processing and settling interbank transactions for lower cost.

DLT is promising. But far more revolutionary than the prospect of DLT increasing efficiencies in the banking industry is that it could also be applied to the market for gold. Indeed, were DLT applied to the gold market, then in principle it would become less costly to process and settle transactions in gold than in the existing fiat currencies of the world today! And DLT also allows for settlements to take place in essentially real time. Real-time settlements (RTS) for securities on exchanges is something that has been mooted as a future application of DLT. There is no reason why the same cannot be done with gold. But the beauty of applying DLT and RTS to the gold market is that you thus enable gold to be used as a hyperefficient money far superior to anything that exists today.

Yes, gold is money. Currently that money is unofficial, but as we have explored in this book, the game theory dynamics of international monetary relations are going to change that in future, perhaps the near future. Gold will be remonetized in time. And the combination of gold remonetization on the one hand, and DLT and RTS technology on the other, will enable a huge, quantum leap in economic efficiency generally. Not only will sound money facilitate superior, more sustainable resource allocation but DLT and RTS will allow payments and settlements to all occur in real time, regardless of point of origin or destination.

If I am right in my predictions, then banks as we know them today, perhaps even central banks, will gradually just fade away, their core functions having been effectively disintermediated and dispersed by all the various aspects of financial technology innovation, including innovation in money itself—digital gold. The monetary cycle of history will have come full circle yet again, but this time at a far, far higher level of economic and social advancement.

Chapter 18: When All Else Fails, Enter the "Gold Vigilantes"

> "I used to think that if there was reincarnation, I wanted to come back as the president or the pope or as a .400 baseball hitter. But now I would like to come back as the bond market. You can intimidate everybody."
>
> —James Carville,
> former political adviser to President Bill Clinton

IT IS OF COURSE POSSIBLE that I am giving too much credit to economic and monetary policy officials. Perhaps there is not a single country prepared to be a first mover in defecting from the dysfunctional fiat dollar reserve standard. Perhaps no consensus can be reached on how to coordinate multilateral action. Perhaps the entire world is going to cling to the inflationary fiat dollar indefinitely, even as this creates ever greater global economic instability. If so, does this imply that the world will not someday remonetize gold?

Not at all. What it does imply is that the world indeed moves back to gold, just not with any official sanction. In other words, the world will eventually end up on a de facto gold standard, not a de jure one.

What do we mean by this? Consider: We have explored how, following a sufficient rise in the price of gold, the excessive, unsustainable debts of today become, in fact, sustainable. The idea that there is too little gold in the world is indeed specious, as Jim Rickards observes. Financial market agents can pay whatever they like for gold. Or looked at in the other way, they can *sell* whatever they like for gold. They can sell currencies. They can sell bonds, government or corporate. They can sell stocks. They can sell houses. There is no limit to how much selling can take place as the supply of money, narrow and broad, credit, government and corporate, equities, and property grows. Financial markets can just continue to bid up the price of gold accordingly, to levels that compensate for this ever-increasing supply of everything else.

For those who haven't noticed, this process is, in fact, already underway. Since 2000, gold has been in a major secular bull market, outperforming currencies, bonds, equities, and property over time, through both the booms and the busts. The retracement since 2011 is fully in line with past secular bull markets, such as that of the 1970s. As our calculations have shown, the gold price remains far below where it needs to be to imply that the overall supply of money and financial assets is not excessively burdensome. But we have already come a long way from the gold bear market that existed through the 1980s and 1990s, years when global productivity growth was quite strong in a historical comparison. Sovereign debt burdens, in particular in the United States, were also far smaller and, it appeared at the time, sustainable. The financial system was better capitalized against potential future losses. The dollar seemed at less risk of falling sharply in value. In sum, there were fewer reasons for investors to protect themselves from excessive debt and leverage by eschewing currencies and financial assets generally and holding gold instead. Into this mix, European central banks were also net sellers of gold accumulated under Bretton Woods decades earlier.

Let us not forget what made the 1980s and 1990s possible: the 1970s. If not for a decade of stagflationary economic deleveraging, culminating in punitive levels of both nominal and real interest rates and the most severe US recession since World War II, a period of US economic renewal would not have been possible. The spectacular rally in gold in the late 1970s thus served an important purpose, helping to place the US economy on a more sustainable path. And it occurred not because of any official policy initiative, but rather because the global financial markets forced the issue through the marketplace itself. (In this regard, it is instructive to note that the rise in the price of gold to over $800/oz. in 1981 implied a narrow money M0 coverage ratio is excess of 100 percent.)

Although looked on as a failure of policy—rightly so, I would add—the 1970s experience demonstrates the ultimate supremacy of the financial markets in the global economy. Sure, governments can distort markets and misallocate resources for a time. The Soviet Union did so for many decades before crumbling amidst soaring monetary inflation in the 1980s. China did much the same, but came to its senses under the hugely underappreciated leadership of Deng Xiaoping in the 1980s, enacting market-based reforms that set the stage for the world's most populous country's spectacular reentry into the global economy. India, the second most populous, flirted with socialism for a time, only to make a similar choice as China eventually. Brazil was arguably just an unusually large banana republic until it got some market-based religion in the 1990s. It is no coincidence that, one country at a time, the market wins out over authoritarian, unsustainable central planning.

Now it is the turn of the United States (and Europe) to learn some harsh lessons, harsher even than those of the 1970s. The United States can do so quickly by acting unilaterally to restore gold convertibility. Another country or group of countries might act first, forcing the issue. Or it might be left to the global financial markets themselves. In any case, gold will play the role it has always played. It will become, either de jure or de facto, the universal, objective reference point for measuring value. As it stands now, this would imply a gold price an order of magnitude higher than it is today. Once this has occurred, it will be irrelevant whether a country or group of countries has officially moved back onto a gold standard. The market-pricing mechanism, enabled by reference to gold, will have reasserted itself.

Investors, therefore, need to prepare. Not only do they need to consider the outlook for the price of gold, or of the implied, sharply reduced purchasing power of paper currencies. They also need to understand what the return to gold implies for interest-rate determination, asset valuation, and investing generally. It is to this we now turn in the following section.

Section IV:
The Economic, Financial, and Investment Implications of the Remonetization of Gold

> "[T]he uncertainty that plagues the investment commitment process is far more pervasive than a decade ago. . . . [T]he most important cause of this uncertainty is inflation, the fear of an increasing rate in the years ahead. An inflationary environment makes calculation of the rate of return on new investment more uncertain."
>
> —Alan Greenspan, "Investment Risk: The New Dimension of Policy," *Economist,* August 6, 1977

ONCE THE WORLD IS BACK on some form of credible gold standard, perhaps a hyperefficient one enabled by digital ledger technology and real-time settlements, the global investment landscape will be completely transformed. Rather than treated as a speculative asset, albeit one with a strong historical track record in providing a store of value, gold will be perceived as the universal, global money, the objective reference point for economic value, relative to which all other values will be measured.

In much the same way that Copernicus placed the sun, rather than the earth, at the center of the universe, thereby simplifying astronomical calculation to the point where Newton was eventually able to explain the movements of both terrestrial and astronomical objects with a single, elegant equation—the law of universal gravitation—placing gold at the center of the global monetary system will greatly simplify economic calculation and asset valuation. By corollary, it will also simplify global commerce and finance generally.

This simplification has a wide range of implications that cut across all aspects of the investment world, in particular, how assets are to be valued vis-à-vis each other and versus gold itself. In the previous section, we explored the outlook for the price of gold relative to the dollar and other currencies, as the world transitions back to some form of gold standard. Regardless of how, exactly, the transition comes about, it is clear that the price of gold, not only in dollar terms but also in terms of any fiat currency, even those regarded as relatively hard, is going to be multiples higher than it is today. Otherwise, the gold standard will simply not be credible or sustainable because the implied legacy real debt burdens will still dwarf economies' ability to service that debt. Currencies will collapse anew, and another attempt will be made to return to gold, at an even higher price, until finally a stable equilibrium is reached. From that point forward, the economy and financial system will be sufficiently deleveraged and sustainable economic growth will be possible.

In this section, we leap forward into the aftermath of the Golden Revolution that lies in our future, taking it as a given that some form of stable, credible global gold standard has been reestablished. We then go about applying traditional financial valuation methodologies and metrics to a wide range of assets. While it is difficult to get too precise, there are certain general estimations that one can make about things such as:

- The level of interest rates and yields on government bonds
- Credit spreads for corporate bonds
- Equity market valuations
- The level of implied volatility and associated options pricing

Once we have a good feel for how to understand the impact of gold remonetization on these topics, we will then be able to consider investment strategy and asset allocation generally. How will investors go about constructing sensible, efficiently diversified portfolios? Where will investors focus when looking for opportunities to outperform? What methodologies or investment styles will be relatively more effective and popular? Each of these questions, and others, will be considered in turn.

This may seem a daunting task. Yet as we shall see, it is not. If there is one thing that the gold standard will do to the investment landscape, it is that it will greatly simplify it. Returning to our astronomical analogy, Newton's single law and equation of universal gravitation replaced a myriad number of far, far more complex equations, requiring more rigorous and time-consuming calculation, only to arrive at an ultimately incorrect result. Under a global gold standard, investors will find that they have fewer sources of uncertainty with which to deal. Thus they will be able to focus and concentrate on a smaller number of variables and make more sensible investment decisions.

The result is likely to be a far more efficient allocation of capital across companies, industries, and countries around the world, with positive implications for economic growth and financial market stability. George Gilder explains at length in his short book, *The Scandal of Money*, why gold is the best known monetary conduit for the essential price information required for an efficiently functioning capitalist economy. The primary reasons are that, as a nonreactive element, gold cannot be consumed and thus has near-zero entropy, and that gold cannot be created at will by an authority in order to dilute or even de facto reverse prior economic transactions.[92]

The efficient flow of information is a good thing for all economic actors, and the extensive benefits of the future global gold standard—economic, financial, and social—are explored in the conclusion of this book. But now let us get down to the task at hand, put on our investor's hat, roll up our sleeves, pull out our calculator, and see what we can learn about investing under a gold standard. To begin, we will consider how a return to gold will all but eliminate the uncertainty associated with inflation.

The Underestimation and Underappreciation of Uncertainty

Uncertainty is a fact of economic life, for households and corporations, at the micro and the macro level. Yet while some may claim to thrive on uncertainty—entrepreneurs come to mind—what they probably mean is that they enjoy the stimulation that uncertainty provides and

92 As Gilder also makes plain, he is an admirer of bitcoin because it is an admirable attempt to simulate the properties of gold. He does, however, regard bitcoin as an experiment whereas gold is tried and tested as the superior information conduit.

the satisfaction that comes from, over time, turning visionary, risky ideas into tangible business plans and, hopefully, success. In this way, success is derived from taking something risky, such as a rather amorphous business idea, and turning it into a practical, cash-generating, going concern, which is far less risky. Entrepreneurs embrace uncertainty and, over time, turn it into something rather more certain, extracting a profit in the process, if and when they succeed.

Economic progress in general can be understood in this way, as moving from rather less to rather more certain conditions. Indeed, as the division of labor and capital underlies all improvements in economic efficiency, with technology an important enabling factor, increasing certainty is critical to sustainable economic growth. Can the mechanic who repairs tractors for a living depend on his farmer customers to grow food, for which he can then exchange his labor at an economically attractive price? If not, there are not going to be any mechanics, and farmers will need to repair their own tractors, implying a loss of farm productivity and lower incomes for all.

Can the miller buy grain, process it into flour, and sell flour to the baker? Can the baker then sell bread to the farmer? What of the transport firm that moves the grain, the flour, and the bread from place to place? Can they depend on the mechanic to repair their vehicles too? And can they depend on the local gas station to maintain a reliable supply of fuel, oil, and other motor fluids? Can the gas station owner rely on the refiner of those products? Can the refiner rely on the oil transporter to deliver the right grade of oil, to the right refinery, at the right time? Can the transporter rely on the well producer? Can the well producer rely on the drilling equipment provider? Can they both rely on their steel provider, and the steel provider on its iron ore miner? If there is no certainty that labor or goods can be exchanged at a reasonable price both today and in the future, then there can be no specialization, no division of labor, and no economic progress.

When taken in aggregate, the division of labor and capital in a modern economy is so complex that it boggles the mind. It is what economists call a complex system in that it cannot, in fact, possibly be modeled in its entirety or understood by any person or even a group of persons.[93] Yet as stated before, economic progress is impossible without a continuing evolution of the division of labor and capital. Economic progress thus depends primarily on a self-regulating complex system commonly called the free market. The more certainty there exists in this free market, the more economic progress becomes possible.[94]

The role of uncertainty in economic life naturally extends into the world of investing. As with all economic agents, from entrepreneurs to laborers, investors seek to reduce uncertainty over time. They can try to mitigate it, to manage it, to model it, to understand it. But naturally they cannot eliminate it.

There can be no investment without uncertainty. Nor can the price for a given investment be determined without consideration of the risks involved. As the risks grow, with other factors equal, investments become

93 While countless academic papers have been written on the topic of the complex division of labor and capital in the modern global economy, a more poignant treatment of the topic is Leonard Read's famous brief essay, "I, Pencil," which describes in some detail how a pencil is made and, in doing so, illustrates how even an apparently simple economic good is the product of myriad processes. Indeed, as the pencil asserts, "Not a single person on the face of this earth knows how to make me." The entire essay can be found at the Library of Economics and Liberty: http://www.econlib.org/library/Essays/rdPncl1.html

94 The reader should note that we are talking about economic progress here, not social. Whether economic progress leads to social progress is a matter of great debate that is beyond the scope of this book. That said, I will offer the following thought: as long as economic progress proceeds in a voluntary fashion, following from choices made free of coercion by the individual members of a society, we consider it at a minimum highly unlikely and most probably impossible for any given set of voluntary economic choices to lead to consistently undesirable social outcomes. Consider this argument in reverse. Should we be confident that involuntary, coerced economic choices would produce superior social outcomes? At the extreme, coerced economic choice is simple slavery. That might produce a desirable social outcome for the masters, but we doubt the slaves would agree.

less attractive. More risk equals less investment, and vice versa. This may seem obvious. Yet it is rather easy to overlook that the uncertain value of unbacked fiat currencies and the associated, unsustainable debt burdens so denominated are the single most fundamental investment uncertainty of all. Remove that, and the task of making sensible investment decisions becomes far easier.

Money, Inflation, and Uncertainty

Whether you produce energy, raw materials, manufactured goods, or widgets or provide services such as health care, hairdressing, or dog grooming, to start or expand a business, you are going to need to invest. Funds are going to need to be borrowed, interest paid, and principal repaid. Operating costs and revenues are going to be estimated, and profits will, hopefully, meet or exceed expectations. But under a fiat currency monetary system, each and every one of these estimates—the cost of borrowing, the costs of production, the revenues, the profits—is subject to the uncertainty of inflation. Extrapolated to the global level, where a number of fiat currencies constantly fluctuate, the uncertainty is all the greater.

The greater the uncertainty around inflation, therefore, the greater the investment uncertainty and, other factors equal, the less attractive any given investment will be. As such, one of the first things that we can conclude about a gold standard is that, by restricting money and, by implication, credit growth, a gold standard is going to reduce the negative impact inflation uncertainty has on investment decisions. Other factors equal, less uncertainty equals more, higher-quality investment. Higher-quality investment equals a higher rate of potential economic growth. This is the single most important benefit of a gold standard, one that positively affects an economy at every level.[95] Yet the economic

95 There are those who believe that economic growth is not necessarily good. They point to things associated with economic growth, such as pollution, for example, that can reduce the quality of life. To deal with such qualitative criticisms of

mainstream generally fails to recognize this. We have lived with unstable money and credit growth and the associated economic bubbles and busts for so long that many no longer appreciate the huge benefits that the greater monetary certainty of the future gold standard will provide.

In the following chapters, as we consider how to value various assets under a gold standard, what will most probably strike the reader is not how complicated things are likely to be but rather the opposite. Just as greater monetary certainty will lead to higher-quality investment decisions, it will also greatly simplify all things financial. We begin our discussion at the heart of the modern financial system and the role that central banks are likely to play—or rather not play, as it were—following the return to gold.

---

growth is beyond the scope of this book. Let me merely point out that, other factors equal, the *potential* for a higher rate of economic growth cannot possibly be a bad thing; whether a society *chooses* to exercise the potential is another matter, a value judgment. Technology can be put to good or evil uses. But it is a mistake to argue against technology itself.

Chapter 19: The Role of Central Banking Under a Gold Standard

> "No central bank is truly independent. If there is a fundamental conflict between the objectives of the government and the behavior of the central bank, the central bank, however independent, will sooner or later give in."
>
> —Milton Friedman, interview published in the *Quarterly Journal of Central Banking,* August 2002

IT IS UNDERSTANDABLE THAT THE economic mainstream takes central banking for granted. After all, there is not a single sovereign issuer of currency today that does not have a central bank.[96] However, banking is far older than central banking, in the United States and elsewhere. The US Federal Reserve System came into existence in 1914. Prior to that, there was no single issuer of US banknotes. Rather, banks issued their own.[97]

Recall that in Section II, we took a look at the origins and history of the US dollar, originally defined as a weight of silver. The dollar has

96 There are instances in which sovereign nations do not have their own central bank, such as the members of the euro area, for example. Also, a handful of countries use another country's currency. But where countries issue their own national currency, a central bank controls the money supply and normally also regulates banks and, in some cases, the broader financial system.

97 The Bank of England, regarded by historians as the model for the Federal Reserve, opened for business in 1694. However, the oldest central bank still in existence today is the Swedish Riksbank, dating from 1668.

subsequently remained the official unit of account of the United States for all domestic commerce, financial and otherwise. Yet the dollar was not associated with any paper money printed by a US government institution prior to the Civil War, when greenbacks came into existence as a means of Union war financing. This greenback episode is instructive in considering the role, or rather the relative lack thereof, of a central bank under a gold standard.

A Brief History of the Greenbacks

Wars are expensive, with civil wars exponentially more expensive to prosecute than foreign. Not only must the war be fought but also financed with far fewer domestic resources than would otherwise have been available, were the country in question in one piece, fighting a foreign enemy rather than a domestic foe. Presumably, the opponents in a civil war do not remit taxes or other official revenue to one another, as would be the case in peacetime. And regardless of who wins or loses a given battle, the very act of fighting on domestic soil is likely to cause some degree of destruction to local commerce and, hence, to the available tax base for either or both sides.

History books on the US Civil War generally make the obvious point that the primary reason the Union eventually won was far superior industrial and other economic resources. The Confederacy had a reasonably well-drilled and well-led army, but time was not on its side. It attempted, in vain, to cause such quick and severe losses on the Union side that the latter would rather settle for peace and recognize separate nations than undergo a potentially prolonged, highly destructive war. As it turns out, the Confederacy underestimated the Union's willingness to completely and sustainably mobilize society for war, under the leadership of President Lincoln. Finally, in 1865, with much of the South in ruins, it was the Confederacy that sued for an essentially unconditional peace, to be followed by years of occupation and reconstruction.

But what the history books tend to overlook as a historical aside is how difficult it was for the relatively prosperous Union to finance the war effort. Not only was the US federal government still tiny at the time, relative to the economy in general, with a correspondingly tiny tax base, but also the tax base itself had now shrunk enormously along with the secession of the Southern states. Indeed, historians generally agree that the proximate cause of the war was not the underlying moral issue of Southern slavery, which had been festering even before the United States formally came into existence in the eighteenth century, but rather the issue of federal tariffs on imports. As Southern states generally lacked a manufacturing base, but were rich in arable land and sunshine, they exported tobacco, cotton, and other raw products to Europe in trade for manufactured products from abroad. As such, the economic burden of the tariffs fell disproportionately on the Southern states and were hugely unpopular in the region.

With Southern tariff revenue suddenly gone with the outbreak of war, yet huge war mobilization costs to pay, the Union had to find alternative sources of financing. This it quickly did by levying an apportioned tax on the Northern states. But the amounts generated were far too small to finance the war, even early on. As such, the Union set about borrowing the funds instead. One way in which this was done was through the issuance of so-called greenbacks, otherwise known as United States notes.

These notes were denominated in dollars yet bore no interest and could not be redeemed in specie. Naturally, they invariably traded at a discount to actual specie dollar coin or gold-backed US Treasury bonds. This was particularly true early on, as it was unclear how long it would take the Union to successfully prosecute the war, demobilize, and redirect resources toward paying off the accumulated war debt, including an eventual redemption of the greenbacks. There was also the possibility that the Union would simply default on the greenbacks, in particular if the war went particularly badly.

As an example of why greenbacks were regarded as risky, on December 16, 1861, prior to the issuance of the greenbacks, gold-backed US Treasury bonds plummeted by over 2 percent in a single day, as rumors spread that the United Kingdom planned on entering the war against the Union, something that would have not only lengthened the war in any case but also made it far less of a foregone conclusion that the Union would win. Not long thereafter, the United States suspended specie redemption for outstanding Treasury bonds, forcing banks and investors to roll them over instead. Needless to say, as the unredeemable greenbacks were by design subordinate to previously gold-redeemable US Treasury notes, their value would have declined by substantially more, had they been trading at the time.

The greenbacks were thus a fiat currency, the first ever issued by the US federal government.[98] Yes, the dollar was still defined in terms of specie at the time, but the greenbacks, although denominated in dollars, were not redeemable. It was only after an unspecified period and with a degree of uncertainty and default risk in the potentially long interim that holders of greenbacks could hope that the federal government would eventually buy them back. How, then, did the government get anyone to accept them as a form of payment? Why, by instituting legal tender laws requiring their acceptance. This is but one prominent historical example of how absent some degree of coercion fiat currencies are not willingly held by the public, given there is a specie-backed alternative.

There were numerous prominent critics of the greenback plan and of the legal tender laws enacted to force their circulation, among them Senator Lovejoy, who said in Congressional debate that:

> It is not in the power of this Congress . . . to accomplish an impossibility in making something out of nothing.

98 The Revolutionary continentals were removed from circulation prior to the establishment of the federal government, following the ratification of the Constitution.

> The piece of paper you stamp as five dollars is not five dollars, and it never will be, unless it is convertible into a five-dollar gold piece; and to profess that it is, is simply a delusion and a fallacy.[99]

Proponents of the legal tender laws responded to such criticism in varying ways. Among their arguments was that the supply of greenbacks would be strictly limited, such that confidence in their reliability as a store of value would be high, perhaps even *higher* than gold. As such, they claimed, the poor historical track record of fiat currencies, including the continentals used to finance the Revolutionary War and the French Revolutionary assignats, would not be repeated with the greenbacks.

Senator Thomas would have none of it, pointing out, "The experience of mankind . . . shows the danger of entering upon this path; that boundaries are fixed only to be overrun; promises made only to be broken."[100] He was joined by Senator Pomeroy, who was more specific in his predictions:

> The same necessity which now requires the amount of inconvertible paper now authorized, will require sixty days hence a similar issue, and then another, each one requiring a larger nominal amount to represent the same intrinsic value.[101]

Proponents also tried a completely different tack, which was to build confidence in the greenbacks by making them convertible into gold-backed US Treasury bonds, for which redemption in specie had already been suspended:

99 Wesley Clair Mitchell, *A History of the Greenbacks* (Chicago: University of Chicago Press, 1903), 56.

100 Mitchell, *A History of the Greenbacks*, 57.

101 IBID.

> Section one of the bill provided that holders of legal-tender notes could at any time exchange them at par for 6 per cent twenty-year bonds. Under this arrangement, it was supposed, the value of the [Greenbacks] could never be less than that of the bonds, and, as bonds could by law not be sold for less than par, it followed that the notes could not greatly depreciate. Unfortunately for the argument, even while Congress was debating the bill, bonds were selling in New York at 90 cents upon the dollar. . . .[102]

This line of argument was somewhat self-defeating, as the entire point of the legal tender laws was to prevent government-issued fiat money from trading at a discount in the first place. If even gold-backed Treasury bonds could trade at a discount—presumably because investors discounted the risk that redemption might be suspended indefinitely—then so could the non-interest-bearing, irredeemable greenbacks.

Proponents thus found themselves in a corner. If it were possible for the greenbacks to trade at a discount to coin specie, then:

> [C]oin would disappear from circulation . . . prices would rise suddenly, fixed incomes would decline, creditors be defrauded, and the widows and orphans would suffer. Senator Collamer showed how depositors in savings banks would lose by depreciation, and Senator Fessenden how labor would be injured by a rise of prices exceeding the rise of wages. Finally, Mr. Crisfield represented forcibly the instability of a paper standard of value and the consequent danger to business. . . .[103]

And finally:

102 IBID.

103 Mitchell, *A History of the Greenbacks*, 59.

> [T]he resort to an irredeemable paper currency was a practical confession of bankruptcy, and would therefore injure the credit of the government, and make less favorable the conditions on which it could borrow . . . the government might as well lose 25 per cent on the sale of her [*sic*] bonds, as to be obliged, in avoiding it, to pay 25 per cent more for everything she buys.[104]

In the end, amid the backdrop of war, the greenback proponents carried the day. The key argument on which they always fell back was that the war made the hitherto repugnant (and arguably unconstitutional) idea of a fiat currency tolerable as a limited, temporary, necessary, emergency measure. Little did they know that, a little over a century hence, an unbacked fiat dollar would be regarded as just the normal state of affairs.

Why fiat currencies require legal tender laws and central banks (and, by implication, why a gold standard does not)

The great greenback debate helps to illustrate just how a fiat currency is differentiated from a specie-backed one and, by implication, how a central bank is naturally more associated with the former.

The most obvious point is that a fiat currency cannot compete with specie absent legal tender laws. Other factors equal, claims on specie will always be in greater demand than those for irredeemable fiat notes. Thus, there must be a central authority that can enforce the acceptance of unbacked notes, or they will be driven out of circulation, as per Gresham's Law.

A fiat currency also requires a central authority as issuer, for two reasons. First, unlike specie coin, which is ultimately a standardized measure of weight not necessarily requiring legal recognition, a

104 IBID.

fiat currency is not going to be accepted for payment unless it is unambiguously genuine legal tender, with a high degree of confidence that it is not simply manufactured counterfeit.

Second, to manage supply, there must be a single authority behind a fiat legal tender. If multiple entities are entitled to issue the same currency, then naturally, each has an incentive to print as much of it into existence as possible, making it impossible to control supply and, by implication, prices.

There is then the issue of interest. The greenbacks were non-interest-bearing and intended to serve as a legal tender currency. However, the debate made clear that, as fiat currency, they were likely to trade at a discount to specie or specie-backed bonds. Something that trades at a discount to face value has an imputed interest rate, which is a function of the size of the discount and the term to maturity.

This brings us to the following: although this was not the case with the greenbacks, in the event that banks are required to accept the legal tender at face value to specie, then they will not be able to earn interest on reserves and will hold as little of it as possible. Specie will be driven out of circulation into private, nonbanking hoards. As this would weaken the banking system, there arises the issue as to whether the government or other authority should set minimum reserve requirements to prevent banks from operating with dangerously low capital ratios.

Now in theory, the government itself, rather than an authorized agency thereof, can be the issuer of a fiat currency. Indeed, this was the case with the greenbacks. The government can also manage the money supply and, of course, can function as the regulatory agent, including setting reserve requirements. But notice that all of these functions, none of which is required under specie standard, are typically given over to a central bank in practice. The simplest explanations are historical ones. Banks were, naturally, the first issuers of banknotes, although these were originally always backed by specie of some kind, as *de facto* receipts for specie stored in a vault. As such, it naturally followed that, when banknote issuance was placed under a single authority, a designated bank would take the role.

Also, central banking predates the general introduction of fiat currencies. Their origin lies in the need of various European crowns to finance wars or other spending. Monarchs and parliaments had varying degrees of taxing authority, yet, by the seventeenth century, found they were increasingly reliant on bank borrowing. By creating a central bank implicitly backed by the sovereign taxing authority, it was assumed that borrowing costs would be lower than otherwise, as sovereigns would in effect be borrowing against their future tax revenues rather than in unsecured fashion through private banking middlemen who would require a higher rate of interest.

As seen in the greenback debate, this was a key argument of the proponents for legal tender laws. As such, both fiat currencies and central banking have their origin in sovereign financing rather than in banking generally, which grew out of private commerce, using specie as a market-based medium of exchange. To the extent that there were legal tender laws, in practice these were enacted to regulate the value of the coin of the realm and to provide the crown with seignorage income, as new coinage was introduced via sovereign mining operations, domestically or via colonies such as those of the New World.

Not incidentally, the detractors' views on how the greenbacks and legal-tender laws would distort the Union's financial system and economy were eventually vindicated by events. Not only were multiple series of greenbacks issued in the following years but the negative impact on commerce was palpable:

> [S]uspension of specie payments threw the monetary circulation of the loyal states into disorder by causing the withdrawal of gold and silver coin from common use as money. . . .

> [T]hough the inconveniences caused by these changes in the medium of exchange were not slight, they were less serious than were the results produced by the change in the standard of value. . . . The legal tender acts substituted the greenback for the gold dollar as this unit. Now the gold dollar had contained 23.2 grains of pure metal, but the greenback dollar that took its place was at no time during the war worth so much as this. A year after the passage of the first legal-tender act a greenback dollar would purchase by 14.5 grains of gold. . . .
>
> It was this depreciation of the money unit that gave rise to the most complicated and interesting economic developments of the war period. Of course, in exchanging commodities for money, men were unwilling to give as much for a dollar worth 9 grains of gold as they had given for the dollar worth 23.2 grains. What is tantamount to giving less goods for the dollar, they demanded more dollars for the goods. The decline in the specie value of the greenbacks, therefore, produced an extraordinary rise of prices. . . .[105]

That the forced introduction of an unredeemable fiat currency into circulation would lead to a surge in price inflation is hardly surprising. As Henry Hazlitt and Milton Friedman reminded us in the 1960s, inflation is always and everywhere a monetary phenomenon.

The greenback episode also demonstrates that, notwithstanding the monetary aspect of price inflation, it is, in fact, ultimately a political phenomenon. Absent politicians' willingness to override markets' monetary preferences, thereby driving gold and silver out of circulation and into hoards, inflation would be a nonissue. In this regard, the historical

105 Mitchell, *A History of the Greenbacks* (Chicago: University of Chicago Press, 1903), 142.

legacy of the greenback episode, associated with what was, ultimately, a triumphant if horribly costly Union victory in the war, led to a more open mind at the federal government level regarding the idea of a fiat dollar and the associated inflation. As we know, in 1971, the United States embarked on another fiat currency misadventure, yet to conclude.

Free Banking:
Why central banking is unnecessary under a gold standard

It should now be clearer why central banking is in theory entirely unnecessary under a gold standard but necessary under a fiat one. First, there need be no single issuing authority. Recall that according to the Coinage Act of 1792, the US dollar originally referred to the Spanish milled dollar or piece of eight rather than to anything issued by the Continental Congress or the federal government that succeeded it. Second, as the supply of specie cannot be arbitrarily inflated, there need not be a central authority to control the supply.

Third, whereas banks are not inclined to hold non-interest-bearing, non-specie reserves, they have a clear incentive to hold gold and silver. Hold too few reserves, and depositors will be reluctant to place money with the bank unless rates of interest on deposits rise. The higher the rate paid on deposits, the less profitable the bank. As such, on a gold standard, market forces can be expected to prevent banks from holding dangerously low levels of reserves. Those that do will find that they are driven out of businesses or taken over by their more sensible competitors.

This brings us to the concept of free banking, in which the financial industry functions more or less as any other, rather than as a tightly regulated, highly concentrated industry dependent on a central authority. It should come as no surprise that many advocates of returning to a gold standard also advocate a form of what is generally referred to as free banking, in which banks operate in an essentially free market, more akin to how most normal industries tend to operate.[106]

Nonfinancial corporations tend to decide for themselves, for example, what products they would like to manufacture or what services they want to provide, using what materials or human resources, priced at what price in which market, and so forth. Those who choose to manufacture products or provide services that customers actually want, at prices they can reasonably afford, and market these effectively, tend to make a profit. Those who don't either change what they are doing or are ultimately forced into bankruptcy and reorganization, freeing up their assets for use in some other, presumably more profitable enterprise.

As we have seen in our discussion of the greenbacks and the nature of fiat currency and legal tender laws, the fact that the world is currently on a fiat dollar standard effectively requires banking to be a highly regulated industry. Yes, there is a degree of competition and freedom of action at the margin, but the vast bulk of what banks do is determined by a set of rules laid down by the central bank or other regulatory authority:

- Banking licenses are normally expensive and time-consuming to obtain, stifling competition and favoring those with political connections.
- Banks are required to use the currency issued by the central bank.
- Banks must maintain a mandated portion of reserves.
- Banks' cost of funding is determined by the central bank, normally in the form of a security repurchase or repo rate, or that for borrowing reserves (i.e., covering a temporary shortfall) from the central bank.
- Banks' lending activities tend to be restricted in various ways or, alternatively, subsidized to benefit defined groups.
- Banks can be summarily suspended or even shut down if they are found to be noncompliant with any given regulation.

106 Among prominent modern advocates of free banking are Lawrence White and George Selgin. Nobel laureate Friedrich Hayek also supported free banking.

Central banking can certainly coexist with a gold standard. The era referred to as the classical gold standard period, 1880 to 1914, began and concluded with European central banks in operation at each step of the way. The point, however, is that the role of central banks is considerably circumscribed. Nowhere is this more likely to be the case than with setting interest rates, something that is taken for granted under a fiat regime but, under a gold standard, is necessarily left largely to the free market, as we shall see. A simple way to illustrate this is to discuss how a so-called currency board functions.

How to disarm a central bank

As discussed before, we take it for granted that central banks, as part of their remit, set short-term interest rates and control the money supply. While this is indeed common, there are exceptions where the central bank leaves interest rates and the money supply to the market to determine. A simple example of this in practice is that of a currency board, such as that operating in Argentina from 1991 to 2002. This is when a country, normally with the central bank acting as agent, decides to peg its currency to that of another, normally much larger country.

As a first step in establishing a currency board, a central bank accumulates some amount of reserves of the foreign currency that is to serve as the peg. The central bank then maintains this peg by allowing the domestic level of interest rates to rise if the foreign exchange markets prefer to sell the domestic currency and, conversely, allow the domestic level of interest rates to fall if the markets prefer to buy. The accumulated reserves are to provide temporary liquidity for these transactions only. The point of the policy is not to accumulate reserves; rather, it is to maintain a stable exchange rate. That said, the country does earn interest on the reserves, a form of seignorage income comparable to charging a premium for newly issued coins of the realm or—perhaps a better comparison if the currency is pegged to an inflating currency—clipping coins as they pass through the Treasury.

In practice, the result is that the country operating a currency board in effect outsources its monetary policy to the issuer of the reference currency. This is because the foreign exchange markets will perceive an essentially risk-free arbitrage opportunity in the event that a credible currency board rate of interest is materially above or below that of the reference currency. As such, they will buy or sell currency in whatever amount is required until the interest rates either converge or, more likely, narrow to a level that represents a small risk or liquidity premium for holding the pegged currency, but nothing more.

The observed risk premium in this case becomes a market-determined barometer of the sustainability of the currency board country's domestic fiscal and other, nonmonetary economic policies, with monetary policy outsourced. This can be a highly useful arrangement for a government seeking to implement painful economic reforms, for example, reducing government expenditures and getting wage inflation under control. Indeed, these are precisely the reasons why Argentina chose to adopt a currency board in 1991, with the peso pegged to the US dollar.

In a way, one can think of a gold standard as the ultimate currency board, with gold itself providing the peg. Gold might pay no interest, but a paper or electronic currency pegged to gold might need to in the event the government of issue was deemed a credit risk. In any event, the role of central banks will be limited to strict mechanical procedures for processing gold convertibility and foreign exchange transactions and possibly also providing temporary, emergency liquidity to distressed banks. Central banks may continue to set interest rates at the margin, but they will have a severely limited ability to set rates far from where the market would place them for any sustained period, as this would drain the gold reserves. It is also entirely possible that central banks will be seen as essentially irrelevant, their core functions having been rendered either obsolete or, if certain functions are still desirable, free-market, technology-enabled solutions may take over in time. Therefore, we now turn to how interest rates, the fundamental building block of all finance, are to be determined under the gold standard.

Chapter 20: Financial Asset Valuation Fundamentals under a Gold Standard

> "The [true rate of interest] is essentially independent of the supply of money and money-substitutes, notwithstanding the fact that changes in the supply of money and money-substitutes can indirectly affect its height. But the market rate of interest can be affected by changes in the money [supply]."
>
> —Ludwig von Mises,
> *Human Action*, Chapter 19, section 6

FINANCIAL ASSETS ARE LEGAL CLAIMS on future cash flows of varying degrees of certainty. Therefore, any methodology for valuing assets must contain an assumption for the time value of money, or rate of interest, as well as a way for estimating, measuring and discounting the uncertainty necessarily associated with anything that lies in the future. In this chapter, we begin with a consideration of these fundamental concepts and subsequently apply them to a range of assets, giving due consideration to the monetary constraints implied by a gold standard.

SAVINGS, INVESTMENT, CONSUMPTION, AND TIME PREFERENCE

Let us return briefly to the topic of economic uncertainty, introduced earlier, from the perspective of an investor. Investors always have a choice of either saving or investing. As uncertainty decreases, other factors equal, investors are willing to invest more, and vice versa. Yet what one investor saves remains available, via the banking and financial system, for others to invest. As such, we recognize one of the fundamental accounting identities of economics, that savings must equal investment:

Savings (S) = Investment (I)[107]

As investment opportunities become more attractive and investors thus want to invest relatively more and save relatively less, the rate of interest on (or price of) savings must necessarily rise, such that savings and investment remain in balance. Alternatively, if investment becomes relatively less attractive for some reason and investors become more inclined to save, then the rate of interest will decline.

Economists refer to this phenomenon as time preference, which also applies to consumption. At any given point in time, a household can either save or consume. What is saved today is consumed in the future, reflecting a preference to do so. As the propensity to consume today increases, households save relatively less, and, to keep savings and investment in balance, the rate of interest on savings must rise. Alternatively, if households become more inclined to save today and consume more in future instead, then the rate of interest will decline accordingly. Looking at the bigger picture, what one household saves out of their income becomes available for investment. As such, we recognize another macroeconomic accounting identity, that income, minus savings (or investment), must equal consumption:

107 It is worth noting here that, due to depreciation of the capital stock, a degree of savings is required simply to maintain what exists. Adding to the capital stock requires commensurately more savings. All productive assets depreciate over time to some degree. As such, the greater the capital stock in relation to the economy generally, the more that will need to be saved to maintain it over time. This is the simplest way to understand why an economy can save/invest too much: it ends up with a capital stock that depreciates at a greater rate than what it produces can be consumed, implying a net economic loss due to overcapacity. Ideally, a capital stock will grow only to the point that what it produces is fully consumed, no production is wasted, and there is no excessive depreciation. For more on this topic, see Robert Solow's growth model, presented in "A Contribution to the Theory of Economic Growth," *The Quarterly Journal of Economics*, volume 70, issue 1 (1956): p. 65–94.

Income (I) – Savings (S) = Consumption (C)

Interest rates are thus properly understood as the prices that keep these identities between income, savings/investment, and consumption in balance.

The concept of the "Risk-Free" interest rate

Economists use the concept of a risk-free interest rate to separate the concept of the time-value of money from that of credit risk. If one person lends money to another, naturally, they expect to get it back. If they perceive zero risk that they will not get it back, then the interest rate charged is risk-free in that there is no default risk included in the calculation.

This is different from saying that there is no interest rate risk, which increases with maturity. For example, if a bank lends money to a business over a ten-year period at a 2 percent risk-free rate, but then, for whatever reason, time preferences change in favor of current investment or consumption over future and the going ten-year interest rate rises to 4 percent, then, if the loan is marked to market, it will have fallen in value, as it earns only 2 percent rather than 4 percent.

This price risk associated with changes in the market level of interest rates is not credit or default risk but pure interest rate risk, and it explains why default risk-free government bond prices move inversely to yields. In the financial jargon, interest rate risk is divided up into *duration,* which for non-coupon-bearing instruments increases linearly with maturity, and *convexity,* which increases exponentially. Thus, as one moves along the "yield curve" from short to long maturities, interest risk rises.

Real versus nominal interest rates

When discussing interest rates, it is important to distinguish between real and nominal, the difference between the two being the rate of inflation. Recall that savings equals investment. But if over any given time period, the amount of real savings is diluted by the creation of new money, then, other factors being equal, the real rate of interest will be lower. And in the event that the money supply shrinks during any particular time period, the real rate of interest will be higher. As real rates are those that represent the real time-value of money, they are the ones that keep real incomes, savings/investment, and consumption in balance.

Whether nominal interest rates rise and fall with inflation depends on whether such inflation is seen or unseen. If financial markets perceive correctly that inflation is rising, then nominal rates will rise accordingly, and vice versa. In practice, this is not always the case. If, for example, financial markets fail to perceive that inflation is rising (i.e., the money supply is growing), the result will be an investment and/or consumption boom that must, by definition, eventually turn into a bust. This is because, over time, real incomes, savings/investment, and consumption must be in balance.

Rational Expectations Theory (RET)

The 1970s was the decade of the dreaded stagflation, something that traditional Keynesian economic models implied could not happen. This is because, within a traditional Keynesian framework, there is a stable relationship between inflation and unemployment known as Okun's law (after economist Arthur Okun). As inflation rises, unemployment declines, and vice versa. This implicitly assumes, however, that nominal interest rates do not respond to inflation ex ante but rather only ex post. Originally posed by economist John Muth, RET was used by other prominent economists, such Milton Friedman and Robert Lucas, to ridicule this assumption as grossly naïve. Financial markets may not be perfect but they are, according to RET, rational enough to discount macroeconomic policies that have traditionally proven to be inflationary. As such, nominal interest rates rise and fall along with inflation expectations, preventing an artificial decline or increase in real rates (via inflation or deflation) from translating into an actual investment boom/bust. The stagflationary 1970s were to an extent predicted by RET and, in retrospect, rather well explained by it. The persistent weakness of the economy amid generally rising inflation from the mid-1970s through early 1980s is thus better explained by structural factors (e.g., that the United States was not energy efficient enough to absorb higher oil prices and had also become relatively less competitive internationally in a number of key industries, such as car manufacturing), and RET postulates further that the stagflation thus ended not only because policy makers decisively reversed inflationary policies via sharply higher interest rates and lower money supply growth in the early 1980s but also because the US economy made some important structural adjustments by the mid-1980s, including becoming generally more energy efficient, and also benefited from increased global trade, in particular with the Pacific Rim, which had become considerably more affluent.

Incidentally, the Nobel Prize in Economics was recently awarded to three economists for their work on RET.

Real versus nominal interest rates in practice

Under a fiat currency standard, with legal tender laws enforcing its use and central banks setting interest rates, there is no free market in money. Interest rates are not set by a reconciliation of supply and demand for savings, investment, and consumption; rather, they are set by a central bank in an attempt to achieve certain policy goals, such as meeting a target rate of growth in a consumer price index. By altering the growth rate of the money supply and arbitrarily setting short-term or even long-term interest rates, they seek to manage economic activity to some end, the most common ostensible reason being to maintain stable growth and avoid recessions, with consumer price stability the most prominent means to this end. But with few exceptions, the history of central banking is not, as we have seen, a history of maintaining price stability at all, much less economic and financial stability more generally. Rather, as demonstrated in Section I, it is a history of facilitating an ongoing series of bubbles and busts and then stepping in where necessary to save the financial system from itself. As this process has critically undermined the current, dollar-centric, global monetary order, a return to a gold standard has become both necessary and inevitable.

Fortunately, once under a gold standard, in which material monetary inflation becomes essentially impossible absent a formal exit or devaluation from that standard, then nominal interest rates are going to fall in line with real. Moreover, it will be impossible for central banks, assuming that they still exist, to hold interest rates at levels other than where a free market in money would place them and still remain on a gold standard. To the extent that they do diverge, they will be an indication that financial markets are concerned that macroeconomic policies are incompatible with adherence to the gold standard, that governments are behaving recklessly, and that there is a growing risk of a currency devaluation or departure from the gold standard at some point in future. Governments, in other words, will find poor policies more difficult to hide and, therefore, more difficult to implement in the first place.

To some extent, this is what is being observed in the euro area today. Euro-area member countries no longer control their respective national printing presses. Of these, several followed expansionary, even reckless fiscal policies during the first decade of European monetary union (EMU), 1999–2009. Euro-area commercial banks took advantage of the low interest rates provided by the German anchor to the system and engaged in all manner of property speculation. In multiple countries, they were bailed out by governments in 2008–9, with the governments de facto assuming the bad debts. However, rather than seeing their currencies depreciate because of poor policies—as would have been the case pre-EMU—they find their borrowing costs are rising. This increase in interest rates is not a function of current inflation, which is contained by the more moderate monetary policies of the European Central Bank (ECB); rather, it reflects the growing risk that these countries will, soon, either default on these debts, exit the euro area and devalue their currencies, or some combination of the two.

The euro area, in this respect, thus functions as a kind of quasi gold standard, imposing market-based interest rate discipline on governments that run unsustainable policies. Greece, Portugal, and Ireland have all restricted their debts in recent years. It is also probable that, at some point in future, both Spain and Italy will require a debt restructuring. Even in Germany and France there are issues, although for now these remain at the commercial bank rather than sovereign level.

The alternative for a country seeking fiscal and monetary autonomy would be to leave the euro area, akin to withdrawing from a gold standard. Without the credible backing of the euro, however, withdrawal will naturally lead to a dramatic currency depreciation, destroying much of the accumulated paper wealth of the country in question. Hyperinflation and a complete collapse of the new domestic currency are entirely possible. The Greeks and others are no doubt aware of this risk, hence their extreme reluctance to ditch the euro and introduce a neo-drachma or other national currencies instead.

Much the same discipline imposed by membership in the euro area would be observed under an actual gold standard. In fact, it would be even stricter. This is because although the ECB, as a supranational central bank, cannot set monetary policy for just one or two member countries in debt trouble; nevertheless, there is the possibility that such countries might be bailed out by other members. Also, as we have seen over the course of the past few years, the ECB has the flexibility to provide temporary emergency financing to members, something that it has been doing with the express intent of buying time so that some sort of comprehensive bailout of weak euro-area sovereign borrowers can be arranged.

Gold, as a nonprintable substance, cannot simply be conjured into existence as desired to provide a temporary source of confidence in a failing financial institution, sovereign or other public entity—or any borrower for that matter. Under a gold standard, financial support, absent the sudden acquisition of additional gold, comes with an immediate, objective cost: an incrementally higher rate of interest. The more one borrows relative to one's ability to service the debt, the higher the interest rate demanded by the financial markets.

Such discipline, in practice, essentially guarantees that attempts by fiscal or monetary authorities to implement clearly unsustainable policies will nearly simultaneously not only be exposed as such but also, as such exposure occurs through the interest rate itself, quickly become prohibitively costly such that they are likely to be abandoned unless other commitments, fiscal or monetary, are scaled back accordingly. Under a gold standard, the authorities will be able to increase spending on only programs that represent the most important priorities, something that, one could argue, is highly likely to result in a sensible rationalization of public policy generally.

Estimating the level of interest rates

As we have seen, absent unsustainable macroeconomic policies, under a credible gold standard, interest rates will be determined by the underlying real supply and demand for funds, both functions of economic time preference. But then what is the interest rate likely to be?

Recall that by placing gold at the center of the economic and financial universe, calculation is greatly simplified. In this case, the interest rate will reflect nothing more than the real time-value of money; it will be a direct, undistorted expression of time preference on the part of investors and households. As savings preferences rise, so will the interest rate. If investment and consumption preferences rise instead, so will the interest rate. As always, the interest rate will be at the level that maintains our macroeconomic accounting identities:

Savings = Investment

and

Income – Savings/Investment = Consumption

The real time-value of money should be a function of the sustainable potential growth rate of the economy. If, as is sometimes assumed, a developed industrial economy can grow sustainably at around 3 percent per annum, then this would probably give an indication of the rough magnitude of the long-term risk-free interest rate under a gold standard. For an economy capable of growing sustainably at a higher rate, the rate would be higher, and vice versa. In Figure 20.1, we see that ten-year US real interest rates have tended to fluctuate around a level more or less in line with that of trend GDP growth, notwithstanding much cyclical volatility from time to time.

Figure 20.1: Ten-Year US nominal and real interest rates through the decades

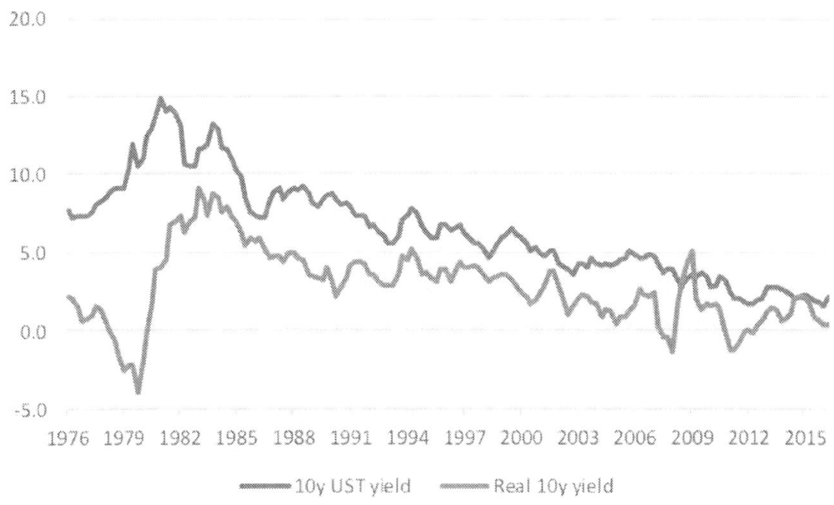

Source: Federal Reserve.

WHY GDP IS A POOR MEASURE OF ECONOMIC GROWTH IN A MODERN ECONOMY

Gross domestic product (GDP) is the most common measure of total economic income used by the economic mainstream today. Unfortunately, it is a highly flawed measure, better designed to measure the available tax base rather than the real economy. It also obscures the quality and sustainability of growth.

The GDP is based on the economic identity that total economic income must equal total economic production. It is then calculated by dividing production up into various sectors, most commonly into private-sector consumption (C), investment (I), government spending (G), and net exports to other economies, and then adding them all together to calculate the total. So a typical GDP equation is the following:

$$GDP = C + I + G + (E - I),$$

with imports (I) subtracted from exports (E) to calculate net exports.

Thus, GDP estimates the total value of all economic transactions during any given period. It does not measure activity for which no transaction takes place. So, for example, if you purchase food at a supermarket but prepare the meal at home, the latter value added will not be captured in GDP. Purchase a ready-made meal, however, requiring no preparation, and the entire value added will be captured by GDP. Whereas the purchase of the ready-made meal is taxable, the final preparation of a home meal is not. As such, GDP captures only visible, not invisible, activity. But consider: is preparing a meal at home somehow less valuable or less desirable than purchasing a ready-made meal? For a household that can get by on one income, regular home meal preparation might be considered a nice luxury, whereas for a family that requires two incomes, the regular purchase of ready-made meals might be seen as an unfortunate necessity of their less affluent financial position.

The GDP also treats all transactions equally, adding them to each other even in the event that they basically cancel each other out. For example, let's say two businesses sue each other over some dispute. On both sides, they pay out substantial legal fees. Perhaps they settle their dispute in the end with neither side benefiting. Yet the legal fees on both sides are added to GDP. Measured in this way, a general increase in litigation would be perceived as economic growth comparable, say, to building new factories and homes. It is highly dubious to assume, however, that society would regard both types of GDP growth as comparable or desirable.

Also, as far as GDP is concerned, there is no difference between growth in private consumption and investment and that of the government. Yet the latter cannot add to growth at all without first taking income away from the private sector, as all government income originates as taxation. (To the extent that the government finances itself through debt issuance, this is a claim on future taxation.) When the government sector is small, so is this distortion. But as a government sector grows relative to the real economy, it becomes significant. What GDP calculates as economic growth could be just a growing transfer of income from the private sector to the government via taxation.

This is the main reason that the Neo-Keynesian economic mainstream is always quick to point out that cuts in government spending will depress GDP growth, at least temporarily. But when they fail to see is that, while GDP may indeed decline as a result, overall, real economic activity may not, in particular when the less visible is included. Referring back to our example, if there were less government spending and thus less taxation, some two-income households might find they can, in fact, get by on one income. As such, one member would be available at home to provide child care and meal preparation. Yes, this would reduce GDP, but would it improve, or worsen, this household's economic position? The question answers itself and demonstrates this major flaw in GDP.

Another shortcoming with GDP is that as economic transactions necessarily take place in nominal values, nominal GDP grows with inflation as well as with the real economy, which grows only in volumes of goods and services. As such, real GDP is derived from nominal values by using a price deflator, which attempts to measure by how much all the various goods and services have risen in price over the same time period.

Although measures of price changes, ranging from consumer price indices (CPI) to GDP deflators, are taken for granted as definitive measures, in practice they are just estimates, subject to various kinds of measurement error. It should be no surprise, for example, that the United States has changed the way it calculates both the CPI and the GDP deflator through the years. If either of these were clearly so definitive, they would not be works in progress.

Lest the reader think that such changes are not material, it is rather eye-opening to learn that the way the CPI is calculated, for example, has changed so much in recent decades that, were the old methodology still in use, it would show CPI currently running at a level as high as during the second half of the 1970s, the years of the dreaded stagflation. Yet the US Federal Reserve, pointing toward the low level of the CPI today, claims it is still concerned primarily by deflation rather than inflation!

It should be clear that, given these various flaws in the GDP methodology, it gives an incomplete and potentially highly misleading picture of an economy, in particular whether the growth taking place is real, healthy, or sustainable. Its widespread use largely reflects the historical legacy of its introduction at a time when economies were primarily production rather than service based, when the government sector was far smaller, and when inflation was much lower, in large part because countries were on a gold standard. As such, it was much less misrepresentative of economic reality back then than today.

Estimating the Term Structure of Interest Rates

As is the case under a fiat standard, under a gold standard short-term interest rates would normally be considerably more volatile than long-term rates. These fluctuations, however, would not reflect changes in inflation or inflation expectations as they would be so stable as to be immaterial. They would, therefore, simply reflect the dynamism of the real economy, that is, the real demand for and supply of savings.

As we are talking about real rates of growth and real rates on savings, there is no inflation calculation to worry about, no potential material loss of purchasing power that must be incorporated into the rate as an inflation risk premium, something that is normally included in interest rate modeling assumptions.

A traditional model for interest rates normally contains the following:

- An assumption for the future path of policy rates
- A risk or term premium to compensate investors for uncertainty, which tends to be higher at longer than at shorter maturities

However, as we have seen, under a gold standard, interest rates are going to be determined primarily by the financial markets rather than by the arbitrary policy of central bankers, who will have limited flexibility, in particular over longer time horizons. Therefore, to understand how interest rates are likely to behave under a gold standard, we simply focus on our basic concepts of uncertainty and time preference and layer these over a reasonable trend growth rate assumption.

If we stick with an assumption of an underlying trend growth rate of around 3 percent but assume regular fluctuations around this of up to, say, 4 percent, then the economy will grow normally at rates ranging from mild contractions of –1 percent to occasional periods of up to 7 percent annual growth. Naturally, when growth expectations are around this elevated level, there will be strong demand for funds to invest and consume, and interest rates will rise accordingly, most probably by a comparable magnitude. Conversely, when expectations are for a period of stagnation or recession, then savings rates will plummet to below 3 percent and might, from time to time, even approach zero.

While under a fiat currency regime, in which some degree of monetary inflation is the order of the day, zero rates might seem highly counterintuitive and result only from the arbitrary actions of central bankers setting rates, under a gold standard, in which material monetary inflation becomes all but impossible, extremely low interest rates, approaching zero, would be entirely normal during periods of economic stagnation or recession.

One important conclusion to draw, regarding the slope of the yield curve, is that absent the uncertainty associated with inflation, the term premium demanded by investors to hold longer-dated paper will decline dramatically, absent signs of rising fiscal deficits. As unsustainable fiscal deficits are the ultimate source of major inflations and devaluations versus other currencies or gold, naturally these would have an observable impact on term premiums under a gold standard.

As seen in Figure 20.2, business cycles have been the primary driver of yield curve slope. On average, the spread between Fed funds and the ten-year US Treasury note yield has been around 2 percent. Under a credible gold standard, volatility in both the level and slope of the curve is likely to be lower absent the uncertainties of inflation. This simplifies economic calculation for businesses and households alike, facilitating long-term investing and financial planning.

Figure 20.2: US 2-10y US Treasury yield curve spread

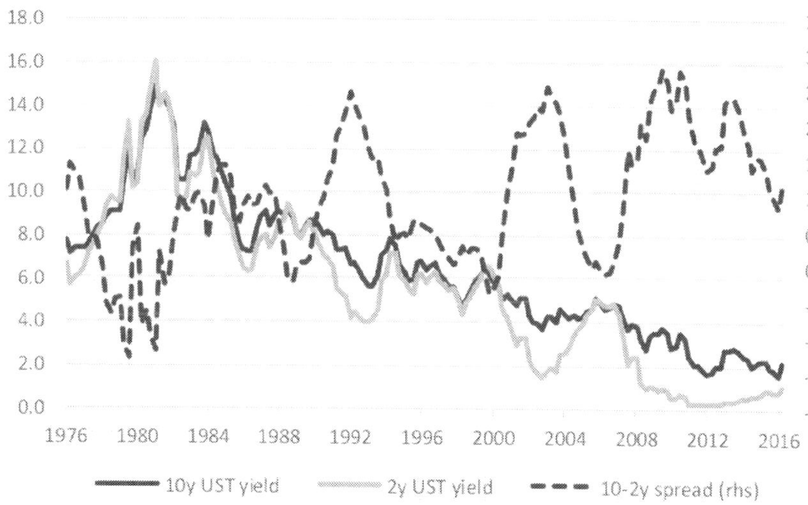

Source: Federal Reserve.

Chapter 21: Estimating Risk Premia under a Gold Standard

> "[Via inflation] they create an abundance of disposable money for which its owners try to find the most profitable investment. Very promptly these funds find outlets in the stock exchange or in fixed investment. The notion that it is possible to pursue a credit expansion without making stock prices rise and fixed investment expand is absurd."
>
> —Ludwig von Mises,
> *Human Action*, Chapter 31, section 5

INTEREST RATES ARE THE FUNDAMENTAL valuation building block common to all assets. Future cash flows must be discounted at some rate to calculate a net present value, or market price, for an asset. Where assets are not risk-free, however, as is the case with government bonds or any theoretical income stream with zero default risk, then the cash flows themselves must be estimated, as they are uncertain in both nominal and real terms. In this chapter, we consider how various risk premia are likely to be affected by the return to gold.

RISK PREMIA WHERE CASH FLOWS ARE RELATIVELY CERTAIN

In cases where the degree of future cash flow uncertainty is relatively low, such as with investment-grade corporate bonds, risk premia tend to be rather small. It is highly unlikely that a mature business in a stable industry with low financial leverage is going to default on its debts. As such, the prices of investment-grade corporate bonds normally move closely in line with those of government bonds. Any spread of the corporate bond yield above that for a comparable-maturity government bond reflects the credit risk of the former, that is, the risk of default and the implied recovery rate on the firm's assets, should that in fact occur.

None of this is going to change under a gold standard. As private-sector entities, corporations will always be at some risk of default. This risk needs to be priced into their bonds in the form of a yield spread over a corresponding risk-free asset such as a government bond. As the risk of default increases, so does the yield spread.

Corporate bond spreads must also incorporate assumed recovery rates on the corporate assets, which will become the property of the bondholders in a default. As the assumed recovery rate on defaulted corporate bonds decreases, the yield spread over risk-free bonds must increase to compensate investors accordingly.

In the case of unsecured bonds for complex multinational companies, recovery rates can be highly uncertain, of course. But this is true of a great many things in finance. While under a gold standard, inflation risk essentially disappears, other forms of risk remain. With corporate bonds, as well as other assets for which the future cash flows are to some degree uncertain, the risk premia implied in a yield spread or other discount to a risk-free benchmark reflect not inflation uncertainty but rather other, real economic forms of uncertainty, for example, the business cycle. In the long-term chart of US corporate bond spreads in Figure 21.1, the impact of the business cycle is clear:

Figure 21.1: US corporate bond yields and spreads

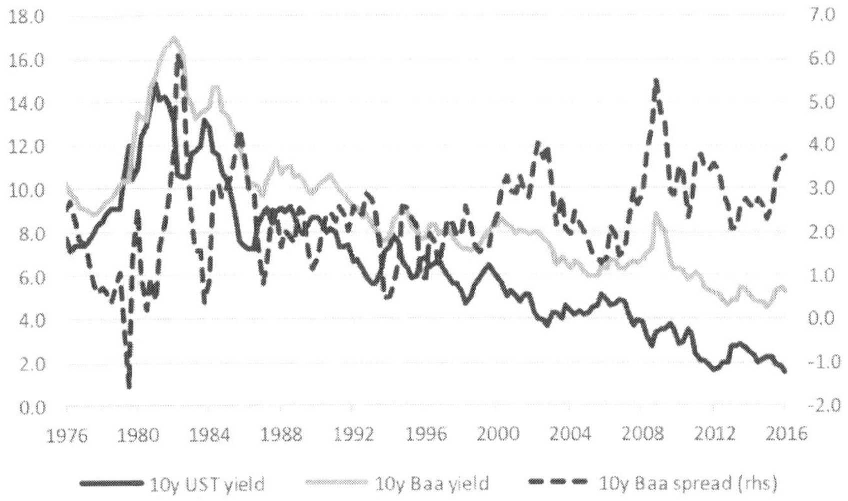

Source: Moody's, US Federal Reserve.

However, whereas with government bonds, inflation uncertainty would show up as a nominal yield in excess of the real yield; with corporate or other assets at risk of default, inflation risk would reduce the relative risk premium. This is because, absent a gold standard, a central bank can lower interest rates, create new money, fuel inflation, and, if necessary, act as a lender of last resort such that, in the event of an economic downturn, corporate default becomes rather less likely. Indeed, there is a natural bias for policymakers to act in this way, absent the constraint imposed by a gold standard. As Ludwig von Mises put it in his magnum opus, *Human Action*:

> [Money] expansion produces first the illusory appearance of prosperity. It is extremely popular because it seems to make the majority, even everybody, more affluent. It has an enticing quality. A special moral effort is needed to stop it. On the other hand, contraction immediately produces conditions which everybody is ready to condemn as evil.

> Its unpopularity is even greater than the popularity of expansion. It creates violent opposition. Very soon they political forces fighting it become irresistible.[108]

As we have seen in the previous chapter, this ability to manipulate interest rates to reduce or prevent corporate bankruptcies is not necessarily good news for an economy at large, as it prevents creative destruction from taking place. However, from the perspective of an investor in a corporate bond, knowing that a central bank stands ready to create money to soften a downturn is seen as a reason for demanding a smaller risk premium over debt that is perceived as free of default risk, such as a government bond.

Other factors being equal, therefore, we should anticipate that corporate credit spreads would be wider under a gold standard than under a fiat standard. But it would be a mistake to conclude that somehow business is fundamentally riskier. On the contrary, it means that businesses' access to debt capital markets is determined by a more rational, disciplined, market-driven process than by investors' speculation regarding whether and under what circumstances central banks will ease credit conditions to support the economy when certain firms, industries, or the entire economy is at risk of recession.

What holds for unsecured corporate bonds will also hold for secured. Recovery rates on bonds secured on specified assets are generally much easier to determine, and risk premia are generally much lower. But here, too, the risk premium should be higher. In the same way that central banks act to create inflation, thereby making corporate defaults less likely in economic downturns, these inflationary policies support asset prices generally, including, of course, those assets that are used to back secured debt, such as receivables of some kind and specified plant or equipment.

---

108 Ludwig von Mises, *Human Action*, (New Haven: Yale University Press, 1949), Chapter 20, section 7.

What holds for secured and unsecured corporate bonds also holds for non-risk-free assets generally. Under a gold standard, risk premia will be higher, other factors being equal. But they will be at a level that corresponds to the real risk assumed by economic actors, rather than distorted by the moral hazard of an implied bailout by a central bank easing monetary conditions. As such, capital is less likely to be misallocated. Firms or industries that get into trouble will spend less time trying to convince policy makers to bail them out and more time considering how best to restructure their operations to return to profitability. They may not always succeed in doing so, but then that is what Schumpeterian creative destruction is all about.

Josef Schumpeter and Creative Destruction

Although not always associated with the Austrian Economic School, Schumpeter was a student of a prominent Austrian economist, Eugen von Boehm-Bawerk, and a contemporary of both von Mises and von Hayek. He is best known for developing his concept of creative destruction, whereby inefficient firms, industries, or even entire economies must, from time to time, undergo periods of economic hardship to reorganize and restructure themselves to adapt to major changes in the underlying economic environment, including the adoption of new technologies that might threaten a dominant firm's market position, a successful industry's profit margins, or an entire economy's competitive advantage vis-à-vis other economies. As old factories are retooled and old industries die and new ones spring up, capital must necessarily be reallocated from one place to another, as fresh capital cannot be conjured out of thin air the way money can be printed.

Indeed, this is one way to understand why inflation can be so harmful to economies in the long run, even if the rate is low and does not cause visible economic damage. What is less visible is that, by creating money out of thin air, a central bank slows the capital reallocation and reorganization process. Firms or industries supported by easy money may be able to resist pressure to modernize or rationalize their operations for years. In the meantime, the entire economy forgoes the opportunity to restructure more aggressively, suffering a recession in the interim perhaps, but then recovering strongly at a higher sustainable growth rate with the advantages of younger, more dynamic firms; new technologies; and workers who have acquired the new skills required to implement them accordingly.

This need to destroy in order to create led Schumpeter to use the term *creative destruction* to describe this important aspect of capitalism. In doing so, he showed how what happens at the micro, firm-specific, and even worker-specific level of an economy cannot be separated from the macro. Monetary and fiscal policy might be used to reduce the volatility of the economic cycle, something that the modern economic mainstream considers sensible, but Schumpeter argued that healthy capitalist economies were arguably more volatile by their very nature, with boom-and-bust cycles serving a critical purpose by creating regular opportunities for creative destruction and, hence, real economic progress.

Risk premia where cash flows are relatively uncertain

As one moves along the risk spectrum, from relatively safe corporate bonds toward speculative-grade bonds, distressed debt, or corporate equities, the risk premium increases. As such, the sensitivity of such assets to the monetary regime also increases. An implied bailout, in the form of artificially low interest rates, can have a dramatic impact on the equity risk premium, for example. As equities are claims on after-tax corporate profits, which tend to grow with inflation, the existence of a credible bailout for firms at risk of default can result in a dramatically lower risk premium. From an investors' point of view, if profits are to grow with inflation, on the one hand, yet default is highly unlikely, on the other, then there is practically no downside to equity investment, whereas by holding bonds instead, the investor receives little, if any, implied protection from monetary inflation.

This asymmetric risk profile perhaps explains why, during much of the 1990s and through the mid-2000s, observed equity risk premia have been generally lower than during the 1950s through the 1980s, notwithstanding generally healthier economic growth during those former decades. Indeed, this observable, policy-driven compression of the equity risk premium in recent years is so significant that it deserves a thorough examination. To do so, we will apply a classic valuation methodology, that of the capital asset pricing model (CAPM).

Using CAPM to reveal how inflation distorts asset prices

Recall our previous discussion of the time value of money: it is to financial asset pricing what the speed of light is to Einstein's theories of relativity. While not a constant in the physical sense, the time value of money, as represented by the term structure of interest rates, is the universal point of reference for discounting the future cash flows on which financial assets represent legal claims.

Financial asset valuation models are, therefore, sensitive to interest rate assumptions, in particular when the cash flows are 1) relatively far out in the future and 2) relatively certain. The shorter the time and the more uncertain the cash flows, the less sensitive a financial asset price is to changes in the term structure of interest rates.

To illustrate this point, consider two financial assets: a long-term government bond and a lottery ticket for tomorrow's $10 million draw. As the cash flows accruing to the government bond are known in advance and extend far out into the future, the price of the bond is highly sensitive to changes in the term structure of interest rates. However, even a large change in interest rates does not have much impact on the value of the lottery ticket. Not only is the cash flow only one day away—not enough time for interest to accrue—but also unknown.

Probability theory can estimate the value of the lottery ticket, but, in practice, the payoff is so uncertain—a binary outcome of either zero or

$10 million—that the actual value of the ticket is really just a function of pure uncertainty, independent of the term structure of interest rates.

Imagine now that the relative certainties of financial asset cash flows are laid out on a spectrum, from the certain to the highly uncertain. It might look something like this:

Certain GBs = CBs = VEs = GEs = VC Uncertain

> where GBs = government bonds, CBs = corporate bonds, VEs = value equities, GEs = growth equities, and VC = venture capital.

As you move from left to right and the uncertainty of the realized size of the cash flows becomes ever greater, the present values (prices) of the cash flows become gradually less sensitive to the term structure of interest rates. As such, investments in equities and venture capital might seem to be relatively insensitive to interest rates. However, it is frequently the case that when it comes to investments in growth equities and venture capital, the cash flows that really matter—that determine whether the investment is going to outperform—are those at least a few years out in the future, perhaps even a decade or more. Due to the long duration of these cash flows, it would be a mistake to conclude that, just because they are relatively uncertain, these assets should not be somewhat sensitive to interest rate assumptions.

Half a century ago, several economists working independently developed the key elements of the CAPM, which has provided a theoretical basis for risky-asset valuation models up to the present day.[109]

---

109 William Sharpe, Henry Markowitz, and Merton Miller jointly received the 1990 Nobel Prize in Economics for the CAPM and modern portfolio theory (MPT), with which it is closely associated, although several others also did essential work in this area. William Sharpe is also well-known for his eponymous measure of risk-adjusted returns. In recent years, CAPM and MPT have come under increased scrutiny in part because they assume that financial market risk is normally distributed. The 2008–2009 credit crisis is just the latest example that this is not the case, although it may appear so from time to time.

In its simplest form, the CAPM model calculates the expected return of a financial asset according to the following equation:

$E(R_i) = R_f + B_i[E(R_m) - R_f]$

where $E(R_i)$ is the expected rate of return, R_f is the risk-free interest rate, B_i is the sensitivity (risk) of the asset relative to the market for comparably risky assets, and $E(R_m)$ is the expected return of the market for comparably risky assets.

While it is obvious that the interest rate R_f plays a role here, notice that, as the measures of risk B_i or $E(R_m)$ approach zero, the expected return on the asset becomes a function entirely of the risk-free interest rate, normally assumed to be that on government bonds. But as B_i and $E(R_m)$ rise, the expected return on the asset becomes less dependent on the risk-free interest rate. If, alternatively, $E(R_m)$ is highly uncertain, the risk-free rate also becomes less relevant.

Regardless, note how the model is based entirely on the concept of relative value: assets are being valued relative to a risk-free asset and relative to the market for comparably risky assets. Now, given that interest rate assumptions have at least a modest impact on relative risky asset valuations, note that if the risk-free rate Rf is being held artificially low by the monetary authority, then this has the effect of increasing the expected returns on risky assets relative to risk-free assets. In other words, risky assets in general will become fundamentally overvalued.

Applied to corporate bonds, this implies that, even absent any explicit or implied government support, spreads to government bonds will become too tight to compensate investors for the fundamental risks they are taking, as we showed earlier in this chapter. And risky equities will become overvalued relative to bonds and to low-beta (low-risk) equities.

This implies that, for any given level of future earnings assumptions, equity P/E ratios will be higher than they would otherwise be, such that investors end up paying more for shares than they can reasonably expect to get back (someday) in the form of actual, after-tax, discounted earnings. By implication, were interest rates allowed to adjust to their natural equilibrium, corporate credit spreads would most likely rise, and share P/Es fall.

Leaving the fundamentals aside for the moment, some might argue that stock market investment is not necessarily investment at all but rather a form of speculation and that what stock market speculators are after is short-term capital gains rather than value-based long-term earnings growth. Warren Buffett and other successful value investors would beg to differ. But Buffett would probably be among the first to acknowledge that a substantial portion of stock market transactions represent the whims of speculators rather than the careful, systematic, value-driven determinations of sensible, value-oriented investors. Indeed, it is the actions of the speculators that move prices to levels that are fundamentally unjustified, which create the very opportunities that value investors such as Buffett seek to exploit.

How distorting interest rates causes real economic damage

This discussion leads us to another way in which the actions of the monetary authority can become so detrimental to the economy at large. By making it more difficult to value risky assets properly and by generally inflating the value of such assets beyond what fundamentals can justify, value-driven investors will be less willing to invest in the market generally. Investment flows will become increasingly dominated by those who are really just speculating and chasing trends rather than making reasoned judgments about which companies offer the best potential long-term value.

But the stock market does not exist in a vacuum. The valuations placed on stocks represent the abilities of companies to raise capital in the form of new shares or debt issues, to acquire other companies through merger or acquisition, to compensate their employees with shares or options—in a word, to grow. If the stock market becomes overvalued, companies are liable to overinvest in their operations.

If speculators rather than value investors are the primary force behind stock price trends, then economic resources generally are being allocated in an inefficient, haphazard way that leads to malinvestments. Such malinvestments, over time, have the effect of reducing the overall economy's potential growth rate, as they divert resources from more productive activities or, alternatively, lead to a general overinvestment in the capital stock such that depreciation becomes a drag on growth.[110]

Consider the tech bubble for example. Notwithstanding the very real technological advances taking place in the 1990s, by 1997 the stock prices of tech firms began to rise out of line with any reasonable assumptions of economic reality. Value investors began to retreat from the market, leaving it more open to speculators. In the wake of the Asian crisis in 1997, which reduced the attractiveness of emerging markets, these speculators moved more aggressively into tech stocks. When the Fed bailed out Long-Term Capital Management (LTCM) in 1998 and eased monetary conditions briefly going into Y2K, speculators became even more aggressive. As tech and other stock prices rose and rose, these companies spent more and more on various expansion plans.

Eventually, it all came crashing down, and the malinvestments were exposed for what they were. Sure, there were real economic advances that had taken place, but valuations, with much help from the Fed, had become so stretched that a bust became inevitable. To compensate for that bust, of course, the Fed eased policy even more aggressively than it had in the wake of the LTCM failure, with the entirely predictable consequence that new bubbles would form elsewhere, this time in residential and

110 It may seem counterintuitive that a capital stock can become too large. After all, the greater the capital stock, the greater the overall productive potential of the economy. But consider: if the capital stock grows relative to the level of the available labor to service and maintain it correctly, then it will depreciate prior to being utilized fully to produce consumer goods, resulting in a net loss of wealth. Just as economies can overconsume, they can also overinvest if interest rates are held at artificially low levels. Take a look at the many empty homes in the United States left in the wake of defaulted mortgages, depreciating away, and this loss of wealth can be observed directly.

commercial real estate and in global credit markets generally, leading to even greater malinvestments, which have subsequently been exposed as such by a commensurately greater bust. As for where the next bubbles are now forming, we believe that the Fed and economic policy makers generally have spun a vast web of financial market distortions and systemic moral hazard that facilitates asset misallocations just about everywhere. Financial history may not repeat, but it certainly rhymes.

A MORE ROBUST CAPM: VALUING FINANCIAL ASSETS AS OPTIONS

Our discussion of valuations so far has been based on a classic interpretation of what qualifies as a risk premium and how it can be imputed from observed financial asset prices and a benchmark risk-free interest rate. There are robust ways of estimating risk premia, however. One of these is to value assets based on the implied optionality of future cash flows.

As mentioned previously, some cash flows are less certain than others. Where cash flows are uncertain, however, one can assume that they are likely to fit a distribution. Classic option pricing theory assumes a Gaussian, or normal, distribution for financial variables. The original options pricing model, which became the basis for the growth of the derivatives industry in the 1980s, was published in 1973 by Fischer Black and Myron Scholes and is known as the Black-Scholes model.

Black and Scholes set out to show that, using Gaussian distribution assumptions, one could place an objective value on randomly distributed outcomes, including movements in stock prices and other financial assets. But one can take a similar set of assumptions and apply it to the cash flows that comprise the given valuation of a financial asset.

Take an oil well, for example, that can produce a barrel of oil for a cost of $80. Naturally, if the price of oil exceeds $80 per barrel, the well turns a profit. Should the price of oil decline below $80, however, it is not profitable to operate the well. As such, the well represents the option to produce oil and should be valued as such. Rather than just assuming an average future price of oil and discounting the implied future cash flows at some risk-free rate to determine the net present value of the well today, it is a more robust process to assume a distribution for the future oil price and to value the well as an *option* to produce oil instead.

Viewed in this way, all productive assets are options. Some might not be as easy as an oil well to turn on or off. But if price swings are large and sustained enough, even the most complex industrial processes are, ultimately, options rather than obligations to produce something.

An investor applying an options-based valuation methodology could possibly determine, for example, that a mature company in a relatively stable industry, was overvalued relative to a younger, riskier competitor. Whereas investors generally prefer stable investments to less stable ones, the implied option value of certain risky operations could, in theory, make the riskier firms more attractive.

This becomes particularly possible, of course, if the riskier firms are perceived as having some form of implied bailout in the form of a proactive central bank easing of policy in response to economic downturns. In this sense, even the disciplined, value-based investor, looking at cash flows from the bottom up, and applying options-based valuation techniques, ends up making investment decisions that are influenced by the central bank, valuing risky enterprises at an artificial premium to less risky ones, thereby misallocating capital in the process, to the broader economy's detriment.

Beyond CAPM: Valuing Assets in a Non-Normal World

As explored at length in Section I, much modern financial theory, including the hugely influential CAPM valuation methodology, and actual practice, is based on Gaussian, normal distribution assumptions. While certainly convenient from a risk calculation perspective, such assumptions are also convenient for those who desire to take excessive risk in investment decisions. Regardless of which motivating factor explains the lingering dominance of Gaussian finance, for years a growing number of prominent intellectuals have been pointing out that financial asset returns are emphatically not normally distributed but follow rather scale-invariant power curve distributions, as described by Jim Rickards in Section II.

The father of the anti-Gaussian rebellion in modern finance was no doubt the late Benoit Mandelbrot. Although he came rather late to finance, his work was to have a profound intellectual impact. Mandelbrot demonstrated that the financial world only appeared Gaussian to observers ensconced within a cave in which financial crises simply did not occur or were deliberately dismissed from the data set outright, as exceptional events. But of course, we know they occur. They occur across time, across economies, and across cultures, and they occur with a regularity completely out of scale with Gaussian assumptions.

What Mandelbrot discovered was the fractal nature of financial markets. That is, what happens frequently on a small scale occurs infrequently on a large scale. The scale itself is determined by the size of the financial system. Other factors being equal, as the system grows, so does the potential future crisis. Like earthquakes, these crises cannot be predicted with respect to timing. Their size, however, can be estimated and capital provisioned against anticipated future losses.

Why is this important to our discussion of risk premia? Recall that the implied bailout of the financial system and economy generally by central banks depresses risk premia to artificially low levels. This in turn implies that too much risk is taken; that is, the financial system and economy grow excessively in size through leverage. From time to time, a generally unforeseen development takes place that exposes that the risk provisioning in the system is inadequate, and a general crash ensues. At this point, the central bank can be relied on to do as it has done before and bail out the system yet again, encouraging it to grow even bigger in the future, thereby sowing the seeds of the next crisis, and so on.

Under a gold standard, this escalating boom-and-bust process becomes impossible, as it becomes prohibitively costly for economic agents to hold misplaced Gaussian assumptions. Low-risk premia that do not reflect reality lead to failed enterprises, plain and simple. There will be no bailout. Financial risk premia will reflect the non-Gaussian reality of the world in which we actually live, not the cave in which the economic mainstream resides, continuing to assume as if financial crises are some sort of aberration.

By implication, under a gold standard, risk premia will be higher. Equity and risky-asset valuations will therefore decline, other factors being equal, relative to their less risky alternatives. Value-driven investing, itself infected by the moral hazard of the current fiat dollar global monetary regime, will heal itself with proper, Mandelbrot-inspired, real-world assumptions and will largely, although never completely, displace more speculative forms of investing in which short-term traders attempt to offload fundamentally overvalued assets on others before they are exposed by future events as such.

This is yet another way in which the return to gold will be salutary for the global economy. There will be a renaissance of value-based investing and a decline in speculation. Financial firms will be forced to greatly derisk their balance sheets, as will highly leveraged corporations that attract capital because of bailout speculation rather than by representing superior fundamental value. The return to gold will thus produce both winners and losers, and it to this that we now turn.

Chapter 22: Golden Winners and Paper Losers

> "The financial sector of our economy is the largest profit-making sector in America... We've become a financial economy which has overwhelmed the productive economy."
>
> —John Bogle, CEO of Vanguard Fund Management, interview with Bill Moyers, September 2007

WHEN CONSIDERING WHICH FIRMS, INDUSTRIES, and asset classes are likely to benefit or suffer most in relative terms from a return to gold, we need to focus on fundamental value rather than speculation. We also must not lose sight of the role that risk-premia adjustments are likely to play. In general, the better-performing assets will be those that will see the smallest increases in risk premia, as risk premia in general are likely to rise somewhat as a trade-off for the essential disappearance of the inflation risk premium from the scene.

Should the transition period to gold prove disorderly, history suggests that valuations may reach levels that are extremely depressed. Yes, earnings are likely to rise in nominal terms if there is a general surge in global inflation associated with the decline in the purchasing power of the dollar and fiat currencies generally. But in real terms, they may not rise at all and could well decline, as global growth is likely to be weak. The rise in economic uncertainty, in general, is likely to favor defensive assets, albeit those that cannot simply be devalued through inflation, such as fixed-interest securities, including, of course, government bonds.

Within equities, which do offer some protection from inflation, value-based investing should do better than growth. High dividend yields will command a valuation premium. Firms providing stable products, services, and infrastructure and offering some global diversification should fare relatively well, but total market equity P/E ratios in the single digits are likely to be observed once it appears that the transition to gold is relatively certain and the temporary surge in inflation and future expectations thereof begin to subside. Should that seem overly bearish to some, consider that the US equity market traded at a single-digit P/E ratio in the early 1980s, the last time there was serious speculation that the United States might be headed back to a gold standard.

What applies to firms, industries, and asset classes also applies to entire countries and financial systems. Notwithstanding massive global linkages, some economies and financial systems are less leveraged than others, and these are likely to fare relatively better following the return to gold.

Financials

Nowhere is the adjustment back to a gold standard going to be as disruptive as within the financial system itself. It follows that the valuation of financial firms is going to change dramatically. As it turns out, this will not be for the better. Arguably, the single biggest financial market implication of a return to gold will be a generally de-rating of financial corporate assets to nonfinancial.

First, consider that the implied bailout in place under the current fiat dollar standard applies first and foremost to the too-big-to-fail firms that reside at the center of the financial system. It is here that risk is concentrated and where risk premia are most compressed relative to those elsewhere. A return to gold will reduce and possibly eliminate the entire too-big-to-fail advantage. By implication, there will be a large relative rise in risk premia in this sector.

Second, consider how financial firms have grown their earnings through various forms of financial engineering that have allowed excessive leverage into the system. Following a return to gold, much of this financial engineering will be seen for the opaque alchemy it is. Much of what happens in finance is related to the origination and subsequent hedging of interest rate risk. As we have shown, much interest rate risk is generated by inflation and expectations thereof. By essentially eliminating the risk of inflation, these activities will become largely unnecessary and uneconomic.

The ability of the financial system to grow faster than the economy generally, as has been the case on average since the dollar's link to gold was severed, will be thrown into reverse. At best, financial firms' profits will keep up with the economy but only after a painful period of downsizing. Originating and then retiring financial instruments only to the extent that these transactions support real economic activity should not be a particularly high-margin business and, absent leverage, should generate reasonable but hardly spectacular profits. Investors anticipating a return to gold should, therefore, strategically underweight financial shares and their risky, subordinated debt.

Industrials

Unlike financial firms, which have been the primary beneficiaries of the fiat dollar reserve standard, industrial firms have been only indirectly affected. Yes, they, too, have enjoyed structurally lower risk premia because of the general implied economic bailout provided by the monetary authorities, but to a much lesser extent. As such, while their risk premia are likely to be higher under a gold standard than at present, the relative increase is likely to be far smaller.

Industrial corporate bonds will also see higher risk premia under a gold standard than is the case today, although the increase will be slight in comparison to that for corporate shares and for financial companies' bonds. However, the transition back to gold is likely to be temporarily highly inflationary, as we discussed in Section II. As fixed-interest securities, industrial corporate bonds are thus not likely to fare as well as shares during the transition phase. Shares, while risky, are likely to rise alongside the inflation even as P/Es compress.

One way to get exposure to the industrial bond sector and avoid the risks of shares without taking much inflation risk is to buy floating-rate notes (FRNs). When interest rates rise as the world moves back to gold, so will the coupons of floating-rate notes. Yet the risk premia associated with FRNs should rise by less than that for industrial companies' shares, for the very same reason as for corporate bonds in general. As such, industrial FRNs, in particular for strong, investment-grade firms, provide investors with an excellent way to avoid the risk premium expansion and temporary inflation risks that are likely to characterize the transition period back to gold.

Industrial subsectors

Within industrials, some sectors are likely to perform better than others during the transition back to gold. Here we take a look at a few sectors that are likely to be most affected.

Mining

An obvious candidate for outperformance is the precious metals sector, the valuation of which is a direct function of the price of precious metals. That said, investors must consider other factors in this sector, in particular the speculative element presented by immature mines or exploration activities, but when it comes to reliable, established operations, it follows that a rise in the price of precious metals leads to rising miners' share prices.

As it stands at the time I am writing, the share prices of major precious metals mining firms, in particular those that employ leverage, are unusually low relative to gold and silver. As such, it could be argued that investors looking to profit from a return to gold should consider an allocation to established gold- and silver-mining firms, where the upside may be substantially greater.

So-called junior miners may struggle to perform as well. In principle, they provide investors with more leverage. However, as risk premia in general expand under a gold standard, relatively riskier mining and exploration operations may see their relative valuations suffer for a time. Once the transition back to gold is complete, however, and the global economy stabilizes, then it is highly likely that the junior miners will offer a range of enticing opportunities, albeit with substantially more risk than their mature counterparts.

Capital Goods

As is the case with consumer durables, the transition back to gold is likely to see a general underperformance of capital goods shares. Naturally, such shares are highly cyclical. Also, these firms tend to have large R&D costs that are recovered only over long periods of time. In some cases, capital goods producers make a profit only from the maintenance, servicing, and provision of spare parts for their equipment, such as with aircraft engines, for example. In certain cases, capital goods producers have financing arms that assist customers with the term financing of these expensive purchases. Like financing activities generally, however, these will be less profitable under a gold standard.

Once the transition is complete, however, and financing activities have shrunk to a more appropriate size, this is one of the sectors that will benefit most from the migration of capital out of speculative financial activities generally and back into the real, productive economy. As the many engineers and scientists who went to work in finance migrate into the capital goods industries, they will become part of an engineering and innovation renaissance.

Utilities

Long regarded as a staid, uninteresting business, utilities may provide one of the most interesting areas for investment, both during the transition back to gold and subsequently. As mature, relatively defensive companies, with relatively high dividend yields, they have the basic characteristics that we have identified as most suitable for outperformance during the potentially disorderly transition back to a gold standard. However, they are also an area ripe for innovation.

Among industrial sectors, utilities are the most heavily regulated. In many cases, they are either owned outright by the government or the government owns a large stake. Many are regulated monopolies, ultimately run by politicians who generally do not seek to maximize shareholder value.

Under a gold standard, in which government involvement in the economy is almost certain to be somewhat less, there exists the potential for substantial deregulation of utilities. The increased potential for innovation as capital is redirected from the financial sector and the arrival of new engineering talent could result in substantial technological innovation and increased efficiency. Profit margins could increase substantially.

While no doubt utilities would become riskier investments in this scenario, the increase in risk would be longer term, after the return to a credible gold standard had already been achieved. As such, they would most likely retain their safe-haven status in the interim.

Technology

As such a huge part of the global economy, the technology sector has become increasingly difficult to treat as a single entity for valuation. However, we can offer a few general thoughts.

First, as with capital goods producers, technology firms will benefit hugely from the migration of both capital and skilled labor from the financial sector. There might well be a surge in technological innovation as a result, although it might take some years for that to materialize.

Second, during the transition period, chances are that there will be relatively less demand for cutting-edge technological infrastructure. This is particularly true for consumer electronics, which represents technology for consumption rather than for productive investment. As such, for the transition period, investors should focus on those technologies that generally help to keep down existing costs for existing economic activities rather than those designed to appeal directly to consumers in the form of fashionable, quasi-luxury products.

Consumer Non-discretionary

It stands to reason that staple products are likely to remain in demand no matter how disruptive the transition back to gold proves to be. Defensive investors normally overweight this sector, and for good reason. Not only is demand relatively stable but it is generally assumed that consumer staple product prices rise with inflation.

The downside, of course, is that the sector normally presents less opportunity for robust growth. But during the transition back to gold, robust growth will remain elusive in many economies.

Although long out of favor, food production, processing, transport, and storage are basic, generally low-risk businesses that represent arguably the most staple of all staple products: nutrition. During the potentially disorderly and inflationary transition back to gold, there is certainly still going to be demand for food. Food infrastructure in general is going to remain absolutely essential, no matter how much disruption there is to the financial system and other industries. Food prices are also likely to rise more or less in line with any interim surge in inflation as gold is revalued and the dollar devalued.

Once the transition period is complete, however, the safe haven aspects of this sector will become relatively less attractive. There will probably remain selective opportunities in certain foods and in certain parts of the world that are becoming more affluent and consuming more and higher-quality food, with higher protein content.

Consumer Discretionary

While normally riskier than consumer nondiscretionary shares, during the potentially highly disruptive transition back to gold, there is likely to be a considerably larger expansion of risk premia for discretionary relative to nondiscretionary shares. Amid huge uncertainty and, for many, loss of purchasing power, discretionary purchases will be postponed.

Demand for durable goods, such as automobiles and appliances, will be particularly hard hit. In addition to the factors just mentioned, these purchases are frequently financed. Like financing activities generally, as any implied bailout essentially disappears and financial risk premia expand under a gold standard, it will become more expensive for households to fund purchases on credit. Rather, they will need to save a greater portion of their income first and, when finally able to afford a sizeable down payment, access to some vendor credit may be available at an attractive interest rate.

It is worth considering, however, how this reduction in demand for durable goods will affect certain other activities. As consumers delay purchasing new vehicles or appliances, for example, they are going to need to extend the practical working lives of those durable goods they already have. Specialty producers of replacement parts and providers of servicing and improvements or upgrades that can be applied to existing vehicles and appliances are likely to be in relatively stronger demand, and this could be one of the best performing sectors during the transition period back to gold.

Some thoughts on diversification

It is often said that diversification is the only free lunch in economies. As such, investors should always prefer more, to the extent that diversification does not adversely affect investment returns over time.

In recent years, as financial markets have become almost exclusively focused on policy makers' actions from one day to the next, as one crisis after another escalates, then calms down, then escalates unexpectedly yet again, financial asset prices have become unusually highly correlated. As the source for most volatility in expectations for growth, inflation, and economic variables generally now resides with the highly activist policymaking community, rather than at a firm- or industry-specific level, it is only natural that the expected fortunes of a given firm or industry rise or fall more or less together. Put another way, the bulk of the risk in the world is now primarily systematic rather than idiosyncratic. As such, there is far, far less diversification to be had in financial assets generally.

Even commodity prices are now unusually correlated to financial markets, although substantially less so than the correlations between financial assets themselves. The point is that the growth in what is quite clearly centralized economic planning, as opposed to firm- or industry-specific initiative, has created an unusually binary investment outlook.

While symptomatic of the final stage of the global experiment of a fiat currency reserve standard and associated asset bubbles and busts, this presents investors not only with a tremendous challenge but also with an opportunity. Where diversification can be found, it is likely to find unusually good demand. It may take a commensurately unusual amounts of detective work, but the new firm, new industry, new technology, or applications thereof in a new country naturally still provide investors with opportunities for diversification at reasonable valuations. No matter how disorderly the transition to gold becomes, there will always be a role for traditional, value-based investing to play in any disciplined investment process. The search for both value and for diversification may be unusually challenging at present, those investors who understand that this is where the focus should lie, rather than on chasing growth or momentum, will fare relatively better.

In the following chapter, we explore the topic of efficiently diversified portfolio construction in more detail.

Chapter 23: The Golden Portfolio

> "Diversification is an established tenet of conservative investment...
>
> There is a close logical connection between the concept of a safety margin and the principle of diversification."
>
> —Benjamin Graham

HAVING DEMONSTRATED EARLIER IN THIS book that there is no "free lunch" in economics, it is now time to mention that, in fact, there most certainly is: diversification. Investors of all stripes, no matter how much expertise or specialization they may have in one or more areas, should nevertheless always keep an open mind with respect to how they might best combine one or more specific investments or strategies into a portfolio. For most investors, lacking specific expertise and the time required to generate it, falling back on portfolio diversification is the single most important thing they can do to make their portfolios robust to the unavoidable uncertainties of real-world investing.

Having placed gold back at the center of the investment universe, where it belongs, let us begin there. For if gold is again going to be the de facto global money, whether this is always recognized as de jure or no, then this becomes the default, defensive core position of a diversified portfolio, rather than just another "asset," which is added to the mix to enhance diversification. By implication, the amount of gold an investor should hold in a portfolio thus increases.

However, let's just leave that aside for the moment and cast a glance back at the past century or so of available data on the investment returns generated by stocks, government bonds, corporate bonds, cash, and gold. The US dataset is the most complete and continuous, and so for convenience purposes we will use US financial data for this analysis.

As these various return streams are not perfectly correlated with one another, by combining them into a portfolio we can extract diversification benefits. How best to combine them into the most efficiently diversified portfolio possible?

First of all, some caution is in order. Analyses such as these ultimately depend on choice of specific market indices and specific starting and ending point. However, when it comes to the long-term dataset there really isn't too much index choice involved, so we take what we have. And as for the starting and ending point, when the dataset is sufficiently long, this has less of an impact on the results. Nevertheless, in order to avoid accusations of spurious accuracy, in summarizing these results I will work in ranges rather than specific percentage allocations.

Second, what one finds when running the numbers is that, perhaps curiously to some, the addition of corporate bonds to a portfolio does not add any material diversification benefit over long-time horizons. Why should that be? The explanation lies in that corporate bonds have elements of interest rate risk and firm-specific risk, which are in fact adequately captured by the government bond and equity components of the portfolio, respectively. Nothing against corporate bonds. There is a time and place to opportunistically purchase them for sure, but that is not a "passive" diversification strategy of the type we are trying to derive here; rather, it is taking a specific view that, from time to time, corporate bonds offer good relative value and should be overweighted.

Third, one also finds that when it comes to government bonds, only the longest-dated bonds should be included. Why? Well, if we are after maximum diversification benefits, then to the extent we are dealing with assets that have only low (or negative) correlation to one another, then we want access to higher volatility assets so as to maximize the benefits of that low (or negative) correlation. In this case, as longer-dated bonds are more volatile than short-dated bonds, we should include the former.

Finally, when taking all of the above points into consideration and creating a passive portfolio for the very long term, one which is rebalanced back to base weights on an annual basis, what then are the base weights that result in the maximum diversification benefits? As it happens—and this might surprise some—the weightings for both stocks and government bonds are roughly equal at around 35–45 percent each. That for cash is around 5–10 percent, as is that for gold. It depends on your specific start and end point as per the above.

However, and this is a most important point, if we simply focus on the post-Bretton-Woods time frame during which the dollar has been unanchored from gold, such that cash and gold are not much the same, as they were under the gold standard, then the numbers shift in favor of stocks and gold. This is because cash has generally failed to produce returns in excess of inflation and the value of bonds has occasionally been severely eroded by inflation as well, such as during the 1970s. Rerunning the numbers from 1971 onward, following the end of the Bretton-Woods system, the ideal weightings are 40–45 percent stocks, 35–40 percent bonds, 10–15 percent gold, and only 0–5 percent cash. Indeed, although it is not realistic, a case can be made that investors should have sought to generally minimize cash holdings to the extent that liquidity requirements would allow. As I have advised numerous investors in recent years, "Beyond mere liquidity requirements, holding cash in a portfolio is simply not a valid long-term investment strategy."

Certainly, from an opportunistic perspective, there are times when investors should reduce holdings of stocks, or bonds, or occasionally both, and sit in cash instead, waiting for a better entry point. But that is to take a view, rather than merely to construct a long-term passive portfolio to maximize diversification benefits. Moreover, in an environment of zero or negative interest rates, with sitting in cash not a valid long-term strategy, gold necessarily re-rates as the "go-to asset" in the event that investors opportunistically prefer to sit on the sidelines and reduce their exposure to stocks and/or bonds.

Living as we do in an age of excessive debt and leverage and the associated uncertainty, gold should thus be over- rather than underweighted in a portfolio. With a 10–15 percent holding, one that is simply implied by the historical data as is, that to me is a floor rather than a ceiling regarding how much gold investors should hold in a well-diversified portfolio of financial assets. A case can be made to hold twice as much. Personally, I know of some people who think along these lines and who have made the highly contrarian decision to hold as much as a third, in some cases a half, of their liquid net worth in gold.

When it comes to extracting diversification benefits alone, the historical data would argue against such a large weighting. But when it comes to taking a view as to whether stocks or bonds are overvalued vis-à-vis gold, then it is an entirely valid way to express the view that bond yields are more likely to rise than fall from here, and that stock market valuations are more likely to fall than rise from here. And rather than sit in cash, which can be summarily devalued (e.g. Great Britain of late), or bailed-in (e.g. Cyprus, Greece), or cancelled outright (e.g. India), gold has reemerged as the more attractive option. Indeed, it provides the only way to simultaneously avoid the twin risks of devaluation on the one hand and some form of bank or government default or redefinition of cash on the other.

Some gold purchase and storage considerations

For those inclined to take the decision to hold substantial amounts of gold in their portfolios, the question then becomes how best to hold it. I can't stress enough that anything that appears to be a form of paper gold governed by securities or banking law is potentially at risk from various kinds of fraud. Moreover, in recent years it has become more expensive to operate under securities and banking law due to the growing complexity of regulatory and compliance issues. Hence, the fees associated with

ETFs and other popular forms of paper gold have remained stubbornly higher than operationally necessary, notwithstanding the tremendous economies of scale, which should, in principle, apply to these large paper gold investment vehicles.

Futures contracts, such as those that trade on the US COMEX exchange, also provide a way to gain exposure to the gold price and are somewhat less expensive than the ETFs. But understand that these contracts may provide for low-cost speculation on the price of gold, but they don't represent an actual claim on physical allocated gold. Indeed, at times the amount of eligible and registered gold held in COMEX vaults is tiny relative to the open interest. Yes, more could almost certainly be made available if required, as the global gold market is extremely liquid. But in a crisis, in which perhaps liquidity declines, or in which holders of long positions in COMEX contracts stand for delivery in large amounts, it is questionable whether enough gold could indeed be made available in a short enough time to avoid a default event of some kind. Although presumably holders of contracts would be made whole in some way, it is not entirely clear at what price or in what time frame this would occur. As one of the key properties of gold is to protect wealth in a crisis, this should give investors pause.

Thus, for the buy and hold investor who desires to acquire a substantial portion of gold to diversify a portfolio of assets, rather than merely to speculate, gold should be held in 100 percent allocated physical form only. While smaller amounts can be secured at home, say in a household safe, larger amounts should be held only in high-security vaults with custodial arrangements provided by a reputable, independent gold custodian. (By independent I mean a non-bank.)

There is also a case to be made that large holdings of gold should be held outside one's country of residence. While I would hardly predict a widespread, general gold confiscation by a major government, it cannot be ruled out. But while governments can and do sometimes confiscate household wealth, including physical gold holdings, they cannot easily do so outside their home jurisdiction without undertaking what could amount to an act of war.

It is for precisely this reason that many Americans have chosen to store their gold in Canada. Many Europeans choose Switzerland. Many Asians choose Singapore. These jurisdictions are relatively low risk and have strong historical traditions respecting property rights. They also provide for varying degrees of client confidentiality that may exceed those provided by most jurisdictions including the country of residence of many.

Highly wealthy individuals tend to spread their gold around multiple jurisdictions in the event that one of them is compromised in some way. The same is true of their property and business holdings. Indeed, diversification takes many forms, including those of geography and jurisdiction. The wealthier one becomes, the more important these qualitative forms of diversification.

As the Golden Revolution approaches, there is likely to be an unusually high degree of financial market volatility. All available financial history suggests that prudent individuals should own at least some gold and perhaps much more than the conventional wisdom would suggest. The historical financial data tell a story and that story is in part one of the essential role of gold in a defensive, well-diversified portfolio. However, regardless of just how disruptive the coming monetary regime change is going to be, it is going to have implications above and beyond those for the economy and financial markets alone. And so it is to the broader social implications of the remonetization of gold that we now turn.

Chapter 24: Some Implications of the Gold Standard for Global Labor and Capital Markets

> "[P]olicies about trade and finance should have as their objective the maximum possible free trade in goods and services and free movement of capital... [A] relatively stable price level ... will generally promote that objective."[111]
>
> —Nobel laureate Milton Friedman, 2001

IT IS IMPORTANT TO GIVE some consideration to the implications of the gold standard for global labor and capital markets, in the highly likely event that the bulk of the globe returns to a gold standard. For example, just because one region might be in recession does not imply that others are, notwithstanding the strong global economic linkages observed today. There will always be regional economic differences, in particular between countries with highly distinct economic characteristics, such as agrarian economies, those associated with mining activities, or those primarily engaged in manufacturing or financial services.

We have seen how, under a gold standard, financial markets, rather than central banks, will ultimately determine the level of interest rates. But in a global economy, the level of interest rates will be determined by global supply and global demand, not local. As such, even if the rate of growth approached zero in one part of the world, were other parts more dynamic, growing in excess of 3 percent, say, then gold would flow from where capital was not in demand to where it was, pulling interest rates in

111 "One World, One Money," Options Politiques/Policy Options, May 2001.

the relatively less dynamic regions higher or, at a minimum, preventing them from falling as much as they otherwise would.

This might seem suboptimal from the perspective of a weak economy. Wouldn't it be better if they had their own currency and central bank and could lower interest rates as required to support growth instead? Perhaps in the short term, yes. But consider: naturally fluctuating interest rates become a sort of automatic stabilizing mechanism. Eventually, they rise to a level that prevents a further outflow of gold and implies a higher domestic savings rate. That savings then becomes available for investment, required for a sustainable economic recovery. Moreover, under a gold standard, wages and other variable costs become by necessity more flexible. If it is impossible to inflate or devalue one's way out of an economic downturn, then by implication, production costs must be flexible on the downside. As wages decline, the weaker economy becomes relatively more competitive internationally.

Capital, too, must be more flexible. If businesses are struggling to make a profit or begin to go bankrupt, then they will need to restructure. Money printing will not be available to bail out shareholders or bond holders, who will be responsible for taking over failed enterprises, restructuring their operations, and perhaps breaking them into pieces and selling them off so that capital can be more efficiently employed elsewhere.

This process of labor and capital flexibility and mobility, corporate reorganization, and renewal is absolutely essential to long-term economic progress. Without it, capital gets locked up in old, less dynamic businesses and outmoded technologies. Labor gets stuck in relatively poor, unproductive regions. Progress becomes more and more elusive. By resorting to lower interest rates and inflation, central banks repeatedly soften the short-term impact of an economic downturn. But there is no free lunch. In doing so, central banks prevent Schumpeterian "creative destruction": real economic restructuring, renewal, and long-term advancement. Economies become ossified as a consequence, fail either to develop new technologies or even to adopt those with proven advantages elsewhere.

Eventually, the gap between stagnant economies and those that allow for the occasional major restructuring becomes so vast that they are considered to exist in different "worlds," as in the "developed" and the "developing." Economic history provides numerous examples of this phenomenon. Recall that, as Europe was stagnating through the early Middle Ages, major economic advances were taking place in China and elsewhere in Asia, only to ultimately be suppressed by inflexible regimes.

However, given a sufficient level of flexibility, eventually a combination of higher rates on savings and lower wages makes labor more attractive and capital more available, precisely the combination that can lay the groundwork for a sound, sustainable economic recovery. Meanwhile, those economies that don't experience higher rates on savings or falling wages become less competitive over time, eventually yielding their dynamism to their previously less fortunate counterparts. Interest rates, so absent from the chronic manipulations of policy makers under today's fiat standard, will better facilitate the efficient allocation of global capital flows under the coming global gold standard.

By implication of wages being necessarily more flexible, up and down, under a gold standard in which inflationary responses to unemployment become for all practical purposes impossible to sustain, labor is likely, in general, to be more mobile. In large part, this will be due to the greater difficulty in providing substantial unemployment benefits for an extended period. Labor will seek to move not only within borders to wherever the better jobs are but also, to the extent allowed by the authorities, across them. While picking up and moving, in particular across borders, can be hugely disruptive for households, it does serve an important economic purpose, both in limiting the duration of unemployment and, thinking longer term, facilitating the movement of labor to where it can be most efficiently employed.

A thorough discussion of the apparent trade-off between economic flexibility on the one hand, and social continuity on the other, is beyond the scope of this book. However, in the conclusion that follows, I offer some thoughts in this area.

Conclusion: The Golden Society

> "I believe that banking institutions are more dangerous to our liberties than standing armies . . . If the American people ever allow private banks to control the issue of their currency, first by inflation, then by deflation, the banks and corporations that will grow up around [the banks] . . . will deprive the people of all property until their children wake-up homeless on the continent their fathers conquered . . . The issuing power should be taken from the banks and restored to the people, to whom it properly belongs."
>
> —President Thomas Jefferson, speaking in opposition to the recharter of the Bank Bill (1809)

As we observed in Section III, a young Alan Greenspan, in his 1966 essay "Gold and Economic Freedom," published in Ayn Rand's *The Objectivist,* made the case for a return to a pure gold standard from the somewhat ambiguous Bretton Woods system in not only an economic sense but also a moral sense, in that gold ownership protects private property rights and, by implication, protects the individual against government tyranny. As such, he explicitly placed gold at the center of the entire Western, liberal philosophical tradition, tracing its way back to the Enlightenment. Indeed, the perennial debate between Hobbesian statists on the one hand and Lockean/Jeffersonian minarchists (or anarchists) on the other is to some extent resolved through gold. Not only does it provide for protection of private property rights, as Locke would have it, but a form of objective social order, a universal point of reference for measuring value, facilitating trade, and the associated economic and social progress. (It is often forgotten that Hobbes initiates his famous essay "Leviathan" with a detailed discussion of the importance of commerce in human affairs.)

The US founding fathers, including Thomas Jefferson, quoted above, sought to resolve this dilemma in practice with the drafting and ratification of the US Constitution, which provided the federal government with a handful of enumerated powers. Among these was the power, given to the Congress, to coin money and regulate the value thereof. The first explicit exercise of this power, the Coinage Act of 1792, defined the dollar as an exact weight of silver and gold. As such, the Congress assumed its constitutional monetary authority in a way that prevented banks from somehow arbitrarily inflating (or, for that matter, deflating) the money supply.

Hobbes's advocacy of a Leviathan state was derived primarily from his wanting to prevent a repeat of the devastating English Civil War. It is perhaps a great irony that one of the proximate causes of the Civil War was in 1638 when King Charles I confiscated some 200,000 pounds of private citizen's gold stored in the Royal Mint for safekeeping. This seizure—officially a "loan" to the crown—was considered unacceptable by many prominent Royalists, who subsequently went over to the Parliamentary side. (As it happens, Charles would default on this "loan" in time, having spent the gold to unsuccessfully prosecute his military campaigns.)

To generalize, Hobbes felt that to organize society under an unambiguous, ultimate authority was the only way in which to prevent a never-ending, anarchic "war of all against all" that would render the life of man "solitary, poor, nasty, brutish and short." Yet he also understood that trade and commerce were essential to satisfying human needs and wants and to the general advancement of civilization. Along these lines, consider that by providing an objective, voluntary, universally accepted medium of exchange, gold allows individuals to trade more extensively with one another, outside the family or tribal unit. Absent gold or increasingly authoritarian, perhaps even slave-labor-based societies, there would be only pure barter and some degree of reciprocal altruism, greatly limiting the achievable division of labor and, hence, economic progress. The life of man would remain relatively poor and probably quite short. As we saw in Section I, unsound money can result in socially destabilizing levels of income inequality, also a potential threat to social stability and progress.

Life in an authoritarian society wouldn't necessarily be solitary, nasty, or brutish, but history demonstrates that with increased trade, war tends to become less frequent. Money facilitates trade. In Section II we observed how unstable money destabilizes trade. Unstable money, thus, threatens to undo the historically significant growth of world trade in recent decades, as indeed it did in Europe during and following World War I. As we know, World War II followed.

It is no coincidence, however, that following the world wars of the first half of the twentieth century, the Western monetary order was restored, albeit in somewhat hegemonic fashion by the United States, with gold at the center. Elsewhere, absent stable money, economic modernization, and trade growth, authoritarian regimes dominated.

With the collapse of the Soviet bloc in the 1990s came, on the one hand, the apparent triumph of the West, yet, on the other, the economic modernization and trade growth associated with progressively less-authoritarian regimes. As we have seen, the BRICS (Brazil, Russia, India, China, South Africa) economies and smaller emerging markets now represent a large and growing part of the global economy. As such, mercantilist growth-oriented policies in the developing world, financed by Western money and credit growth, have more than outlived their usefulness, as has the fiat dollar global reserve standard. They are now destabilizing the very economies they previously enabled to grow.

In a sense, the wheel has come full circle. With the erosion of authoritarianism around the world has come the rebalancing of economic power away from the hegemonic monetary order previously provided by the fiat dollar. As is often the case with history, it may seem ironic that in the triumph of the Western liberal economic and political traditions over authoritarianism lay the seeds of the dollar's eventual demise. Yet it has always been gold, rather than an unbacked fiat currency, that has presided over a multipolar world.

A useful historical parallel with today might be the decline of Spain and the emergence of a multipolar European world in the early seventeenth century. As long as Spain remained the monetary hegemon, bringing a seemingly endless supply of gold and silver from the New World to Europe, it could finance wars on demand and dominate much of the continent, including the economically powerful low countries. Yet what seemed endless was anything but, and, as the mint gradually emptied out, Spain sued for peace and Europe's most destructive war to that point came to an end, to be followed by a century and a half of relative peace and growing prosperity, inaugurated by the Peace of Westphalia in 1648. (Incidentally, this relative peace came to an end with the French Revolution and the rise of Napoleon. In my opinion, it is no coincidence that the revolution against Louis XV followed on a period of highly inflationary policies that were not curtailed but rather expanded by the revolutionaries. Large inflations tend to precede, to coincide with and to follow major wars and revolutions.)

Returning to the present, the hegemonic post–World War II economic order has long since given way to a more multipolar one. Now, following the global credit crisis that began in 2008, the already fragile fiat dollar reserve equilibrium has become terminally destabilized. Gold will soon resume its normal, historical role for a non-hegemonic, multipolar world.

We have already discussed at length some of the more important economic and financial market implications of a return to a gold standard.

Along the way, we have occasionally touched on some associated societal implications. It remains to draw some firmer conclusions in this area.

As a young Greenspan observed, gold helps to protect private property rights, which, alongside natural political rights, provide the basis of the Western, liberal, democratic, commercial tradition. If governments cannot confiscate wealth through deficit spending and inflation, they will be able to do so only through taxation. With each generation having to pay for government as it goes along, rather than passing that burden onto some number of future generations, it stands to reason that there will be greater scrutiny over government spending, which will more closely reflect societal preferences.

There is also a larger moral question here in whether it is right for one generation to borrow from another. I do not believe this to be the case absent a clear, present, existential danger to a society. Yet alongside the rise of the modern, deficit-funded welfare state has come a general acceptance of the immoral practice of leaving future generations with the bill for current consumption. A return to gold will put an end to that practice in short order.

In Section IV, we touched on how labor and capital will necessarily be more mobile under a gold standard, as policy makers will be less able to support poor economic regions at the expense of more affluent ones. While no doubt disruptive for a time, labor and capital mobility are part and parcel of Schumpeterian creative destruction, without which significant economic progress becomes all but impossible.

Once again, there is a moral argument to be made here: is it right for people in one location to be subsidized indefinitely by people in another location just because the former cast a greater number of votes? This is akin to the majority voting to appropriate the wealth of the minority. Such a tyranny of the majority, so feared by the US founding fathers and specifically addressed in the limited federal powers and various checks and balances of the US Constitution, would not long last under a gold standard, in which uneconomic transfers of wealth would be met with an outflow of gold and higher interest rates.

But it is not just the tyranny of the majority that will be curtailed by a return to gold. Any organized group that seeks rents from the government in exchange for political contributions or votes will find it is up against stiffer opposition. With greater fiscal restraint implied by the tether of gold, there will be far fewer political favors to give away. Fewer favors will lead to less rent-seeking activity in the first place. Firms will spend less time lobbying governments and more time rationalizing their operations, developing and implementing new technologies, and so on, to the benefit of all.

As gold also protects wealth and prohibits its confiscation through inflation, the simple virtue of saving will be strengthened. While there will always be those inclined to speculate, no doubt some of whom get lucky and wealthy as a result, it is the simple saver who benefits most from gold, not the speculator. As we have seen, risk premia for financial assets in general are likely to be higher under a gold standard. This implies that, not only will savers be better compensated for saving, but also value-based investors will be able to a better job allocating capital across industries, to the benefit of all.

Yes, this may imply that corporate CEOs and other top executives find it more difficult to secure outsize pay packages for substandard performance, but a rebalancing of power from corporate insiders to shareholders will not only help to ensure that the owners of the corporations—the shareholders—are the primary beneficiaries of profit growth but also dissuade CEOs from excessive risk taking, as it will become more difficult to extract huge payouts from a company, short of a long and successful tenure. Control fraud, endemic to the corrupt practices of crony capitalism documented by David Stockman and Nomi Prins, among others, will become less common, to the benefit of corporate employees and their customers.

Looking at the financial sector specifically, in a noninflationary world with no implied bailout for financial firms, there will be far less financial risk appetite relative to the desire to take operational risk. Profits will migrate from financial to operational activities. And where profits migrate, so does capital and labor. Resources being poured into financial activities today will be poured into operational ones instead. Many of those engineers, scientists, mathematicians, and other intelligent, highly trained quants who were drawn to finance in recent years due to the apparent promise of huge salaries and bonuses will find their way into productive enterprises, seeking to build a better mousetrap or widget, or whatever. Fresh graduates will join over time. Together, they will develop new technologies and run more efficient firms for the benefit of the broader economy.

Although I could go on, this list is already rather extensive. Gold protects private property and political rights, by limiting the power of government to tax or inflate away the former, while constraining the government's ability to give away political favors to organized rent-seeking groups. Gold prevents monetary inflation from exacerbating income inequality. Gold helps prevent one generation from taxing the next via excessive government borrowing; it helps prevent one region from taxing another just because it delivers more votes; it redirects resources from financial speculation toward value-driven, productive investment; it helps to prevent insider abuse and control fraud from wrecking otherwise profitable corporations; and it returns the basic virtues of thrift, savings, and good old-fashioned hard work to the center of society, thereby strengthening the moral compass and mutual trust required for the advancement of civilization.

Thus, the Golden Revolution promises to be not just monetary, economic, and financial but also societal. And while the transition may be painful for most, it will become only more so the longer it is pushed back. We should, therefore, not only embrace gold and gold-backed money as arguably the best way to protect wealth in uncertain times but embrace it as the best way to place the global economy back on a sustainable path and, in so doing, strengthen the societal bonds that lie at the heart of Western liberal, democratic traditions. If undermined by unsound money and inflation, these traditions are at risk of being displaced by authoritarian traditions instead. As I am an optimist in this regard, in my view the present, elevated level of global monetary instability represents golden writing on the wall.

Bibliography

ARTICLES

Barro, Robert J. "Money and the Price Level under the Gold Standard." *Economic Journal* 89 (March 1979).

Barro, Robert J. and David B. Gordon. "A Positive Theory of Monetary Policy in a Natural Rate Model." *Journal of Political Economy* 91 (August 1983).

Bordo and Jonung. "A Return to the Convertibility Principle? Monetary and Fiscal Regimes in International Perspective." (Nov 2000). Paper prepared for the International Economic Association conference in Trento, Italy, September 4–7, 1997. Online: http://swopec.hhs.se/hastef/papers/hastef0415.pdf.

Bordo, M. D. and F. E. Kydland. "The Gold Standard as a Rule: An Essay in Exploration." *Explorations in Economic History*, Vol. 32 (1995), pp. 423–464.

Bordo, M. D. and H. Rockoff. "The Gold Standard as a 'Good Housekeeping Seal of Approval.'" *Journal of Economic History*, Vol. 56 (1996).

Crafts, N. and P. Fearon. "Lessons from the 1930s' Great Depression." *Oxford Review of Economic Policy*, Vol. 26 (2010), pp. 285–317.

Davidson, Laura F. "The Causes of Price Inflation and Deflation: Fundamental Economic Principles the Deflationists Have Ignored." *Libertarian Papers* 3, 13 (2011).

"Dollars, Deficits and the International Monetary System," *Review of the Federal Reserve Bank of St. Louis*, July 1971.

Eichengreen, Barry. "The Dollar Dilemma." *Foreign Affairs* September/October 2009. The Council on Foreign Relations. Online: http://www.foreignaffairs.com/articles/65241/barry-eichengreen/the-dollar-dilemma.

Eichengreen, Barry and Michael Bordo. "Crises Now and Then: What Lessons from the Last Era of Financial Globalization?" National Bureau of Economic Research Working Paper No. 8716 (January 2002).

Eichengreen, B. and R. Portes. "Debt and Default in the 1930s: Causes and Consequences." *European Economic Review*, Vol. 30 (1986), pp. 599-640.

Farchy, Jack. "Dollar Seen to Lose its Reserve Currency Status." *Financial Times* (June 27, 2011).

Flandreau, Marc and Mathilde Maurel. "Monetary Union, Trade Integration, and Business Cycles in the 19th Century." *Open Economies Review,* Vol. 16 (2005), pp. 135–52.

Frankel, Jeffrey. "The Effect of Monetary Policy on Real Commodity Prices," in John Campbell ed. *Asset Prices and Monetary Policy* (Chicago: University of Chicago Press, 2008).

Frankel, Jeffrey. "Peg the Export Price Index: A Proposed Monetary Regime for Small Countries." *Journal of Policy Modelling* (June 2005).

Friedman, Milton. "Commodity-Reserve Currency." *Journal of Political Economy* 59 (June 1951).

Friedman, Milton. “The Resource Cost of Irredeemable Paper Money.” *Journal of Political Economy* 94 (June 1986).

Gallarotti. “The Rise of the Classical Gold Standard: The Role of Focal Points and Synergistic Effects in Spontaneous Order.” *Humane Studies Review* (2001).

Herbener, Jeffrey M. “After the Age of Inflation: Austrian Proposals for Monetary Reform.” *The Quarterly Journal of Austrian Economics* Vol. 5 (4) (Winter 2002).

Kydland, Finn and Edward C. Prescott. “Rules Rather than Discretion: The Inconsistency of Optimal Plans.” *Journal of Political Economy* 85 (June 1977).

Laffer, Arthur B. and Charles W. Kadlec. “The Point of Linking the Dollar to Gold.” *Wall Street Journal* (October 13, 1982).

McCallum, Bennett T. “Robustness Properties of a Rule for Monetary Policy.” *Carnegie- Rochester Conference Series for Public Policy*, 29 (Autumn 1988).

McCallum, Bennett T. “Alternative Monetary Policy Rules: A Comparison with Historical Settings for the United States, the United Kingdom, and Japan.” *Federal Reserve Bank of Richmond Economic Quarterly*, 86 (Winter 2000).

McKinnon, R. “The Rules of the Game: International Money in Historical Perspective.” *Journal of Economic Literature*, Vol. 31 (1993), pp. 1–44.

Meissner, M. Christopher and J. Ernesto López-Córdova. “Exchange-Rate Regimes and International Trade: Evidence from the Classical Gold Standard Era.” *The American Economic Review.* Vol. 93, No.1 (Mar., 2003), pp. 344–353.

Meissner, C.H. "A New World Order: Explaining the Diffusion of the Classical Gold Standard." National Bureau of Economic Research Working Paper No. 9233 (Sept. 2002).

Morys, Matthias. "The Emergence of the Classical Gold Standard." Economic History Society Annual Conference, Exeter (March, 2007).

Mundell, Robert M. "Gold Would Serve into the 21st Century." *Wall Street Journal* (September 30, 1981).

Obstfeld and Taylor. "Sovereign Risk, Credibility and the Gold Standard: 1870–1913 versus 1925–1931." National Bureau of Economic Research Working Paper 9345 (2002).

Ohanian, Lee. "What, or Who, Started the Great Depression?" *Journal of Economic Theory*, Vol. 144(6) (November 2009).

Ohanian, Lee and Harold Cole. "Stimulus and the Depression: The Untold Story." *Wall Street Journal* (September 26, 2011).

"Reserve Accumulation and International Monetary Stability." International Monetary Fund Working Paper, Strategy Policy and Review Department (April 13, 2010).

Reinhart, Carmen and Belen Sbrancia. "The Liquidation of Government Debt." NBER Working Paper 16893 (2011).

Salerno, Joseph T. "The Gold Standard: An Analysis of Some Recent Proposals." *CATO Policy Analysis* 16 (September 9, 1982).

Sargent, T. and N. Wallace. "Rational Expectations, the Optimal Monetary Instrument and the Optimal Money Supply Rule." *Journal of Political Economy*, vol. 83, no. 2 (April 1975).

Schularick and Steger. "International Financial Integration and Economic Growth- New Evidence from the First Era of Financial Globalization." Center for Economic and Policy Research.

Selgin, George and Lawrence H. White. "Credible Currency: A Constitutional Perspective." *Constitutional Political Economy* 16 (March 2005).

Taylor, John. "Monetary Policy During a Transition to Rational Expectation." *Journal of Political Economy*, vol. 83, no. 5 (October 1975).

Taylor, John. "Discretion Versus Policy Rules in Practice." Carnegie-Rochester Conference Series on Public Policy, vol. 39 (December 1993).

Wanniski, Jude. "A Job Only Gold Can Do." *New York Times* (August 27, 1981).

White, Lawrence H. "Is the Gold Standard Still the Gold Standard among Monetary Systems?" *CATO Briefing Papers* 100 (February 8, 2008).

Wolf, N. "Europe's Great Depression: Coordination Failure after the First World War." *Oxford Review of Economic Policy*, Vol. 26 (2010), pp. 339–369.

BOOKS

Bayoumi, T., B. Eichengreen, and M. P. Taylor, M.P. (eds.) *Modern Perspectives on the Gold Standard.* Cambridge University Press, 1996.

Bernstein. *Capital Ideas Evolving.* Wiley and Sons, 2007.

Bordo, M. and B. Eichengreen, (eds.) *A Retrospective on the Bretton Woods System*. University of Chicago Press, 1993.

Brandeis, Louis. *Other People's Money—And How the Banker's Use It.* 1914. Reprint by BiblioLife, 2009.

Bresciani-Tirroni, Constantino. *The Economics of Inflation*. London: George Allen and Unwin, 1937.

Cochran, P. John and R. Fred Glahe. *The Hayek-Keynes Debate- Lessons for Current Business Cycle Research*. The Edwin Mellen Press, 1999.

Dorn, A. James and Anna J. Schwartz (eds.) *The Search for Stable Money: Essays on Monetary Reform*. University of Chicago Press and the Cato Institute, 1987.

Ebeling, M. Richard (ed.) *The Austrian Theory of the Trade Cycle and Other Essays*. The Ludwig von Mises Institute, 1996.

Eichengreen, Barry. *Exorbitant Privilege*. Oxford University Press, 2011.

Eichengreen, Barry and M. Flandreau (eds.) *The Gold Standard in Theory and History, 2nd Edition*. Routledge, 1997.

Friedman, Milton and Anna Schwartz. *A Monetary History of the United States, 1867-1960*. Princeton University Press, 1963.

Garet, Garrett. *The Bubble That Broke the World.* Little, Brown, and Company, 1932. And the Ludwig von Mises Institute, 2007.

Garrison, Roger. *Time and Money: The Macroeconomics of Capital Structure*. Routledge, 2001.

Geisst, Charles R. *Wall Street: A History: From Its Beginnings to the Fall of Enron*. Oxford University Press, 2004.

Gilder, George. *Knowledge and Power: The Information Theory of Capitalism.* Regnery, 2014.

Gilder, George. *The Scandal of Money: Why Wall Street Recovers but the Economy Never Does.* Regnery, 2016.

Gouge, William M. *A Short History of Paper Money and Banking.* Ludwig von Mises Institute, 1835.

Guindley, Guillaume. *The International Money Triangle: Myths and Realities*, trans. Michael L. Hoffman. White Plains, NY: ME Sharpe, Inc., 1977.

Hayek, F. A. *The Fatal Conceit: The Errors of Socialism.* The University of Chicago Press, 1988.

Hayek, F. A. *Denationalisation of Money: The Argument Refined.* The Institute of Economic Affairs, 1990. The Ludwig von Mises Institute, 2009.

Hazlitt, Henry, ed. *The Critics of Keynesian Economics.* Princeton, NJ: D. van Nostrand Co., Inc., 1960.

Hazlitt, Henry. *The Inflation Crisis and How to Resolve It.* The Ludwig von Mises Institute, 2009.

Hazlitt, Henry. *What You Should Know About Inflation.* Princeton, NJ: D. van Nostrand Company, Inc., 1964.

Hazlitt, Henry. *From Bretton Woods to World Inflation: A Study of Causes and Consequences.* Regnery Gateway, 1984. The Ludwig von Mises Institute, 2008.

Hazlitt, Henry. *Economics in One Lesson.* Harper & Brothers, 1946.

Heilbroner, Robert. *The Worldly Philosophers: The Lives, Times and Ideas of the Great Economic Thinkers.* New York: Simon and Schuster, 1953.

Higgs, Robert. *Crisis and Leviathan: Critical Episodes in the Growth of American Government.* Oxford University Press and the Pacific Research Institute for Public Policy, 1987.

Huerta De Soto, Jesus. *Money, Bank Credit and Economic Cycles.* Auburn, AL: Ludwig von Mises Institute, 2006.

Issing, Otmar, Gaspar Vitor, Angeloni Ignazio, and Tristani Oreste. *Monetary Policy in the Euro Area.* Cambridge University Press, 2001.

Jastram, Roy W., with updated material by Jill Leyland. *The Golden Constant.* Edward Elgar Pub, 2009.

Kindleberger, Charles P. *Manias, Panics, and Crashes: A History of Financial Crises.* 4th Ed. John Wiley & Sons, 2000.

Lehrman, Lewis R. *A Monetary Reform Plan Without Official Reserve Currencies: How We Get from There to Here.* The Lehrman Institute, 2011.

Lewis, Hunter. *Where Keynes Went Wrong.* Axios, 2009.

Litan, Robert. *What Should Banks Do?* The Brookings Institution, 1987.

Lowenstein, Roger. *When Genius Failed.* Random House, 2000.

Maier, S. Charles and N. Leon Lindberg (eds) *The Politics of Inflation of Economic Stagnation.* The Brookings Institution, 1985.

Mandelbrot, Benoit. *The (mis)Behavior of Markets: A Fractal View of Financial Turbulence.* Basic Books, 2004.

Markopolos, Harry. *No One Would Listen: A True Financial Thriller.* John Wiley & Sons, 2010.

McCloskey, Donald N. *If You're So Smart: The Narrative of Economic Expertise.* Chicago: University of Chicago Press, 1990.

Melzer, Allan. *A History of the Federal Reserve, vol. 2, book 2, 1970–1986.* Chicago: University of Chicago Press, 2010.

Mises, Ludwig von. *Economic Policy: Thoughts for Today and Tomorrow.* Auburn, AL: The Ludwig von Mises Institute, 2006.

Mises, Ludwig von. *Human Action.* New Haven: Yale University Press, 1949.

Mises, Ludwig von. *The Theory of Money and Credit*, trans. H. E. Baston. New Haven: Yale University Press, 1953.

Murphy, P. Robert. *The Politically Incorrect Guide to The Great Depression and The New Deal.* Regnery, 2009.

Murphy, P. Robert. *The Politically Incorrect Guide to Capitalism.* Regnery, 2007.

Price, Tim F. *Investing Through the Looking Glass.* Harriman House, 2016.

Prins, Nomi. *All the Presidents' Bankers.* Nation Books, 2015.

Obstfeld, M. and A. M. Taylor. *Global Capital Markets: Integration, Crisis, Growth*. Cambridge University Press, 2004.

Odell, John S. *U. S. International Monetary Policy: Markets, Power and Ideas as Sources of Change*. Princeton: Princeton University Press, 1982.

Powell, Jim. *FDR's Folly: How Roosevelt and His New Deal Prolonged The Great Depression.* Three Rivers Press, 2003.

Prins, Nomi. *All the Presidents' Bankers*, Nation Books, 2015.

Reinhart and Rogoff. *This Time is Different: Eight Centuries of Financial Folly*. Princeton University Press, 2009.

Reisman, George. *Capitalism: A Treatise on Economics.* Ottawa, IL: Jameson Books, 1996.

Rickards, James. *Currency Wars: The Making of the Next Global Crisis.* Portfolio/Penguin, 2011.

Rickards, James. *The Death of Money.* Portfolio/Penguin, 2014.

Rizzo, Mario and Lawrence White. *Foundations of the Market Economy.* Routledge.

Rothbard, Murray N. *A History of Money and Banking in the United States: The Colonial Era to World War II.* The Ludwig von Mises Institute, 2005.

Rothbard, Murray N. *The Mystery of Banking.* The Ludwig von Mises Institute, 2008.

Rothbard, Murray N. *The Case Against the Fed.* The Ludwig von Mises Institute, 1994.

Rothbard, Murray N. *The Panic of 1819.* The Ludwig von Mises Institute, 2007.

Rothbard, Murray N. *What Has Government Done to Our Money?* The Ludwig von Mises Institute, 2005.

Rothbard, Murray N. *America's Great Depression.* The Ludwig von Mises Institute, 2000.

Rothbard, Murray N. *The Case for a 100% Gold Dollar.* The Ludwig von Mises Institute, 2005.

Rueff, Jacques. *The Age of Inflation.* trans. Roger Glemet. New York: Macmillan Co., 1964.

Rueff, Jacques. *The Monetary Sin of the West.* trans. Roger Glemet. New York: Macmillan Co., 1972).

Salerno, Joseph T. *Money, Sound and Unsound.* Auburn, AL: The Ludwig von Mises Institute, 2010.

Samuelson, Paul and William Nordhaus. *Economics.* New York: McGraw Hill, 2009, first published 1948.

Sargent, Thomas J. *Rational Expectations and Inflation.* New York: Harper & Row, 1986.

Scammell, W. M. *International Monetary Policy: Bretton Woods and After.* New York: John Wiley & Sons, 1975.

Schumpeter, Joseph. *Capitalism, Socialism, and Democracy.* New York: Harper & Row, 1950.

Schlichter, Detlev. *Paper Money Collapse.* Wiley, 2012.

Senholz, Hans F. *Age of Inflation.* Western Islands, 1979.

Selgin, George A. *Less Than Zero: The Case for a Falling Price Level in a Growing Economy.* London: Institute for Economic Affairs, 1997.

Selgin, George A. *The Theory of Free Banking: Money Supply Under Competitive Note Issue.* Rowman & Littlefield, 1988.

Shelton, Judy. *A Guide to Sound Money.* Washington, DC: Atlas Economic Research Foundation, 2010.

Shiller, Robert. *Irrational Exuberance.* Princeton University Press, 2000.

Shiller and Akerlof. *Animal Spirits: How Human Psychology Drives the Economy and Why It Matters for Global Capitalism.* Princeton Univ. Press, March 2009.

Smith, Adam. *An Inquiry into the Nature and Causes of the Wealth of Nations,* Ed. Kathryn Sutherland. Oxford: Oxford University Press, 1998.

Sornette, Didier. *Why Stock Markets Crash: Critical Events in Complex Financial Systems*. Princeton University Press, 2003.

Stoerfele, Ronald and Mark Valek. *Austrian Economics for Investors*. Mises Institute of Austria, 2016.

Studenski & Krooss. *Financial History of the United States*. New York: McGraw-Hill, 1952.

Sylla and Sydney Homer. *A History of Interest Rates, 4th Edition*. John Wiley & Sons, 2005.

Treaster, Joseph B. *Paul Volcker, the Making of a Financial Legend*. John Wiley and Sons, 2011.

White, Lawrence H. *Competition and Currency: Essays on Free Banking and Money*. New York University Press, 1989.

Printed in Great Britain
by Amazon

56060780R00218